COAST &
COUNTRYSIDE
HANDBOOK

 THE NATIONAL TRUST

Photographic credits:

1. South-West England
Penberth Cove in Cornwall, looking towards Logan Rocks (NTPL/Rob Matheson)

2. Southern England
Early morning sun on the Seven Sisters in East Sussex (NTPL/David Sellman)

3. London, Thames Valley & Chilterns
The avenue in autumn at Morden Hall Park, London (NTPL/David Magee)

4. Eastern Counties
The lighthouse at Orford Ness in Suffolk (NTPL/Joe Cornish)

5. Central England
View towards Wolfscote Dale in the Peak District, Derbyshire (NTPL/Joe Cornish)

6. North-West England
The lake at Grasmere in Cumbria's Lake District (NTPL/Joe Cornish)

7. North-East England
View of Cowside on the Malham Tarn Estate in North Yorkshire (NTPL/Joe Cornish)

8. Wales
Part of the spectacular Snowdon range in Gwynedd (NTPL/Joe Cornish)

9. Northern Ireland
Strangford Lough in County Down, looking towards Peasland Point (NTPL/Joe Cornish)

Front cover: The headland at Braich y Pwll on the Llŷn Peninsula, Gwynedd (NTPL/Joe Cornish)

Back cover: Young visitor enjoying a 'bug hunt' at Wicken Fen (NTPL/David Levenson)

© The National Trust 1999
ISBN 0 7078 0143 5

First published in Great Britain in 1993
Reprinted 1995, revised 1999
This edition first published 2000
by The National Trust (Enterprises) Ltd,
36 Queen Anne's Gate, London SW1H 9AS

Designed by Pardoe Blacker Ltd, Lingfield, Surrey (2422)
Phototypeset in Monotype Photina Series 747
by SPAN Graphics Ltd, Crawley, West Sussex (SG1581)
Printed by Wing King Tong Ltd, Hong Kong/China

Contents

About the National Trust

The National Trust

- is a registered charity
- is independent of government
- was founded in 1895 to preserve places of historic interest or natural beauty permanently for the nation to enjoy
- relies on the generosity of its supporters, through membership subscriptions, gifts, legacies and the contribution of many thousands of volunteers
- owns more than 248,000 hectares (612,000 acres) of the most beautiful countryside and almost 600 miles of outstanding coast for people to enjoy
- looks after forests, woods, fens, farmland, downs, moorland, islands, archaeological remains, nature reserves, villages – for ever, for everyone
- now protects and opens to the public over 200 historic houses and gardens and 49 industrial monuments and mills
- has the unique statutory power to declare land inalienable – such land cannot be voluntarily sold, mortgaged or compulsorily purchased against the Trust's wishes without special parliamentary procedure. This special power means that protection by the Trust is for ever
- spends all its income on the care and maintenance of the land and buildings in its protection, but cannot meet the cost of all its obligations – four in every five of its historic houses run at a loss – and is always in need of financial support.

Making the most of your visits

This handbook is designed to help you plan and enjoy visits to some of the most outstanding areas of National Trust coast and countryside in England, Wales and Northern Ireland. Public access is central to our work and over 50 million visits are made to our open space properties each year. More than 40 different recreational activities take place on our land and we do our utmost to ensure that these do not conflict,either with each other or with our overriding commitment to protect the land and its wildlife for future generations. We therefore ask you to please show consideration to other users (both human and otherwise!) at all times and to read carefully the section entitled 'Visitor safety in the countryside' on page 7.

The book is divided into nine geographical regions: South-West England; Southern England; London, Thames Valley & Chilterns; Eastern Counties; Central England; North-West England; North-East England; Wales and Northern Ireland. Each section is opened by a full colour divider, on the back of which you will find discussion on a particular feature of that region or aspect of the Trust's work in the countryside generally. Telephone numbers are given for the network of National Trust Regional Offices, your main point of contact should you need further information about any of the properties covered in this book. Public transport infolines are listed for those counties with properties featuring in the book.

Within each section the entries are arranged by name in alphabetical order. Each individual entry contains a brief description of the main physical features of the site, whether man-made or natural, together with interesting historical information. Details are also given of the main wildlife interest present locally, and we welcome news of unusual sightings – please forward your records to the relevant Regional Office.

Practical information about each property is listed under the relevant symbols, as follows:

⚐ Access

Access within the countryside has long depended on traditional routes linking communities together – green lanes, drove roads, bridleways and footpaths. This network of paths is now identified on Ordnance

Survey maps as definitive rights of way. When the National Trust acquires a property this includes the statutory rights of access. In many instances the Trust has also established additional routes, usually permitted (where the owner has given consent for the path to be used by the public), to provide greater variety and to enhance your visit.

Each entry specifies how accessible the property is, listing footpaths, bridleways and waymarked paths, access for disabled visitors and, wherever possible, local stations and bus services. It is worth noting the following points when visiting a property:

- Access is free, but in some cases there may be a charge for car park facilities or information leaflets.

- On Trust farmland please follow footpaths, whether statutory or permitted, close gates and keep dogs on a lead at all times. Please prevent your dogs from fouling paths, or clear up after them.

- Please pay attention to local information; for example, avoid walking on crops, disturbing livestock or ground-nesting birds.

P Parking

At most properties car-parking facilities are provided. Some car parks have a car entry charge – the money is used for the upkeep of the property. Where roadside parking is permitted, visitors are asked not to obstruct gateways or the main highway.

★ Facilities

All properties in this handbook are open throughout the year, although some facilities may be closed during the winter. For detailed information about opening times, please refer to the annual *National Trust Handbook* (issued free to all National Trust members and also available from National Trust shops and bookshops). Information boards, viewpoints and education facilities are indicated, as well as leaflets, which can be obtained from the relevant Regional Offices.

For leaflets on bed and breakfast accommodation and camping facilities, please send a first class stamp to our Membership Department (see page 10). Leaflets are also available at some Trust properties. For a full colour brochure of National Trust cottages, please call our 24-hour brochure line 01225 791133.

⚠ Important information

At some properties there are access restrictions or potential hazards of which visitors need to be aware. Please be sure to read this section before setting out on a visit.

⬛ Location and map reference

The extent of each property is given in both hectares (ha) and acres, together with a brief location description giving distances from nearby towns (ml = miles). An Ordnance Survey map reference is provided for every entry and in most cases represents the main point of public access to the property. All map references relate to the OS Landranger series (1: 50,000). The location of each property is shown on the maps towards the back of the book.

Visitors with disabilities

This handbook identifies those properties where access is available. A free 64-page booklet (also available in large print and on tape), supported by Railtrack, is available from the National Trust Membership Department, FREEPOST MB 1438, Bromley, Kent BR1 3BR (please send a stamped addressed adhesive label, 31p in 1999). It is advisable to check details of on-site facilities with the relevant Regional Office before your visit.

Visitor safety in the countryside

The information given in this book will help you prepare your visits in advance and learn what facilities are available on site. We endeavour to ensure a safe and healthy environment for visitors to our properties and you can help us by observing all notices and signs on site and by following any instructions or advice given by Trust staff. We rely on all visitors to act responsibly and take necessary precautions when out and about. Weather conditions can of course change very quickly, so please always ensure that you are wearing appropriate clothing and footwear, especially in upland areas or on marshland. When walking in coastal areas it may also be necessary to take note of tide times, and if visiting very remote or exposed countryside it is advisable to carry a compass, map and first aid kit.

Protected areas in the United Kingdom
Reference is made in the text to a wide range of landscape and countryside designations, as follows:

- **Areas of Outstanding Natural Beauty (AONBs)** The 50 AONBs include
  many scenic areas of England, Wales and Northern Ireland. English
  and Welsh AONBs were created by the same legislation that led to the
  formation of our National Parks (The National Parks and Access to the
  Countryside Act 1949) and the first ten were designated in the 1950s.
  While an essential objective of National Parks is the provision of
  outdoor recreation, the primary purpose of AONBs is to conserve
  natural beauty. Many AONBs include stretches of Heritage Coast (see
  below).

- **Environmentally Sensitive Areas (ESAs)** In ESAs farmers are offered
  financial incentives to farm in a traditional way for the benefit of the
  landscape, wildlife and the historic interest of these areas. There are 22
  ESAs in England, covering 10% of agricultural land, and a further four
  in Northern Ireland.

- **Heritage Coasts** Local authorities, the Countryside Agency and the
  Countryside Council for Wales have designated 35 per cent of English
  and Welsh coastline as Heritage Coasts, large areas of which are in
  Trust ownership. These coasts are managed for their natural beauty
  and for visitor access. It was only in 1973 that the first Heritage Coasts
  were designated, eight years after the National Trust had first raised
  the alarm by launching its own campaign to save Britain's coastline,
  'Enterprise Neptune'. Due to different legislation, there are no Heritage
  Coasts in Northern Ireland.

- **National Nature Reserves (NNRs)** In England, Wales and Northern
  Ireland nearly 100,000 ha have been designated as NNRs. They were
  established in order to protect Britain's most important areas of wildlife
  habitat and geological formations. Approved bodies such as the
  National Trust manage NNRs that are not owned or controlled by
  government conservation agencies. Of the 300 NNRs, 31 include
  Trust land.

- **National Parks** There are 11 National Parks in England and Wales
  designated by the Government to include areas of unspoilt beauty.
  They are mainly in upland or coastal areas, although the Norfolk

Broads park diverges from this original concept and includes a populated lowland area. Land ownership varies, with much being privately owned. Development control is strict to ensure that the traditional appearance of the landscape is protected. Due to different legislation, there are no National Parks in Northern Ireland.

- **Ramsar Sites** These are wetlands designated by governments in accordance with the provisions of the Convention on Wetlands of International Importance signed at Ramsar, Iran, in 1971.

- **Scheduled Monuments (SAMs)** Scheduled Monuments (also commonly known as Scheduled Ancient Monuments) are sites of national importance, protected from damage and disturbance by the current monuments legislation: the Ancient Monuments and Archaeological Areas Act 1979 in England and Wales, and the Historic Monuments and Archaeological Objects Order 1995 in Northern Ireland. There are approximately 20,000 Scheduled Monuments in England, Wales and Northern Ireland, of which about 1200 are on Trust land.

- **Sites of Special Scientific Interest (SSSIs)** SSSIs are areas of land or water identified as being of outstanding value for their wildlife or geology. They are designated by the Government's statutory conservation agencies under the Wildlife and Countryside Act of 1981. About nine per cent of all SSSIs in England and Wales include Trust land. In Northern Ireland these sites are termed Areas of Special Scientific Interest (ASSIs) or Areas of Scientific Interest (ASIs); 12 include Trust land.

- **Special Areas of Conservation (SACs)** SACs are designated for habitats and species other than birds under the European Habitats Directive. There are 209 in England, Wales and Northern Ireland, of which 86 include Trust land.

- **Special Protection Areas (SPAs)** SPAs are designated for the protection of breeding or wintering birds under the European Birds Directive. There are 95 in England, Wales and Northern Ireland, of which 26 include Trust land. SACs and SPAs together form the Natura 2000 network of sites which is intended to promote the conservation of habitats, wild animals and plants, both on land and at sea throughout Europe.

- **World Heritage Sites** Natural and cultural sites of exceptional interest and universal value are drawn up on a World Heritage List under the UNESCO World Heritage Convention of 1972. The Giant's Causeway in Northern Ireland is an example in the 'natural' category. National Trust sites on the 'cultural' list include Stonehenge, Avebury, Hadrian's Wall, Fountains Abbey & Studley Royal, and Prior Park.

Getting involved

National Trust Membership

As a member of the National Trust you will contribute to our conservation work and the protection of the countryside, gardens and historic buildings in the Trust's care. Your membership card will give you free entry to most Trust properties, and each year you will receive the Members' Handbook, three colour magazines and two regional newsletters. Please see the application form opposite or contact the National Trust Membership Department, PO Box 39, Bromley, Kent BR1 3XL (tel. 020 8315 1111, fax 020 8466 6824, or email enquiries@ntrust.org.uk).

Volunteering

Volunteers provide an important resource for the National Trust: over 38,000 people of all ages and from all walks of life assist each year with the management of the Trust's coast and countryside properties. Voluntary tasks range from the highly skilled or professional to those where energy and an enthusiasm for the National Trust are the most important qualifications. The Trust's developing volunteer programme offers a constructive partnership of volunteers and staff working together to achieve the Trust's aims.

Tasks undertaken by volunteers range from wardening, archaeological and woodland surveys, and conservation work, including scrub, pond or litter clearance, footpath repairs, educational projects or the provision of access for disabled visitors. Some tasks call for a regular commitment while others require short-term or occasional assistance. There are a

Application for annual membership

TO: THE NATIONAL TRUST, FREEPOST MB1438, BROMLEY, KENT BR1 3BR

☐ **Individual:** £30 and, for each additional member living at the same address, £21. One card for each member.

☐ **Family group:** £57 for two adults and their children or grandchildren under 18, living at the same address. Please give names and dates of birth for all children. **Two** cards cover the family.

☐ **Family one adult:** £43 for one adult and his/her children under 18, living at the same address. Please give names and dates of birth for all children. **One** card covers the family.

☐ **Child:** £14.50 Must be under 13 at time of joining. Please give date of birth.

☐ **Young person:** £15 Must be 13 to 25 at time of joining. Please give date of birth.

Please contact our Membership Department for details of life membership and educational group membership.

SOURCE D296			DATE		
FULL ADDRESS					
				POSTCODE	
TITLE	INITIALS	SURNAME		DATE OF BIRTH	VALUE £

AMOUNT ATTACHED:
CHEQUE/POSTAL ORDER £ ____
Delete as appropriate

Credit/debit card payments can be made by telephoning 020 8315 1111 (office hours)

We promise that any information you give will be used for National Trust purposes only. We will write to you about our work and will occasionally include details of products by third parties developed in association with the Trust. We would also like to send you separate details of such products but should you prefer not to receive these separate mailings, please tick this box. ☐

Please allow 21 days for receipt of your membership card.

The National Trust is an independent registered charity (no. 205846)

growing number of opportunities for long-term volunteers and in some cases, accommodation is provided.

The Trust also organises over 400 inexpensive week-long and weekend residential working holidays for all ages from sixteen years. For more information about the opportunities open to volunteers, including local volunteer groups and more than 400 Working Holidays, please send a first class stamp to our Membership Department (see above).

Working Holidays

The Trust hosts some 400 working holidays on coast and countryside properties throughout England, Wales and Northern Ireland. The opportunities range from repairing hurdle fences at a Welsh castle to footpath improvements on Lundy Island and dry-stone walling in the Peak District. Each holiday is run by Trust staff and trained leaders, so experience is not necessary – just plenty of energy and enthusiasm! There is a wide variety of holidays for all ages from 17 to 70. For a brochure please call 020 8315 1111 or send two second class stamps to The National Trust, PO Box 84, Cirencester, Glos GL7 1ZP.

Making contact

We welcome contact from our members and visitors and do our best to respond to queries and comments promptly and efficiently.

For further information about specific properties covered in this book and the opportunities and facilities they offer, please contact the relevant Regional Office, for which details are listed on the regional dividers.

General enquiries should be addressed to the National Trust Membership Department, PO Box 39, Bromley, Kent BR1 3XL (tel. 020 8315 1111; fax 020 8466 6824; email enquiries@ntrust.org.uk).

Our London Head Office is at 36 Queen Anne's Gate, London SW1H 9AS (tel. 020 7222 9251; fax 020 7222 5097).

National Trust Countryside Books

The National Trust publishes a wide range of books promoting our work and the great variety of properties in our care. Over seventy exciting titles are currently available and can be purchased through our website at **http://bookshelf.nationaltrust.org.uk**, at National Trust shops, by mail order on 01225 790800 or at good bookshops worldwide. Many of these superbly illustrated books feature some of the Trust's finest coast and countryside properties. Highlight titles include:

Coast with photography by Joe Cornish, Paul Wakefield and David Noton, hardback, £14.99. A stunning glimpse of some of Britain's greatest coastline scenery, from the granite columns of the Giant's Causeway to the great horizons of the East Anglian shore.

Countryside with photography by Joe Cornish, Paul Wakefield and David Noton, hardback, £14.99. A tour of some of the most beautiful places in England, Wales and Northern Ireland, from the dramatic fells of the Lake District to the rolling commons of Surrey.

Landscapes by Margaret Willes, paperback, £4.99. An exploration of how Man has left his mark on the landscape over the centuries to produce the varied countryside that we cherish today. A beautifully illustrated book featuring a range of National Trust properties.

Hadrian's Wall: An Historic Landscape by Robert Woodside and James Crow, paperback, £16.99. The first illustrated scholarly account of one of Britain's most important historic landscapes, examining the impact of human activity in the area.

For a catalogue containing details of all our books, please send a second class stamp to Publications, The National Trust, 36 Queen Anne's Gate, London SW1H 9AS.

THE NATIONAL TRUST ON THE NET

A wide range of information is available on the Trust's main website, which is located at

www.nationaltrust.org.uk

Here you can find updates on the Trust's work across England, Wales and Northern Ireland, together with details of places to visit, access to our on-line bookshop and hotlinks to our two education websites and to our environment and conservation site, which has interesting information on the Trust and wildlife, land use, archaeology and other green affairs! The news is always changing, so be sure to keep up to date by paying regular visits. You can also email us on **enquiries@ntrust.org.uk**

Arlington Court
Devon

This is a large and historic estate in the deeply incised and wooded valley of the River Yeo, with views across to Exmoor and north to the coast. The house was built in the nineteenth century and is surrounded by parkland in which pockets of 'wilderness' were created as part of the original design, contrasting with the extensive mature broadleaved woodlands that adjoin the estate farmland.

There was a medieval deer park here and the woods are ancient semi-natural. As a result the lichen, bryophyte and invertebrate communities are very rich, with many rare species found only in sites associated with the wildwood. The parkland consists of ancient oak, beech and Corsican pine trees, which support rare and nationally important lichens and invertebrates. Shetland ponies and Jacob sheep can be seen grazing in the park.

A lake, made at the same time as the house, is an important habitat for an interesting variety of birds such as teal, pochard and tufted duck.

The Trust is controlling the invasive rhododendrons in the mature oak woods along the valley sides, where there are numerous wet areas, rich in mosses, lichens and ferns. Red deer can be seen grazing in the woodland glades. Many plants and butterflies (including marsh and silver-washed fritillaries) can be seen in the grassy pockets and meadows along the edges of the woods. Pied flycatcher, tawny owl, redstart and treecreeper nest among the trees, and dipper and kingfisher feed along the river. There is a large heronry in the woods near the lake.

[🚶] Grounds open daily during daylight hours; house open seasonally; network of footpaths from house along river valleys; longer walks on west side of river giving views of house; walks to local hamlets, including Loxhore and Arlington Beccott; circular walks; local station at Barnstaple and Barnstaple–Lynmouth bus service.

[P] Car park at house.

[★] NT shop and refreshments; WCs; leaflet; information boards; birdwatchers' hide over lake; limited disabled access.

[▦] 1125 ha (2780 acres) 7ml NE of Barnstaple, off A39.   [180:SS611405]

Avebury
Wiltshire

This much celebrated and impressive megalithic monument, part of the Stonehenge and Avebury World Heritage Site, includes the largest prehistoric stone circle in Europe. Surrounded by an immense bank and ditch, and approached from the south by an avenue of stones, the West Kennet Avenue, the circle partly envelops the village of Avebury, which dates back to Saxon times.

The surrounding landscape, bounded by the sweeping arable fields, grassland and prominent beech clumps of the Marlborough Downs, is strewn with archaeological remains. Largely crossing land owned by the Trust, a network of paths enables these great monuments to be explored without a car. Barrows can be seen nearby on Overton Hill, and there is evidence of prehistoric, Roman and medieval field systems. Among the ancient routes is the post-Roman Herepath and the Ridgeway. Windmill Hill, to the north-west of Avebury, has a famous Neolithic causewayed enclosure on its summit. Also notable is the sixteenth-century Avebury Manor and a seventeenth-century threshing barn.

Most of the land is intensively farmed, although much has been converted to grass. Remnants of chalk grassland on the earthwork slopes support a wide variety of plants such as round-headed rampion, ox-eye daisy, thyme and stemless thistle. The sarsen standing stones are encrusted with lichens, many characteristic of this unusual environment.

[🚶] Open daily; network of paths; stations at Pewsey and Swindon, and bus service from Swindon, Devizes and Salisbury.

[P] Car and coach park; limited parking for cars only at Windmill Hill.

[★] NT shop; restaurant and inn (not NT); WCs (including disabled); Alexander Keiiler Museum contains archaeological displays (free to NT and English Heritage members); walks leaflet pack; children's guide.

[▦] 638 ha (1576 acres) 6ml W of Marlborough, 1ml N of A4.

[173:SU099697]

Bath Skyline   Bath & NE Somerset

Adjacent to Prior Park Landscape Garden, this farmed and wooded landscape is owned by the Trust, the Mallett family and the City of Bath, with the intention of protecting the open skyline above the historic city from development. Celtic field patterns of banks and lynchets can be detected in the surrounding fields, particularly on and around the golf course on Bathampton Down (not owned by the Trust). Limestone walls, hedgerows, scattered trees, pastures and woodland blocks make up this pastoral scene, while steep slopes overlook the valley of the River Avon.

The underlying limestone leads to a great diversity of plants and associated wildlife. Trees on the estate include pedunculate oak, beech, hawthorn, holly, cherry, hornbeam and yew, with woodland plants such as ramson, hart's tongue fern, wood melick, dog's mercury and bluebells. Badger paths dissect some of the woods, and tawny owl, nuthatch, jay, willow warbler and green woodpecker can be seen.

Some of the meadows are rich in flowers, with salad burnet, dwarf thistle, ox-eye daisy, fairy flax, self-heal, cowslip and lady's bedstraw attracting butterflies such as meadow brown and common blue. The field boundaries of hedges and drystone walls are also havens for wildlife.

[⚐] Footpaths and permitted ways; station at Bath (park-and-ride).

[P] Roadside parking nearby.

[★] Walks leaflet; NT shop in Bath.

[▦] 172 ha (424 acres) on Claverton Down, 1ml SE of Bath. [172:ST777630]

Carnewas, Bedruthan Steps (not NT) *and Park Head*   Cornwall

This is a wild, convoluted stretch of coast with dramatic cliffs, isolated rock stacks and secluded coves and beaches. Bronze Age burial mounds, Iron Age cliff castles and prehistoric earthworks scattered along the cliffs and on the plateau of Park Head promontory are evidence of previous civilisations that have defended the forbidding coastline. There are also remains of a nineteenth-century iron mine.

A steep flight of steps is the only descent to the popular beach at Bedruthan, but please note that swimming is not permitted because of dangerous currents. The coast path follows the line of the cliff and passes Diggory's Island, a classic example of a sea stack or pinnacle of rock separated from the mainland.

Wildlife includes grey seals in the secluded coves, marine life in rock pools and seabirds breeding on the cliff ledges. Plants growing in the rock crevices and on the maritime grassland include rock samphire, wild thyme, thrift, kidney vetch and the rare Babington's leek, a tall and striking plant. Gorse scrub is important for birds such as linnet, stonechat and yellowhammer. The cliffline is backed by fields bounded by traditional Cornish hedges of small stones and cushions of thrift and stonecrop.

[⚐] Coast path along the cliffline (part of the South West Coast Path).

[P] Car parks at Carnewas and Pentire Farm.

★ NT shop (originally the counting house for the iron mine) and café; WCs (seasonal); leaflet; information board; emergency telephone at top of steps and in Carnewas car park.

▨ 114 ha (282$\frac{1}{2}$ acres) SW of Padstow, W of B3276, 8ml NE of Newquay.
[200:SW849692 and 845710]

Boscastle Harbour and the Valency Valley Cornwall

Boscastle's position at the end of a sheltered, sinuous channel, one of the few natural inlets in a tortuous stretch of coastline, led to its development as a port serving this remote part of Cornwall. Several of the buildings are owned by the Trust, and it is an area of historic and ecological importance. Beyond the outer breakwater, at certain tides a blow hole throws a plume of spray across the harbour entrance from beneath Penally Point. Iron Age earthworks are visible across the neck of the promontory at Willapark, and there is a nineteenth-century whitewashed look-out tower on its summit.

A path follows the steep, wooded Valency Valley to the church of St Juliot, noted for its Victorian restoration with the young Thomas Hardy as architect. Peter's and Minster Woods, to the south of Newmills, have some interesting ferns and invertebrates under a dense coppiced oak canopy and are an important feeding area for bats.

To the north of the village stand the cliffs of Pentargon, with coastal grassland and heath, and nesting razorbill, guillemot and fulmar. To the south, on Forrabury Common, can be seen surviving medieval strip fields, still in use, with forty-two curving plots or stitches. Traditionally, tenants may crop the stitches individually from Lady Day (25 March) to Michaelmas (29 September), with grazing permitted in winter. The banks between the strips support many species of wild flowers.

Grey seal breed in the sheltered caves along the coast, and there are other important areas of coastal grassland and heath.

⎈ Cliff and valley walks; coastal path leads up from village to headlands; South West Coast Path.

P Car parks at Boscastle.

★ NT shop and information (seasonal); WCs; leaflets; guidebooks; guided walks; viewpoints.

▨ 190 ha (468 acres) 3$\frac{1}{2}$ml NE of Tintagel, on B3263 Bude road.
[190:SX097914]

Branscombe, Salcombe Regis and Sidmouth Devon

Lying within a stretch of Heritage Coast, this area of flat-topped hills, deep-cut valleys leading to the sea, copses and hedges, shingle beaches and thatched buildings is one of the most spectacular parts of the east Devon landscape. On the high ground are pockets of scrub and heath behind cliffs which are unstable and liable to landslip.

The undercliff system, dry calcareous grassland slopes, deep combe sides and marshland pockets are of immense nature conservation importance. A number of rare flowers grow, including Nottingham catchfly, several orchids and a local abundance of blue gromwell. Three species of violet-feeding fritillary butterfly occur, and colonies of the scarce wood white occupy the combe bottoms and adjoining undercliff slopes. A number of extremely rare mining bees occur, making Branscombe a top national site for these insects. The bands of woodland add further diversity, offering a delightful spring ground flora and habitat for numerous small birds. Buzzard soar overhead.

The landscape also contains evidence of past industries, including lime kilns and pits, potato-growing and milling, particularly in Branscombe village where there is an old smithy, baking-room (now a museum) and a gypsum mill (now a café) where traces of a wheel-pit are still visible. The stone quarries at Beer date back to Roman times.

Over the cliff tops towards Sidmouth, Weston Cliff falls away to Weston Mouth, a secluded wooded combe. Salcombe Hill to the east and Peak Hill to the west of Sidmouth are also protected by the Trust. There is a prehistoric enclosure at Berry Cliffs.

[🏃] South West Coast Path linking all Trust properties; connecting paths inland.

[P] Car parks at Peak Hill, Salcombe Hill, Weston Mouth, Branscombe Mouth and in Branscombe village.

[★] NT shop in Sidmouth; leaflet and information panels at Branscombe, Weston Mouth, Salcombe Hill and Peak Hill; information centre at Branscombe Bakery.

[▦] 338 ha (835 acres) S of A3052, 3ml E of Sidmouth.

[192:SY208882 and 148877]

Brean Down   North Somerset

This dramatic headland of hard limestone is joined to the mainland by a narrow neck of low-lying marsh, one of the main landmarks of the Bristol Channel. At one time it was suggested as the point for the proposed Severn Barrage.

The peninsula (designated an SSSI and an SAM) has been used as a site of settlement, ritual and defence for thousands of years. Sites include Bronze Age barrows, Bronze and Iron Age settlements and field systems, an Iron Age promontory fort and a Roman temple. There are also some medieval 'pillow' mounds. The tip of the promontory is dominated by a Palmerston fort built in 1867 as part of the Bristol Channel defences, and there are also some twentieth-century gun emplacements.

The continual process of erosion in the sand cliff adjoining the beach is endangering the Bronze Age and early Christian remains, and blocks have been placed along the beach in an effort to contain the problem. The sand cliff has also revealed evidence of mammals dating from the Ice Age.

The narrow promontory is also of great geological and ornithological interest, and is used as a landing-stage (together with nearby Sand Point) for migrant birds. Oystercatcher and dunlin can be seen along the fore-shore and estuary, and the scrub is important for migrant birds such as thrush, redstart, brambling, redpoll and reed bunting. Resident popula-tions include dunnock, robin, whitethroat and linnet. The south-facing slope is particularly attractive to butterflies, such as chalkhill blue, grayling and dark-green fritillary.

Exposure to wind, rain and salt spray, and the shallow soil, have strongly influenced plant communities. A number of scarce plants occur, often in unusual juxtaposition. Sea lavender and rock samphire grow in the more saline areas. The open grassland supports rare plants such as white rockrose and Somerset hairgrass (which is unique to the Mendip area), as well as more typical calcareous grassland species. Unusual lichens occur on the foreshore rocks.

🚶 2 footpaths with steep steps.

🅿 Car park at Tropical Bird Garden.

★ Information boards at steps and gate.

♿ 64 ha (159 acres) 2ml SW of Weston-super-Mare, S of Weston Bay, via Brean village.   [182:ST297588]

Brownsea Island Dorset

Although located within one of the largest natural harbours in the world, Brownsea Island is far removed from the commercialism of the boating marinas and maritime traffic. Its charm lies in the great diversity of its wildlife and its unusual historical remains.

Expanses of heath are relics of the extensive heathland once wide-spread across the county, and provide a habitat for heathland butterflies such as silver-studded blue, common blue and small copper, as well as for common lizard.

The woodland, which now covers a large part of the island, is a mixture of pine and deciduous trees, in which red squirrel can sometimes be seen.

Part of the island is leased as a nature reserve to the Dorset Wildlife Trust. The heronry is one of the largest in Britain, and many other waders and seabirds are attracted to the lagoon, with great and lesser black-backed gulls, shelduck, curlew, oystercatcher, dunlin, greenshank, avocet, wigeon, teal and pintail. Sandwich and common terns nest on the specially created small gravel islets, and the reedbeds and alder carr attract many small birds, including reed and sedge warblers.

[▲] By boat from Poole Quay, Sandbanks and Bournemouth; private boats may land at Pottery Pier, at the west end of the island; seasonal access to nature reserve; station at Poole and foot ferry from Sandbanks to Poole.

[P] Car parks in Poole.

[★] NT shop; café; WCs; leaflets (including Braille and large print); guide-books; information panels; public birdwatchers' hide with views over lagoons; wheelchair access (paths hilly and uneven); battery cars; baby buggies; nursing parent room; NT holiday cottage.

[▦] 202 ha (500 acres) 1ml SE of Poole, in Poole Harbour. [195:SZ032878]

Buckland Devon

Set within the tranquil valley of the River Tavy, Buckland Abbey has a rich 700-year history dating back to its establishment as a Cistercian monastery in the thirteenth century. In the sixteenth century it was converted to a country house for the Grenville and, later, the Drake families; on display are the period rooms and exhibitions on monastic life, Sir Francis Drake and the development of the estate. There is also a massive barn, other medieval buildings and craft workshops in the ox sheds.

The Abbey stands on the eastern side of an extensively wooded valley, with the ecologically important Fishacre Woods (under the management of the Forestry Commission) stretching for two miles along the western side of the Tavy. In the woodlands of sessile oak the damp conditions are ideal for rare mosses, lichens, liverworts and ferns, with other ground plants such as the great woodrush, bilberry, bluebell, yellow archangel, sweet woodruff and wood anemone flourishing under the dense canopy. The dead wood provides a habitat for many beetles, snails, woodlice and other invertebrates.

Flowers thrive along the side of the streams where there is more light, and the alder carr and marshlands along the alluvial flats are rich in wetland plants, with marsh violet, flag iris, valerian, meadowsweet, sedges and grasses. Butterflies, such as silver-washed and pearl-bordered fritillaries and purple hairstreak, flourish in the glades and along the woodland edges. Buzzard are often seen circling overhead, and blackcap, chiffchaff, willow warbler and wren are some of the many birds nesting in the woodlands.

🚶 Abbey and estate open seasonally and at weekends during winter; walks and circular paths; Forestry Commission paths through Fishacre Woods (not directly accessible from NT property); site steep and difficult for disabled; bus service from Yelverton.

🅿 Car park at the Abbey; special car park for disabled.

✴ NT shop, refreshments; WCs (including disabled); workshops; scented herb garden; audio-visual introduction; education centre; museum with period display rooms; motorised buggy (sometimes) and wheelchairs (for lower floors of house only) available; Braille guide and special leaflet with disabled facilities available on request.

🏞 116 ha (287 acres) 6ml S of Tavistock, 11ml N of Plymouth.

[201:SX487667]

Bude to Morwenstow   Cornwall

The Trust owns three tracts of this dramatic west-facing Cornish coast near the Devon border. Here Celtic Cornwall merges with Saxon England, with small fields bounded by earth banks, old farmsteads, hamlets and isolated churches. Between Henna Point and Higher Sharpnose near Morwenstow the contorted rocks (the cause of several wrecked vessels) form a rugged, uncultivated cliffline of maritime grassland, gorse, heath and woodland, with thrift and other cliff plants clinging to the ledges.

To the south Sandy Mouth, Duckpool and Maer Cliff surround beaches and a boulder-strewn shore with access along narrow lanes. Inland, wild herbs on sheltered grassy slopes and yellow flag growing in damper locations attract a variety of butterflies, including blues, gatekeeper and speckled wood. The heathlands are of particular ecological interest, supporting many insects, and the woodland of the Tidna Valley is renowned for its unusual lichens. Other places of interest include Hawker's Hut, where Parson Hawker (a well-known local figure in the nineteenth century) meditated and wrote his poetry; and St John's Well at Morwenstow.

[†] Difficult to get to by road; narrow lanes; coast path.

[P] Car parks at Sandy Mouth, Northcott Mouth, Duckpool, Morwenstow and Crooklets Beach.

[★] Seasonal refreshments at Sandy Mouth and Morwenstow; WCs at Crooklets Beach, Sandy Mouth and Steeple Point car parks; disabled WCs at Crooklets Beach and Sandy Mouth; viewpoint at Steeple Point; leaflet; information board at Morwenstow.

[▦] 443.5 ha (1096 acres) off A39(T).   [190:SS205153 and 202085]

Castle Drogo and Teign Valley Woods   Devon

This imposing granite 'fortress' was designed by the architect Edwin Lutyens at the beginning of this century. It overlooks the wooded gorge of the River Teign, which flows down from the granite massif of Dartmoor National Park.

Riverside, hilltop and woodland paths lead from the estate. Hunter's Path, following the north side of the Teign, passes through heathland and overlooks the gorge and across to the Iron Age hill fort of Cranbrook Castle (not owned by the Trust). Nearby Fingle Bridge was the site of skirmishes during the Civil War. On the heathy slopes, ivy-leaved bellflower and flax-leaved St John's wort can be found, as well as stonechat and grayling butterfly. The Trust has introduced pony grazing to help counter the development of scrub and to conserve the important heathland. Riverside wet flushes are rich in sedges, *Sphagnum* moss, marsh pennywort and tormentil.

To the south of the river, Whiddon Park House is surrounded by farmland, ancient oak woodlands (once coppiced for tanning bark and wood for local industries such as charcoal) and a medieval deer park, where the remains of a 2.7-metre high granite surrounding wall dating from the sixteenth century, earlier drystone walls and a seventeenth-century deer-culling hut can still be seen. The parkland consists of ancient oak, ash and beech trees set in open bracken and wet grasslands. The woodlands are rich in wildlife and the mature trees within the park support nationally rare communities of lichen and moss.

There are good views across the valley from the outcrops of rock breaking through the dense oak canopy, and many plants typical of these ancient woodlands are found, including greater woodrush, wood sorrel, wood anemone and primrose, with impressive displays of wild daffodil and bluebell in the spring. Species of warbler, treecreeper, pied flycatcher, nuthatch, redstart and tawny owl nest in the woods, and green woodpecker can be seen often eating the wood ants which make movable nests out of piles of twigs and leaves. Dipper and kingfisher frequent the river, and raven nest on the crags of Sharp Tor. Buzzard soar above the valley.

[🚶] Castle open seasonally; paths from Castle Drogo; circular walks starting from Fingle Bridge along and above river valley; other paths to the west; local station at Yeoford and bus service from Exeter.

[P] Car-parking at Castle Drogo, Drewsteignton village and Fingle Bridge, Steps Bridge and south entrance to Meadhaydown Woodland on Dunsford and Drewsteignton road.

[★] NT shop and refreshments at Castle Drogo; WCs (including disabled) at Castle Drogo, also at Drewsteignton and Fingle Bridge; leaflet; viewpoint; fishing by permit only (details from regional office or at Castle Drogo).

[⛺] 247 ha (611 acres) at Drewsteignton, 4ml NE of Chagford, 4ml S of A30 (signposted from A30 at Cheriton Bishop turning and off A382 from Sandy Park); Teign Valley Woods 8ml W of Exeter, 3ml NE of Moretonhampstead, both sides of B3212.

[191:SX725902 and 199:SX802883]

The Cheddar Cliffs   Somerset

Much of the land around one of Britain's most spectacular and popular sights is managed by the Trust for its superb nature conservation interest. The dramatic limestone gorge, famous for its potholes and caves, has evidence of palaeolithic and neolithic occupation. The road winds down between high vertical cliffs, with outstanding views from the top (on a clear day) of the Somerset Levels, the Quantock Hills and across the Bristol Channel to Wales.

The cliffs and scree slopes have recently undergone an extensive rock-safety and scrub-clearance programme, grant-aided by English Nature, to conserve the complex mosaic of open habitats so beneficial to the geological, entomological and botanical interest of this sssi. Specialist plants found here include the famous Cheddar pink (also found in south-east France but nowhere else in Britain), three endemic hawkweeds, and good populations of green-winged orchid and autumn lady's tresses. Also present are butterfly rarities such as green hairstreak and marbled white.

Black Rock and Black Rock Drove are leased to the Somerset Wildlife Trust. A circular walk from the B3135 road at Black Rock Gate passes through plantations, natural woodland and rough downland.

[⅄] Footpath from Black Rock car park to permitted path along top of property down to Cufic Lane; station at Worle.

[P] Car parks at Cheddar end of gorge; small car park at Black Rock.

[★] Local facilities and information at Cheddar; walks leaflets.

[⬛] 174 ha (429 acres) 8ml NW of Wells, on B3135.   [182:ST468543]

Cherhill Down and Calstone Coombes   Wiltshire

This ancient downland landscape overlooks the Vale of Pewsey, with a series of deeply incised sheltered coombes supporting a herb-rich chalk grassland with characteristic clumps of beech trees. At the summit of the chalk ridge is the Iron Age hill fort of Oldbury Castle and the recently restored Lansdowne Monument, built in 1845 by the 3rd Marquis of Lansdowne in memory of the economist Sir William Petty.

A white horse (not owned by the Trust) is carved into the flank of the downland, one of the many man-made features in this striking landscape, which also has Bronze Age bowl and long barrows, a cross-ridge dyke, ancient routeways, tumuli, strip field systems, earthworks and old mineral workings.

The steeper slopes facing the west and south are best for chalkland flowers, with bastard toadflax, burnt and other orchids, round-headed rampion and tuberous thistle. Butterflies include adonis and chalkhill blues, dark green and marsh fritillaries, dingy skipper and brown argus. The uniform mounds left by the yellow meadow ant are typical of a long-unploughed grassland. Skylark and meadow pipit are common in summer, when peregrine falcon may also be seen, and hen harrier and short-eared owl visit in winter.

[⅄] Footpaths and bridleways.

[P] No formal car park.

[★] Local facilities.

[⬛] 204 ha (504 acres) on A4 between Calne and Beckhampton.
                                        [173:SU046694]

Cley Hill　　　　　Wiltshire

This chalk hill, some six miles to the west of Salisbury Plain, consists of unimproved downland of SSSI status which supports a good range of characteristic flora and fauna, including a wide variety of rarer species. It is famous as a habitat of the chalkhill blue butterfly, and several orchids.

Like so many hilltops in Wessex the summit is crowned by an Iron Age hill fort, with two Bronze Age bowl barrows inside. It was the site of an Armada beacon, and there are some medieval strip lynchets and a disused nineteenth-century quarry.

From the summit there are fine views overlooking the Longleat Estate and, in especially clear conditions, towards the Brecon Beacons.

[🚶] Open access; station at Warminster.

[P] Car park.

[★] Information panel; facilities at nearby Longleat House (not NT).

[≗] 27 ha (66 acres) 2ml W of Warminster, N of A362.　　　[183:ST838443]

The Corfe Castle and Purbeck Estate　　　　　Dorset

This extensive estate essentially comprises a section of the Dorset coastline from Poole Harbour to Seacombe Valley, including Studland Bay, Old Harry Rocks, Ballard Down and Belle Vue. It contains an extraordinarily diverse landscape and habitats such as reedbed, saltmarsh, lowland heath, limestone pasture, chalk downland, ancient woodland and ancient commonland.

Studland and Godlingston Heath National Nature Reserve is one of the largest remaining tracts of lowland heath in Britain and home to many endangered heathland species. These include all six species of British reptile, scarce birds such as the hobby and Dartford warbler, as well as a host of Red Data Book insects. Dragonflies are also prominent here. Interesting plants include marsh gentian, sundews and pale butterwort. In winter up to 3000 duck use the Little Sea lagoon and can be watched from the numerous hides.

Corfe Castle Common, one of Dorset's largest traditionally managed commons, has not been ploughed for centuries and has abundant wild flowers, including orchids. It is also the site of several Bronze Age burial mounds. Nearby Hartland Moor lies between the village of Corfe Castle and Wareham. Reminiscent of the New Forest, this extensive tract of lowland heath has deer, ponies and cattle roaming freely. Here the Trust is undertaking an ambitious project to convert 160 ha (400 acres) of farmland back into heath.

The area between Seacombe Valley and Durlston Head contains quarries from which is drawn the famous Purbeck stone, used for centuries both in local houses and in more prestigious buildings such as Westminster Abbey. Many of the quarries remain in Trust ownership and extensive repairs have been carried out to the traditional dry-stone walls which are such a hallmark of the area. Limestone pasture is the dominant habitat and contains many rare species, such as early spider orchid and spring gentian. At Seacombe Valley the traditional pastures are grazed by the Trust's wild herd of Exmoor ponies. Birds on this stretch of coast include puffin, guillemot, razorbill, kittiwake, peregrine and raven, all of which nest on the cliffs.

The chalk grassland on Old Harry, Ballard Down, Ailwood Down and Godlingston Hill is rich in orchids and butterflies, including the chalkhill blue, adonis blue and Lulworth skipper. Ancient barrows dot the top of the ridge between Studland and Corfe Castle. Ailwood Down and Old Harry have some oak, ash and hazel woodland, possibly of ancient origin.

Studland Bay comprises four miles of sandy beach and an extensive area of coastal sand dunes, with smaller areas of saltmarsh and inter-tidal mudflats. The constantly shifting dune complex is one of the largest in England and supports a wide range of vegetation. In winter great northern diver and slavonian grebe can be seen offshore.

[🚶] Network of footpaths; South West Coast Path starts/finishes at Studland; disabled access at Hartland Moor; stations at Poole and Wareham; good local bus service for walkers.

[P] Car parks in Corfe Castle at Castle View and in West Street (not NT); extensive car parks at Studland and small facilities in the villages of Acton and Langton Matravers.

[★] NT shop and café at Studland; NT shop and tea-room at Corfe Castle; leaflets and guidebooks; bird hides at Little Sea and Hartland Moor; information boards at Spyway Farm; dog restrictions apply on Studland beach in summer.

[⛴] 3240 ha (8000 acres), broadly straddling the area between Swanage and Wareham, with access via the A351.   [195:SY959824]

Cotehele   Cornwall

Among the wooded fringes of the River Tamar stands one of the best preserved medieval houses in the country, surrounded by an estate which has substantial remains of a former working landscape centred on a riverside quay. Now renovated by the Trust, with small tea-rooms, a maritime museum and the restored Tamar sailing barge, *Shamrock*, the quay has witnessed the passage of barges carrying various cargoes, from soft fruit grown on the rolling sheltered slopes of the river valley during the late nineteenth century to copper and arsenic from inland mines, and limestone brought in to supply the local lime kilns. Several of these kilns can still be seen near the quayside, and were once an important part of an intensively industrial scene.

In the Morden Valley, close to the quay, are an eighteenth-century corn mill, wheelwrights and carpenter's shops, a cider press, forge and saw pit, plus extensive mining remains in the nearby Danescombe Valley. These all bear witness to what was once a self-contained community housed in small hamlets nearby, such as the small village of Bohetherick which has good examples of vernacular buildings.

Some important wildlife habitats are to be found in this exceptionally mild part of the country. Damp and shaded oak woodlands are of interest, with some areas thought to be ancient woods, and harbouring a rich variety of plants, mosses, insects and lichens. Sparrowhawk, barn owl and lesser spotted woodpecker can be seen. The brackish marsh along Morden Mill stream supports an unusual combination of freshwater and coastal plants, with associated birds sheltering in the reedbeds. The thick hedge banks along the old lanes are lined with wild flowers attracting butterflies and birds.

🛉 House and mill open seasonally; garden open all year; walks throughout the estate; local station at Calstock.

P Car parks at quay and house.

🟊 NT shop at house; gallery on quay; refreshments on quay (all seasonal); WCs (including disabled); limited facilities for disabled (only quay and part of gardens level enough for wheelchairs); leaflet; information board.

🗺 522 ha (1289 acres) on W bank of the Tamar, 2ml W of Calstock by footpath, 9ml SW of Tavistock.   [201:SX422685]

Crackington Haven   Cornwall

On either side of the tiny port of Crackington Haven is a distorted cliffline of fractured rocks (the cause of several shipwrecks) with spectacular fissures, landslips, caves and arches, and geologically important contorted folding visible in the cliff faces.

To the north, Dizzard Point is of note for its wind-clipped thicket of twisted sessile oaks, wild service and holly trees, which struggle to reach a height of six metres. They support an internationally important variety of lichens and mosses. There are many areas of coastal grassland and heath all along the cliffs and undercliffs, which must provide some of the best examples of natural vegetation, unmodified by man, in the South West.

The possible remains of an Iron Age castle can be detected at Castle Point, St Gennys, and there is much of prehistoric interest in the area, with earthworks and barrows, as well as signs of medieval strip field systems, particularly near St Gennys Church.

The headland of Cambeak projects west from Tremoutha Haven and commands outstanding views along the coast beyond the natural rock archway of Northern Door. Behind the coastline, small hamlets and farms are scattered around the valleys. Trevigue Farm is an example of a building style typical to north Cornwall, with its large locally quarried random slates. Penkenna and Castle Point are dominated by heath, with wind-blown shrubs of heather and bell heather attracting linnet, white-throat and stonechat.

[i] Via small roads (crowded in peak season); footpaths along cliffline.

[P] Car parks at High Cliff, Strangles and Rusey Cliff (very limited), and Crackington Haven.

[★] WCs at Crackington Haven; leaflet; information board; viewpoints.

[▣] 329 ha (814 acres), 6ml NE of Boscastle, 8ml SW of Bude.

[190:SX142968]

Crantock Beach to Holywell Bay   Cornwall

Sandy beaches, headlands with deep inlets and collapsed caves, common-land, stream valleys, broad expanses of dunes and the tidal estuary of the Gannel make up this varied and more sheltered stretch of Cornish coast, which is steeped in historic associations and curiosities. The Gannel lies between the headlands of Pentire East and West Points, where sailing vessels used to travel up the inlet with cargoes of limestone and coal. Notable populations of waders and wildfowl can be seen on the saltings and mudflats of the Gannel, part of a complex estuarine and dune habitat; over 700 curlew overwinter here, along with other species such as oystercatcher, lapwing, ringed and golden plovers, turnstone, bar-tailed godwit, redshank, dunlin and heron.

The sand dunes rise to the plateau of Rushy Green, an area of sandy grassland rich in lime-loving plants. Kelsey Head, where the low bank and shallow ditch of a cliff castle can be seen, is backed by a series of historic field boundaries known as the Outer, Middle and Inner Kelseys. Fulmar, shag, herring gull and kittiwake nest along the cliffs of Kelsey Head, an important site for the passage of birds, and many auks, including razorbill and puffin, can be seen just offshore on Carter's Rocks (not owned by the Trust). Fulmar nest on the Chick, off Kelsey Head, and grey seal are found along the coast.

Porth Joke is a beautiful, secluded beach, isolated from the intrusion of cars, and small fields in the Porth Joke valley support a rich variety of flowers and grasses, including one of the most important populations of arable 'weeds' and birds in the county. A walk follows the stream to Treago Mill. The fragile and unstable dune system (the largest within the Trust's Cornish holdings) behind the broad expanse of Holywell Bay is colonised by plants such as sea holly, sea bindweed and henbane, and between the more stable dunes a rich grassland supports many flowers such as thyme, eyebright, cowslip, hairy violet and pyramidal orchid, with butterflies, including the uncommon dark-green and silver-washed fritillaries.

Cubert Common is an undulating stretch of sandy grassland which contains lime-loving plants such as cowslip. There is a fine Bronze Age barrow on the southern side of the common.

[🚶] The Gannel can be reached from road S of Newquay; free access to beach at Crantock; waymarked paths through Holywell dunes; no right of way from Trevemper to Penpol Creek on S shore of the Gannel, but footpath through Treringey to head of the creek.

[P] Car parks at Crantock, Cubert Common, Treago Mill, Holywell and West Pentire.

[★] Seasonal refreshments at Crantock and Holywell; WCs; leaflet; information boards at Porth Joke and Holywell; viewpoint from Kelsey Head.

[!] The Gannel may be crossed at low tide by both tidal bridges between end May and mid-September, in winter by Trethellan Bridge only; crossing at high tide by Fern Pit ferry in summer, otherwise only by rounding from Trevemper; wading is not recommended; bathing is unsafe at the Gannel end of Crantock Beach.

[⊞] 460.5 ha (1138 acres) SW of Newquay, W of Crantock.

[200:TW790610, SW7961 and 7760]

The Dodman and Nare Head   Cornwall

These two prominent headlands between Falmouth and Fowey can be explored on spectacular circular walks with dramatic views of coves, beaches, rock archways and crumbling cliffs covered with relict heath, coastal grassland and scrub. Small marshes and reedbeds in the valleys are the habitat of damp-loving plants such as meadowsweet, yellow flag and sedges, and there are a few areas of unimproved grassland in enclosures with magnificent stone-faced hedgebanks.

Covered with archaeological remains, this unspoilt coastline has a great feeling of history. On Dodman Point a massive earthwork defines an Iron Age cliff castle, and within the enclosure can be seen traces of a medieval strip field system. There are also Bronze Age barrows, a stone cross and an eighteenth-century watch house. Walks radiate from the hamlet of Penare to the Dodman, Hemmick Beach, Vault Beach and Maenease Point.

To the west of Nare Head, Pendower Beach merges with Carne Beach, and the irregular pattern of fields, bounded by traditional Cornish stone walls, extends to the cliff edge. The valley behind Pendower Beach is wooded and can be explored on a sheltered walk. The Trust has worked closely with local tenant farmers to ensure that the modern farming methods on Nare Head do not intrude on this beautiful part of the country.

Near Nare Head can also be found Veryan Castle on the side of a steep valley, an Iron Age settlement on an oval platform cut into the hillside, and Carne Beacon, a Bronze Age barrow. Gull Rock, to the south-east, was the film set for *Treasure Island* in the 1950s, and is now a sanctuary for nesting seabirds, including guillemot, cormorant and shag. Kiberick Cove is backed by landslips, including Slip Field, thought to have moved as recently as the nineteenth century.

[⚇] Nare Head accessible from both sides; network of circular paths at Nare Head and Dodman Point.

[P] Car parks at Nare Head, Carne Beach and Pendower Beach, Penare and Lamledra.

[★] Leaflet; viewpoint path with access for wheelchairs at Nare Head; beaches suitable for families (no steep slopes except at Kiberick and Paradoe coves).

[⚏] 210 ha (518 acres) 10ml SW of St Austell and 4ml S of Megavissey.
[204:SX916370 and SX0039]

Dunsland
Devon

Dunsland is a pre-Norman manor, with a remarkable survival of ancient woodland and pasture, and an interesting ecological system associated with the wildwood. The Tudor house, altered and enlarged in the seventeenth century, was tragically destroyed by fire in 1967 after extensive restoration work by the Trust, but the park still carries the historic interest of the site, one of the best in England for lichens of the Lobarion community.

Outhouses remain, including a coach house, stables and a generator shed. Cadiho Well, a spring covered by a well-head, is where the first Cadiho, the Norman owner of the house, reputedly killed the previous Anglo-Saxon incumbent. There are some overgrown and disused fishtanks (possibly medieval) which now provide a valuable habitat for wildlife.

The present park landscape was planted in 1795, and includes an area of flower-rich grassland, and a pocket of tall plants where the dominant meadowsweet supports a varied population of invertebrates, including damselflies and dragonflies. In the woods, the ancient oak, ash, beech, aspen and willow trees are encrusted with lichens, with many rare species. Broadleaved helleborine can be found in the valley woodlands. Ponds, where willow carr is beginning to be established around the margins, provide a valuable habitat for newts and many invertebrates including springtail.

🚶 Footpaths.

🅿 Car park and informal parking.

★ Local facilities.

🏞 25 ha (62 acres) 4½ml E of Holsworthy, 9ml W of Hatherleigh to N of A3072.   [190:SS409051]

Failand
North Somerset

Situated within an area of small valleys with intervening hills, this rural landscape is characterised by small fields, orchards, sunken lanes, streams and small deciduous woodlands. Despite being so close to Bristol, the area has a wide range of wildlife, and visitors can enjoy some classic walks.

Summer House Wood is one of five main woodlands on the estate and contains some interesting plants, including ragged robin and lady's smock in marshy hollows beside the streams, and rushes, water forget-me-not, marsh pennywort, gipsywort and butterbur on the wooded banks. Another wood, dominated by alder, has a rich flora of marsh marigold, golden saxifrage and rushes. The hedgebanks include plants characteristic of the woodland edges, with herb robert, clematis, hawthorn, blackthorn, red campion and woundwort.

[🏃] Footpaths.

[P] Limited parking.

[★] Local facilities.

[♿] 147 ha (363 acres) 4ml W of Bristol, S of A363, E of Lower Failand, overlooking River Severn.   [172:ST518736]

Fontmell and Melbury Downs   Dorset

This estate covers an important stretch of ancient chalk downland within the Cranborne and West Wiltshire AONB. The downs, which include Fontmell Down, Melbury Beacon and Melbury Down, are cut by steep-sided valley coombes, and the surrounding hamlets have witnessed little change in the land-use pattern over the years. Sheep-grazing continues the traditions of local farming, with cattle in some areas. There is much of historical interest, notably two Iron Age cross-ridge dykes, Celtic field systems, medieval strip lynchets and a Saxon trackway. On Melbury Down is a Bronze Age barrow and an Armada beacon.

Fontmell Down, with its magnificent views over the Blackmore Vale and Cranborne Chase, was bought by the Trust to commemorate the evocative landscapes of Thomas Hardy. It is now partly leased to the Dorset Wildlife Trust. All three downs are of great importance for their butterfly populations.

A great diversity of chalk-loving grasses and flowers reflects the downs' long standing as an area of unploughed and largely unimproved grassland, and species include cowslip, milkwort, stemless thistle, clustered bellflower, horseshoe vetch, bastard toadflax, squinancywort and quaking grass. The wide range of butterflies feeding on the grassland plants includes chalkhill and adonis blues, silver-spotted skipper, Duke of Burgundy and dark-green fritillary.

In places, scrub is invading the downland, with blackthorn and wayfaring trees smothered in wild clematis (old man's beard), attracting many birds. Over fifty-five species have been recorded, including nightingale, grasshopper warbler, sparrowhawk, kestrel and buzzard. The hedgerows are lined with wild arum, primrose, cow parsley, yellow archangel and herb robert.

[🚶] Path from car park.

[P] Small car park at Spread Eagle Hill on B3081.

[★] Facilities at nearby Compton Abbas Airfield; information panels in car park.

[♿] 295 ha (730 acres) 6ml S of Shaftesbury, between Shaftesbury and Blandford.   [183:ST884187]

Fowey and Lantic Bay to Sharrow Point   Cornwall

The Trust owns a number of properties around the historic harbour of Fowey and along the coast to Sharrow Point. On and around the secluded Fowey Estuary they include Gribbin Head with its distinctive daymark, Pont Pill, St Saviour's Point at Polruan, St Catherine's Point which is crowned with a castle (English Heritage), Coombe, a coastal farm west of St Catherine's Point, and Station Wood. The strategic Enterprise Neptune acquisition of Townsend Farm helped to save the valuable landscape by effectively containing the village of Polruan, which was in danger of engulfing this beautiful estuary. Behind St Catherine's Castle is Covington Wood, a hanging wood with many ferns, mosses and liverworts.

This busy commercial harbour includes a mosaic of estuarine and coastal habitats, with scrubby woodlands of oak, ash and hazel growing in old field sites fringing the estuaries, small areas of unimproved grassland, and in places a narrow fringe of herb-rich maritime grassland on the cliffs where thrift, sea campion and ox-eye daisy thrive. Traveller's joy is a distinctive plant of the woodland edge. Along the secluded shores heron, redshank, oystercatcher and occasional kingfisher can be seen.

This is a quiet and gentler coastline of scattered hamlets, sheltered sandy coves and both high and low cliffs which provide a home for raven, peregrine, kestrel and jackdaw. Pencarrow Head separates Lantic and Lantivet Bays, and commands impressive views of the coast. Inland, behind a tiny cove on Lantivet Bay, the isolated hamlet of Lansallos nestles above a wooded coombe. Lanes and paths connect the scattered communities, and the cliffs at Polperro conceal the well-known fishing village, adorned with colourful gardens. Stories of smugglers and maritime tales add to the rich history of this coastal landscape. From Polperro, Downend Point and Hore Point enclose Talland Bay, which is the site of one set of large black and white panels used by the Royal Navy to mark out the length of a nautical mile.

The cliffs in the Pencarrow Head area have a characteristic bevelled profile. Except on the Head itself, they have not been grazed for many years, so that much of the cliff-slope vegetation is dense bracken, blackthorn scrub and even incipient sycamore woodland. Since these cliffs are more sheltered than those on the north coast, maritime vegetation associated with salt spray and wind is found only along the very edge of the coast. There are some interesting features, however. Sand and shingle beaches, including some fine examples of raised beaches (indicating intertidal periods of higher sea levels), have local plants such as sea holly, sea bindweed, sea kale and the nationally rare shore dock. Brackish pools on the wave-cut platform at the foot of the cliffs are also of interest.

Grasslands in the fields above the cliffs have a rich flora which includes wild thyme, pale flax, centaury and the hairy, slender and common bird's-foot trefoils. The striking tree mallow, a Cornish speciality, grows in rough or waste ground along the coast.

Sunken lanes and paths to the beaches were once used by pack horses carrying sand and seaweed up to the fields. Not only was grazing once much more extensive, but so was cultivation: old bulb fields occur at Polperro, now filled with scrub.

🏃 Via small roads; footpath along Pont Pill and at Coombe Haven; Hall Walk opposite Fowey; steep climb down to Lantic Bay; access to Polperro cliffs difficult (narrow path); network of paths linked to coast path and inland.

🅿 Car parks at Coombe, Fowey, Pencarrow Head, Lansallos, Sharrow Point, Hore Point, Talland Bay and Polperro.

★ Local facilities at Fowey, Polperro and Polruan; leaflets; 3 viewpoints at Lantic Bay, also at Nealand Point, Downend Point and Hore Point.

🛏 151 ha (374 acres) surrounding village of Fowey (accessible from both sides of estuary) and from mouth of River Fowey to Looe.
[200:SX127545 and 140510, and 201:SW390525]

Glastonbury Tor   Somerset

Renowned for its ecclesiastical, secular and legendary associations, the unmistakable profile of Glastonbury Tor is a dominant feature in the landscape with splendid views over the Somerset Levels, once a wide area of lake and marshland surrounding the tor. The conical hill, made up of horizontal layers of rock, has been a defensive stronghold throughout history. Built on the site of at least two former places of worship, the fifteenth-century St Michael's Tower on the summit, scheduled as an SAM has now been restored.

On the slopes of the tor, the terraces are the strip lynchets or cultivation terraces of medieval farming (there are fields on the east side of the tor still called Lynches). Wild thyme grows in places on the slopes, and hedgerows, trees and small orchards create cover for a variety of birds.

[i] By foot only from SW and NE; summer park-and-ride from the town.

[P] Limited parking at top and bottom of Wellhouse Lane.

[*] Interpretation panels at both access points; leaflet.

[▣] 29 ha (73 acres) SE of Glastonbury, off A361.   [182 and 183:ST512386]

Godrevy to Portreath   Cornwall

The Trust owns most of the coastline from Godrevy round to Navax Point, east of St Ives Bay, and along the cliffline of Hudder and Reskajeage downs to Western Hill, west of Portreath Beach. The cliffs are high and sheer, and their tops support gorse and some of the best maritime heath in the country, indeed in Europe, with heather, bell heather, western gorse, yellow rattle, sheep's bit, golden rod, devil's bit scabious, betony, dyer's greenweed and the unusual pale dog violet, with many other species. Royal fern, primrose, bluebell and sea spleenwort grow in the cliff gullies and on the rocks. Guillemot, razorbill, fulmar, cormorant and shag breed on the cliffs. The area is rich in wild flowers, and interesting species also occur along old hedgebanks.

The sand dunes at Gwithian (not NT), a place popular with surfers, are known as 'towans', and have preserved a string of archaeological remains of settlements from the Mesolithic era onwards. The more stable dunes, despite excessive pressure from holiday-makers, support a great range of maritime plants such as blue fleabane, sea fern grass, sand cat's tail and field madder.

Behind the coast is the country park of Tehidy Woods, which is managed by the County Council. Other points of interest are an Iron Age cliff castle and localised quarries. Godrevy Lighthouse (not owned by the Trust) was the inspiration for Virginia Woolf's novel *To the Lighthouse*. The local names spell out the curious maritime history of the area (eg Ralph's Cupboard, Deadman's Cove, Hell's Mouth), and the traditional stone walls, gateposts, stiles and buildings all add to the sense of a historical landscape, but sadly the unspoilt nature of the coastline is being affected by the removal of sand and the effects of waste from tin extraction discharged into the river.

🚶 Footpath routes linked with Tehidy Country Park; coast path.

🅿 Car parks at Gwithian, Godrevy, Portreath and along coast road.

★ Seasonal refreshments; WCs; leaflet; viewing platform for disabled at Reskajeage.

⛺ 304 ha (751 acres) N of B3301.   [203:SW651453 to 585423]

Golden Cap   Dorset

This eight-mile stretch of coast, part of the dramatic west Dorset coastline of blue lias clays capped with sandstone, contains the highest cliff on the south coast. At 188 metres, Golden Cap is so called because of the 'cap' of golden sandstone which can be seen on the cliff face.

The estate is made up of a number of long hills, covered in gorse and trees, and incised with coombes which run down to the cliffs. Small fields of mainly permanent pasture and herb-rich meadows are linked by ancient hedgerows. The stone and brick farmsteads and the partly deserted village of St Gabriel's, with the ruins of its thirteenth-century chapel, nestle among these windswept valleys, protected by gnarled hedges and trees.

There are other interesting historical sites, including some Bronze Age bowl barrows on the Cap, a Roman road, medieval pillow mounds, old lime kilns, an Admiralty signal station dating from the Napoleonic Wars and listed farmhouses.

The landscape of undulating hills and valleys is a maze of more than twenty-five miles of footpaths and bridleways, meandering over the gorse and heather, down through some of the most extensive herb-rich neutral meadows owned by the Trust, and along the coastline. In the unimproved meadows plants such as adder's tongue fern, green-winged orchid, dropwort and pepper saxifrage can be found. The scrubby hedgebanks are fringed with flowers and ferns.

The cliffs are highly unstable and decidedly hazardous. They contain a large number of fossils, although their extraction is discouraged. The landslip terraces and dangerous mid-flows along the undercliff sections are important for a great range of specialist insects, mainly beetles, semi-aquatic flies, mining bees and digger wasps, including many national rarities.

Tangled thickets of willow and thorn scrub below the cliffline attract many migrant birds, and pockets of remnant heath provide important habitats for Dartford warbler, stonechat and linnet. There are several small woods with evidence of old ash and hazel coppicing (now being reintroduced) and some ancient boundary banks.

[ℹ] By minor roads; some open access; South West Coast Path; extensive network of footpaths and bridleways.

[P] Car parks at Stonebarrow Hill and Langdon Wood; public car parks at Lyme Regis, Charmouth, Seatown and Eype.

[★] NT shop and WCs (including disabled) at Stonebarrow car park; information panels; viewpoints at Stonebarrow, Langdon and Golden Cap; Dorset Heritage Fossil Centre at Charmouth Beach; fossil code of conduct; base camp for volunteers; camping (tel. 01297 489628).

[⌗] 1011 ha (2500 acres) between Lyme Regis and Bridport, off A35.

[193:SY413931 and 383934]

The Helford River   Cornwall

The estuarine channels and the northern entrance of the Helford River around Mawnan Smith are of great marine ecological importance. The rich, muddy intertidal belt is exposed at low tide, and many birds can be seen feeding on the mudflats, including heron, cormorant, shelduck, mallard, curlew and kingfisher. A network of ancient natural woodlands lines the creeks, with abundant ground flora. From Tremayne Wood, which encompasses Vallum Tremayne Creek, there are attractive views across to Merthen Wood (not owned by the Trust), an ancient woodland of particular interest. Frenchman's Creek also has notable oak woodlands.

Many of these ancient woodlands, with their old boundary banks still visible, have been coppiced over the years for firewood, charcoal, ship-building and bark for leather-tanning. They support a variety of ground plants such as bluebell, bilberry, wood anemone, mosses, ferns and lichens, and many woodland invertebrates, as well as great spotted woodpecker, buzzard and treecreeper. Rosemullion Head has interesting coastal grassland, with early purple and green-winged orchids. The valley garden of Glendurgan lies behind the quiet hamlet of Durgan, and Mawnan Church overlooks the mouth of the river, linked to Rosemullion Head (the possible site of a prehistoric fort) by a footpath. There is a Bronze Age settlement at the Herra, on Gillan Harbour; beyond, on the prominent headland of Nare Point, a redundant 1950s naval tracking station is a rare remnant of the Cold War.

🚶 Access to Helford River by small roads and paths, with several circular paths running inland; network of paths around Mawnan Smith; path from Helford running W to Pengwedhen and Frenchman's Creek; foot ferry from Helford Passage to Helford.

🅿 Car parks at Mawnan Church, Bosveal, Glendurgan, St Anthony-in-Meneage and Helford.

★ Local facilities at Helford, Manaccan, Helford Passage and Mawnan Smith; leaflet; viewpoints.

♨ 332 ha (821 acres) SE of Helston, off A3294, and 3ml S of Falmouth.
[203:SW716130, 204:SW770165, 797278 and 728257]

Hentor, Willings Walls, Trowlesworthy Warrens and Goodameavy
Devon

This area covers a large tract of open moorland above the River Plym, cut by steep-sided brooks and lying within the Dartmoor National Park. Numerous archaeological remains exist, including settlements comprising hut circles and surrounding enclosures, and burial chambers or cists dating back to the Bronze Age. The underlying granite of the Dartmoor massif is visible in this rock-strewn prehistoric landscape, formed through a combination of cooling molten rock, receding seas and weathering.

The distinctive outline of the tors and worked granite blocks dominate the warrens where rabbits were extensively bred for fur and meat from the Middle Ages to the nineteenth century. Lee Moor leat is crossed by stone bridges used by the warreners. Medieval farmsteads can be seen at Hentor and Willings Walls. The area was important for the extraction of high quality granite, and there are old quarries at Trowlesworthy, Dewerstone and Cadworthy Woods, with the remains of old tramways once used for haulage now followed by footpaths.

Heaths occur on the mineral soils and shallow peat, supporting a variety of plants such as purple moor grass, heather, bog cotton, *Sphagnum* moss, lesser spearwort, sedges, bog pimpernel, marsh pennywort and bog asphodel. Goodameavy, to the south west, is an important prehistoric moorland and wooded landscape. Rising above the Plym is the Dewerstone, the highest granite outcrop in the south west. It is surmounted by an Iron Age hill fort and other prehistoric remains. In the woods are many birds such as treecreeper, jay and green woodpecker. Skylark, meadow pipit, wheatear and stonechat can be seen on the moors, with raven, crow and jackdaw inhabiting the rocky outcrops.

The woods are rich in wildlife, and are especially important for the rare mosses and lichens which flourish in the damp air.

🚶 Open access.

🅿 Parking at Shaugh Bridge, Cadover Bridge and Blackerbrook.

★ Local facilities; leaflets.

🛏 1513 ha (3739 acres) reached by narrow minor roads off A38, 6ml NE of Plymouth, 2ml S of Yelverton.   [202:SX575645/600655/615680]

The Holnicote Estate   Somerset

There can be few estates of such landscape variety as Holnicote. The gentle Vale of Porlock, with its fertile farms and attractive villages, separates two dramatic upland areas. To the north, the coastal heathland of Bossington Hill and Selworthy Beacon (305 metres) stretches for three miles between the mouth of Grexy Combe in the east and Hurlstone Point in the west.

The rugged, north-facing cliffs with their 'hog's back' profile fall steeply to the Bristol Channel some 244 metres below. To the south, an extensive stretch of wild heather moorland rises to the skyline, dominated by Dunkery Beacon, at 520 metres the highest point of Exmoor. Virtually the whole of the Horner River system is within the estate, from high-level moorland springs down to the sea. It emerges on Bossington Beach, one of the best examples of shingle storm beach in the country.

One of the largest blocks of entirely semi-natural woodland in England lies on the steep valley sides of the Horner Water. In contrast, nearby are beautiful conifer plantations established by Sir Francis Acland in the 1920s.

Such diversity of land forms ensures a wide variety of habitats, supporting rare and locally specialised flora and fauna. One third of the estate was declared a National Nature Reserve in 1995. The predominantly sessile oak woods of Horner support a lichen flora of international importance; more than 330 types are present, including many rarities. A rich birdlife includes breeding populations of pied flycatcher, wood warbler, redstart and dipper. The open nature of the wood allows the growth of violets, the food plant for an abundance of silver-washed fritillary butterflies.

The vast expanse of heather moorland represents the most important heathland remaining on Exmoor. Plant species of national and regional interest include lesser twayblade, Cornish moneywort, fir club moss, cranberry, crowberry, ivy-leaved bellflower and dodder. The dwarf shrub supports six nationally rare spider species and the largest British colonies of the rare heath fritillary butterfly. Nesting moorland birds include red grouse, ring ouzel, wheatear, stonechat, whinchat, raven and buzzard. Britain's smallest bird of prey, the merlin, regularly nests here. Herds of wild red deer wander freely over the uplands.

Signs of man's early history are evident throughout the landscape in the form of Bronze Age barrows, tumuli, cairns, beacon sites and Iron Age hill forts. The development of agricultural life can be appreciated by the mills and accompanying leats, the dovecote at Blackford, the remnants of old cider orchards, packhorse bridges and signs of the tanning industry in Horner Wood. The estate includes the majority of the attractive stone or colourwashed houses and buildings of Selworthy, Luccombe, Allerford, Bossington and Horner. Over 125 buildings are listed.

[i] Open access.

[P] Car parks and lay-bys on moorland. Car parks with WCs at Horner, Bossington, Allerford, Selworthy and Luccombe.

[★] NT shop and information centre at Selworthy Green; tea-rooms at Selworthy, Bossington, Allerford and Horner; information boards; pack of walks leaflets; educational study centre at Piles Mill (tel. 01643 862452 for information about booking).

[▨] 5036 ha (12,443 acres) 4ml W of Minehead, each side of A39.
[181:SS920467]

Ilfracombe to Croyde   Devon

Despite their popularity as seaside resorts, the coast between Ilfracombe and Woolacombe (mostly in Trust ownership) remains unspoilt. From Ilfracombe the South West Coast Path overlooks the coastline to Morte Point, thought to be one of the most dramatic headlands in the West Country. From Lee Bay the path rises to Damage Cliffs, renowned for its flowering primroses and orchids in the spring and a number of prehistoric remains, including some standing stones on Lee Down. At the top of the Tors Walk is a disused lime kiln, dating from the late nineteenth and early twentieth centuries. There are also signs of medieval strip field systems.

The tranquillity of Combesgate Valley offers a refreshing contrast to the windswept coastline, and the extensive sands of Woolacombe Beach are also sheltered by dunes and grassland where autumn lady's tresses and yellow wort grow (much work has been done to control the erosion caused by walkers, and to rescue the flower-rich grassland by clearing the privet scrub). At Morte Point sea thrift, rock samphire, bird's foot trefoil, heather and plantain grow, and rock pipit, wheatear and stonechat are frequently seen along the cliffs, nesting among the scrub and heath. The uncultivated grassland along the cliff edge supports a wide variety of plant species, with associated insects, and the inlet of Bennett's Mouth is one of an important series of habitats along the Bristol Channel for migrating, breeding and overwintering birds.

Baggy Point, best approached from Croyde Bay, is unlike Morte Point in appearance because of the different rock structure, and its vertical cliffs, popular with climbers, provide nesting ledges for numerous sea-birds, including fulmar, shag and cormorant.

[🚶] Network of walks along coast.

[P] Car parks at Ilfracombe, Mortehoe village, Croyde and Marine Drive, Woolacombe.

[★] Local facilities; WCs by Marine Drive; leaflet; viewpoint; blue flag beach; swimming; climbing; part of coastal path from Croyde car park accessible to wheelchairs.

[▣] 541 ha (1336 acres) NE of Barnstaple, access off A361 Barnstaple to Ilfracombe road, via B3231 to Croyde and B3343 to Woolacombe.
[180:SS443457 (Morte Point) and 432396 (Baggy Point)]

Ivythorn and Walton Hills   Somerset

This wooded, south-facing scarp lies on a ridge known as the Polden Hills, above the Somerset Levels. Walton Hill is covered with an ash-scrub woodland, chalk grassland and oak woodland, probably of ancient origin.

Part of the woodland, an SSSI, on Ivythorn Hill is of particular interest for its ancient oak coppicing, and traditional methods of woodland management are now being reintroduced to maintain the original character of the wood. Standard and mature trees are scattered throughout the coppice.

In the woods there is evidence of badgers, and in pockets of blackthorn on the margins the elusive brown hairstreak butterfly can be seen. Blue-bell, dog's mercury, violet, lords and ladies, primrose and wood aven grow among the trees. There are some old boundary banks in the woodlands.

The woodland merges with scrub and a limestone grassland, rich in flowers and grasses, which provides a valuable habitat for a variety of unusual butterflies among plants such as pyramidal orchid and woolly thistle. In the old and overgrown quarry pits are sheltered corners with lime-loving plants.

⚹ Network of footpaths.

P Car park at Walton Hill; 2 car parks at Ivythorn Hill near youth hostel.

★ Information panels in the car parks at Walton Hill and Ivythorn Hill near the youth hostel.

⬛ 36 ha (88½ acres) 1ml S of Street, W of B3151.

[182:ST466352 and 482346]

Killerton   Devon

Set within the fertile river landscapes of the rivers Clyst and Culm, this large estate encompasses an eighteenth-century house and gardens, deer park and parkland originally designed by John Veitch, the famous nurs-eryman and landscape designer. There is a nineteenth-century chapel. Killerton Clump, a prominent volcanic hill sheltering the house and the site of the Dolbury Iron Age hill fort, is part of the estate. Also of interest is Marker's Cottage, built in the fifteenth century and containing some mid-sixteenth century paintings on a wooden screen. An arboretum is laid out on the slopes, with some rare and unusual trees introduced by Veitch. The surrounding farmland is bounded by hedges and woodland.

White Down Copse was planted in the nineteenth century, and Ashclyst Forest includes ancient woods as well as nineteenth-century plantings on the former open commonland. The woods are now a mixture of broadleaved trees and conifers, with ancient oak pollards supporting rare lichens and invertebrates. Some areas of conifer are being restored to open heath, and other areas are being converted to woodland dominated by oak and ash. Roe deer can be seen grazing in the forest glades. Over thirty-five different species of butterflies breed here, includ-ing many hairstreaks, skippers, fritillaries and browns. Birds such as redstart, wood warbler, woodpeckers, treecreeper and buzzard can be seen, as well as many wild flowers including bluebell, primrose, bugle and orchids.

Forest Cottage housed a gamekeeper in the second half of the century, and other cottages were for the use of foresters. The tracks for shooting were cut between 1876 and 1879.

[↟] Park and garden open all year during daylight hours; house open seasonally; open access to Ashclyst Forest, White Down and Paradise Copse; waymarked trails through forests; footpath through estate and along wooded slopes; stations at Pinhoe, Whimple, Exeter Central and St Davids, and regular local bus service from Exeter.

[P] Car parks at Killerton House, Columbjohn and Killerton chapel; 4 car parks on road running N–S through Ashclyst Forest and Paradise Copse; special parking for disabled.

[⊠] NT shop and refreshments; WCs (including disabled); information centre at house car park; motorised buggies.

[≋] 2585 ha (6388 acres) 7ml NE of Exeter, each side of B3181 Exeter to Cullompton road.   [192:SX977001]

The Kingston Lacy Estate, including Badbury Rings
Dorset

This substantial agricultural estate surrounds the historic seventeenth-century mansion of Kingston Lacy. Located in low-lying chalk downland between the River Stour and its tributaries, the property encompasses fourteen farms, parts of the villages of Shapwick and Pamphill, Holt Heath National Nature Reserve and to the north-west the Scheduled Ancient Monument of Badbury Rings.

The house is set in an eighteenth-century naturalistic landscaped park, where historic records show that there was once a medieval house and deer park. The mature trees support good lichen and inverte-brate communities typical of a long-established woodland site. Small copses and woods are scattered over the farmland, and the marginal woodland belts also include some ancient sites with interesting ground flora.

The slow-moving river is the haunt of kingfisher, mute swan and little grebe, and some of the unimproved riverside meadows on the wide allu-vial plains are rich in wild flowers, with the few remaining areas of permanent pastures providing good feeding grounds for wading birds such as lapwing and redshank.

The chalk grasslands over the Badbury Rings are rich in plants such as the greater butterfly, frog and bee orchids, bastard toadflax, adder's tongue fern and knapweed broomrape, and support a number of butterflies. The Rings themselves form one of the best-known Iron Age hill forts in Britain. The circular, grassy mound with its wooded clump shows signs of the different stages of the fort's construction, with three concentric ramparts and ditches.

Also of historical interest on the estate are some prehistoric round burial barrows, a Roman road and settlement, and evidence of Celtic field systems.

[i] Network of footpaths and bridleways; access to estate all year; house and park open seasonally; station at Poole and local bus service to Wimborne Square.

[P] Car park at house; other small informal car parks around estate; large car park at Badbury Rings.

[★] NT shop and restaurant at house; WCs (including disabled); wheelchair access to garden only; leaflets; dogs allowed on leads in park and on woodland trails; picnics in north park only.

[⬛] 3559 ha (8795 acres) 2ml NW of Wimborne Minster, on each side of B3082 Blandford road.   [195:SY978014]

The Lacock Estate   Wiltshire

Lacock is one of the best-preserved medieval wool villages in England. The cottages, barns and houses vary in architectural styles dating from the thirteenth to the nineteenth centuries, but many have medieval timber-framed cores. The River Avon meanders close to the thirteenth-century nunnery of Lacock Abbey, of which the cloisters still exist and which was converted into a house in 1539 after the Dissolution of the Monasteries. It later became the home of the Talbot family, who gave the Abbey and village to the Trust in 1944. A museum at the Abbey entrance commemorates the achievements of William Henry Fox Talbot, the famous early Victorian pioneer of photography.

The surrounding countryside contains a network of footpaths as well as traces of field cultivation, historic boundaries, pack-horse bridges and features associated with the former monastic communities.

The steep-sided riverbanks, with occasional pollards, are the haunt of kingfisher, dipper and sand martin, and owls, jackdaw, nuthatch and spotted flycatcher can be seen among the ornamental parkland trees around the Abbey. In places, the grassland of Bewley Common supports a variety of plants including yellow rattle and ragged robin.

[i] Abbey open seasonally; museum open daily in season and weekends in winter; open access to village; station at Chippenham and local bus service from Chippenham and Trowbridge.

P Car park; special parking for disabled.

★ NT shop in village; WCs (including disabled) at Abbey; guidebooks for Abbey and village; wheelchairs available from museum.

⊞ 131 ha (324 acres) 3ml S of Chippenham, E of A350.   [173:ST919684]

Lanhydrock   Cornwall

This delightful Victorian house, a Grade I listed building of monastic origins with a seventeenth-century wing and gatehouse, is set in a medieval deer park enclosing remains of the ancient woodland overlooking the valley of the River Fowey. The boundaries of the park can be seen along the Maudlin Valley, and an old gate post on the way to Brownqueen Farm. Station Drive follows the line of the original carriage-drive from Bodmin Parkway Station to the house. A network of paths leads from the shrub gardens of magnolia, rhododendron and camellia through the luxuriant natural woodlands to the river.

Lanhydrock is approached by a famous avenue of beeches and sycamores, some of the latter planted as long ago as 1648. The oak woodlands, together with individual trees within the park, are of great nature conservation importance. Despite recent storm damage, they represent a long history of woodland continuity and support many interesting insects and lichens. The woods are also important for flowers and ferns, including royal fern. Birds include all three species of woodpecker, as well as dipper, grey wagtail, owls (little, barn and tawny), nuthatch and treecreeper. There are badger setts, and otters use the River Fowey.

Evidence of tin-streaming can be seen throughout Higginsmoor.

⚡ Free public access to park; network of footpaths and circular walks; house and garden open seasonally; local station at Bodmin Parkway.

P Car parks at Respryn and Lanhydrock.

★ NT shop and restaurant at house (seasonal); WCs (including disabled); NT regional office within park; information boards in car parks; leaflet; education material; disabled visitors may be driven to house (special parking available through car park attendant).

⊞ 369 ha (911 acres) 2½ml S of Bodmin on Lostwithiel road.

                                              [200:SX085636]

Lanyon Quoit
Cornwall

One of several quoits in the South West, this trio of granite uprights supporting a huge granite slab (the remains of a megalithic chamber tomb dating from 4000 to 3000BC) is one of the most famous prehistoric sites in Cornwall. Rising prominently from the open moorland, Lanyon Quoit was probably the ceremonial tomb for a local community. The stones were re-erected in 1824 after collapsing in 1815.

[†] Short footpath.

[P] Small lay-by beside road.

[★] Leaflet.

[▣] 0.5 ha (1½ acres) 4ml NW of Penzance, 2ml SE of Morvah on N road between Morvah and Penzance.   [203:SW430337]

Leigh Woods
North Somerset

Located on the west side of the Avon Gorge, with the southern portion of the woods a designated National Nature Reserve. The plateau above the gorge is covered by a diverse woodland, comprising a mixture of old pasture woodland with pollards and an area of old coppice with oak standards and an understorey of small-leaved lime and hazel. Two species of whitebeam also occur here. Peregrine falcon and raven nest in the old quarries on the gorge side, which is also home to several notable plant species, including Bristol rock-cress and western spiked speedwell.

The Iron Age fort of Stokeleigh Camp provides excellent views across to Bristol, with the Clifton Suspension Bridge in the foreground.

[†] Network of footpaths.

[P] Car park on neighbouring Forest Enterprise site.

[★] Information panel; leaflet; two waymarked trails.

[▣] 64 ha (159 acres) 2ml W of central Bristol, NE of A369.
[172:ST555730]

The Lizard (East): Lizard Point to St. Keverne
Cornwall

The Trust owns a number of properties along the dramatic coastline of the Lizard, a prominent and broad, flat-topped peninsula which terminates at Lizard Point, the southernmost extremity of mainland Britain.

The Point was acquired through specific legacies and the Enterprise Neptune appeal.

To the east of the Point is a spectacular collapsed sea cave called The Lion's Den. The Lizard peninsula is unique for its complex geology of serpentine, gabbro, granite and gneiss. Serpentine was once worked at Carleon Cove (see below), and there are still stiles made of this smooth, polished rock. The soil overlying these rocks, together with the very mild oceanic climate, result in a flora unlike that of any other in the country. The cliffs in the area have been invaded by the rampant Hottentot fig, imported from South Africa at the turn of the century, which threatens to swamp the finer native plants for which the Lizard is internationally renowned. On Pen Olver is a simple building that was Marconi's experimental wireless station in 1900/1; beyond, on Bass Point, is an 1872 Lloyd's Signal Station.

Cadgwith is a fishing cove with some charming examples of Cornish vernacular buildings (many of thatch in a county where slate is more common) and old pilchard cellars. An unusual wood of dwarf elms, thought to have been planted originally for cheap fuel, covers the promontory to the Devil's Frying Pan, a collapsed cavern through which the sea crashes at high tide.

At the seaward end of the Poltesco Valley, where Babington's leek was first identified, are the ruins of a nineteenth-century serpentine stone-cutting works at Carleon Cove. Further along the coast, on both sides of the tiny harbour of Coverack, are Beagles Point, Chynhalls Cliff and Point, and Lowland Point. Of particular interest are the 'lazy beds' (man-made cultivation ridges in areas of thin or poor soil) in the Downas Valley, the flowers of the maritime heathland on Chynhalls Cliff and the Iron Age cliff castle on Chynhalls Point.

🚶 Coast paths on the Lizard linked to inland paths to Lizard Town and to villages of Cadgwith, Coverack and St Keverne.

🅿 Car parks at Lizard Town (footpath link to the Point), Landewednack Church, Inglewidden, Cadgwith, Poltesco, Coverack and Dean Quarry.

★ Local facilities at Lizard Town, Cadgwith and Coverack; leaflets; information boards; viewpoints.

▣ 317 ha (783 acres).   [203:SW698117 to 803196]

The Lizard (West): from Poldhu Cove to Kynance Cove   Cornwall

The coastline on the west of the peninsula is more exposed than the gentler east side, with rocky coves, sea stacks, blow holes, cliffs and beaches, structures unique to the Lizard of schist, gneiss, gabbro and serpentine. These rocks, the soil derived from them, the oceanic climate and historical land use have led to a remarkable mosaic of heaths, grasslands and cliffs.

The Lizard has been a mecca for botanists for a long time. The serpentine, in particular, supports plant species not found on any other rock type and many not found elsewhere on mainland Britain. The Cornish heath, a robust, bright pink heather found commonly on the heaths, cliffs and hedgerows, is one such speciality. Many other plants are found in the grasslands and heaths, such as kidney vetch, common milkwort, thyme, bloody crane's bill, lady's bedstraw, dropwort, great burnet and burnet rose. The large, uncultivated tracts of heath on the Lizard plateau and cliffs are one of its main features, and one of the largest surviving areas of heathland in lowland Britain.

Heathland plants include bell heather, gorse, saw wort, prostrate dyer's greenweed, heath spotted orchid and devil's bit scabious, as well as the Cornish heath already mentioned. Unusual rushes (such as the black bog rush, and some very rare dwarf rushes), sedges and royal fern can be seen in damp areas, valleys, cart tracks and around pools on the heath. Small migrant birds nest among the thickets of scrub, and the variety of invertebrate species is also of international importance. Much of this heath is now in National Nature Reserves, or is managed primarily for its wildlife and historic landscape value by conservation organisations, and in parts by the Ministry of Defence, who own the largest helicopter station in western Europe at Culdrose.

From the cliffs above Poldhu Cove (which is backed by a series of eroded sand dunes), Guglielmo Marconi transmitted the first wireless message across the Atlantic on 12 December 1901. Further south, Mullion Cove provides a harbour for the local fishing community, where there are good examples of vernacular buildings and an old net store. Iron Age field systems can be seen on the Predannack cliffs, and the farm, with typical vernacular buildings, has field boundaries unchanged at least since the Lanhydrock Atlas of 1695.

The rocky clefts and ledges around Predannack are ablaze with cliff flowers, such as blue spring squill, in April and May, and thrift, sea campion, green-winged orchid, dropwort, kidney vetch and patches of Cornish heath cover the Mullion cliffs. Kynance Cove has been a destination for day trips since the the eighteenth century's fascination for the picturesque. The characteristic, multi-coloured, metamorphic serpentine rocks have been cut and polished for many years, now mainly for the local craft and souvenir industry. The secluded cove is also of great interest to the ecologist for its variety of plants and invertebrates, particularly moths and unusual spiders in the grasslands, and a great range of plants on the cliff edges and in the heath behind.

[🏃] Coast path; linking paths across farmland; path from clifftop car park (past viewpoint for disabled visitors) descends to Kynance Cove via Goose Curtain Brook.

[P] Car parks at Carrag-a-pilez, Poldhu Cove, Mullion Cove, Predannack and Kynance.

[★] Seasonal café and WCs at Kynance Cove and Poldhu Cove; leaflets; information boards; viewpoints (wheelchair access to viewpoint at Kynance Cove).

[!] Care should be taken when bathing at Kynance Cove, which is cut off at high tide.

[♿] 345 ha (853 acres) S of Helston, minor roads off A3083, A3293 and A3294. Kynance Cove 1ml NW of Lizard Town, reached on foot or by toll road (A3083).   [203:SW665199 to 690133]

The Loe and Gunwalloe   Cornwall

Loe Pool is an elongated freshwater lake, the largest natural lake in Cornwall, with flooded river valleys forming creeks round its edge. It is renowned for its populations of water birds, including mallard, tufted duck, mute swan, coot, wintering wigeon, teal, shoveler, red-throated diver and red-necked grebe.

At the mouth of the River Cober where it flows into the lake is Loe Marsh, a rich wetland of alder and willow, which can be crossed by a causeway following a historic route. It provides an important habitat for many invertebrates (particularly damselfly and dragonfly), for marshland birds such as sedge and reed warblers and water rail, and for its variety of wetland plants (yellow flag, valerian, hemlock water dropwort, marsh marigold and many sedges). Gentle wooded slopes partly fringe the margins of the lake, which is separated from the sea by a shingle bar linked to Porthleven Sands. Sea bindweed and sea rocket thrive along the shingle.

To the east the beach rises to a cliffline (with a colony of sand martins) from Gunwalloe Fishing Cove (used by local fishermen), Hazelphron Cliff, Castle Mound and Gunwalloe Church Cove (where there is an Iron Age cliff castle). Other sites of historical interest are Bronze Age barrows on Pedngwinian, the pattern of an ancient strip-field system at Chyvarloe, the fourteenth-century church with detached tower at Gunwalloe and old silver and lead mine workings at Wheal Pool. To the east of the Loe, in the surrounding undulating farmland, lies the Penrose estate, which has had a significant influence on the area with notable plantings of tall palms, tree ferns, bamboo groves and exotic conifers in the nineteenth-century landscaped park.

[⚡] Footpaths round lake, behind shingle bar, and along cliffs beyond Loe Bar to Gunwalloe Church Cove.

[P] Car parks at Helston, Penrose, Highburrow, Degibna, Chyvarloe and Gunwalloe.

[★] Leaflets; information boards; birdwatchers' hide accessible for wheelchairs at Helston Lodge; patrolled swimming at Gunwalloe (summer months); excellent sea fishing from Loe Bar to Gunwalloe; emergency telephone at Bar Lodge.

[!] Bathing, boating and other water sports are not permitted on Loe Pool in the interests of the wildlife. Bathing off Loe Bar is dangerous because of strong currents.

[▦] 629 ha (1554 acres) 2ml S of Helston, 1ml E of Porthleven.
[203:SW645250]

Lydford Gorge   Devon

This well-known deep, wooded ravine in the Dartmoor National Park was gouged out by the erosive powers of the River Lyd, the result of 'river capture', earth movements which diverted the flow of the river. A series of smooth potholes have been carved out by the water, and a tributary stream plunges over twenty five metres down White Lady waterfall, which can be reached by a circular walk returning along a narrow and dramatic path leading to the Devil's Cauldron, a spectacular amphitheatre of rock. Footbridges cross the river, with views of the steep-sided gorge and its mantle of trees enveloped in mosses, lichens and ferns.

The oak woodlands surrounding the river and falls have delightful names indicating their historic origins – Smalland, Lambhole and Old Cleave. Their maturity is reflected in the variety of plants to be seen from the wetter margins to the valley tops. Lady, male and hart's tongue ferns, woodrush, ramson and ivy cover the gorge, as well as more unusual plants such as pink purslane. The rocks and trees are covered with many types of rare mosses, lichens and liverworts. Kingfisher, heron, grey wagtail and dipper feed along the river, and the great spotted wood-pecker, treecreeper, pied flycatcher and nuthatch can be seen among the trees.

The nearby village of Lydford with its castle is of interest as a 'burh' dating from the time of King Alfred. The remains of the Anglo-Saxon town bank, an earth rampart, and a Norman fort embankment can be seen. There is a disused railway line to the south.

[🚶] Entrances at Lydford Bridge and on Brentor road (seasonal opening); stations at Okehampton and Bere Alston; local bus service to Lydford.

[P] Car parks at both entrances.

[★] NT shop; refreshments; WCs; leaflet; guidebook; viewpoint.

[!] The gorge is often slippery and steep in parts; stout footwear essential and unsuitable for disabled visitors.

[⬛] 47 ha (117 acres) W of Lydford village, off A386 Okehampton to Tavistock road.   [191 and 201:SX509846]

Lynmouth: Watersmeet and Countisbury   Devon

This is an extensive and varied property around the deeply incised valleys of the East Lyn River and Hoar Oak Water, descending from Exmoor to the sea near the Somerset border. The fast-flowing peat-stained rivers, waterfalls and steep hillsides covered with oak woodlands are within Exmoor National Park.

The coastline is backed by open hill country, and the uncultivated cliff edge of heath, gorse and grassland contrasts with the agricultural land. Foreland Point is Devon's most northerly point, and site of the Foreland lighthouse. The land rises inland to over 300 metres at Countisbury Hill above the hamlet with its charming stone buildings, while to the east of Chubhill Combe, above the sheer cliff tops, a predominantly oak wood-land covers the coastline.

Of archaeological interest is the massive earthwork on Wind Hill, known as Countisbury Camp. There are also prehistoric barrows on Countisbury Common, and a standing stone, possibly Bronze Age, west of the footpath crossing Myrtleberry North Camp. The latter, together with Myrtleberry South Camp, is the remains of Iron Age enclosures. Lloyds Signal Station, on Butter Hill, is now used to house electrical equipment and as a shelter for walkers. Other interesting historical features are the two disused nine-teenth-century lime kilns which can be seen at Watersmeet.

The woodlands are of particular ecological interest, with birch, rowan and ash among the sessile oak, as well as a number of scarce trees including some species of whitebeam (*Sorbus devoniensis, S. subcuneata* and *S.vexans*). The flora is rich and varied with some unusual plants such as Irish spurge, Wilson's filmy fern, wood vetch, wood stitchwort and nettle-leaved bellflower. Ferns and rare woodland mosses and lichens thrive in the moist and unpolluted atmosphere, and the woods provide important cover for buzzard, redstart, pied flycatcher and wood warbler. Woodland butterflies are common along the paths and in openings among the trees, and dark-green fritillary can be seen on the bracken-covered slopes. In July silver-washed fritillary feed on the brambles.

On the deep river pools and waterfalls a keen eye may spot dipper, grey wagtail, kingfisher and salmon.

🚶 South West Coast Path; network of paths along coast and inland; high-level paths above valleys.

🅿 Car parks at Watersmeet, Hillsford Bridge, Countisbury, Lynmouth and Barna Barrow.

⭐ Shop; refreshments; WCs; leaflet; information point and self-service restaurant at Watersmeet House (seasonal opening); viewpoints; fishing permits obtainable locally; riding; Exmoor base camp (used for conservation projects and holidays) at Countisbury.

🏞 607 ha (1500 acres) E of Lynmouth, each side of A39, access from A39.
[180:SS7449]

The Mendips: Crook's Peak, Wavering Down and Shute Shelve Hill   Somerset

On the western slope of the Mendip Hills, this extensive area of downland rises above the Somerset Levels. The Trust owns the southern steep slopes, coombes and spurs of this rolling limestone landscape, which is an SSSI and has been grazed for centuries as commonland, largely by sheep. As well as the grassland, habitats include heathland, woodland and scrub, containing an immense variety of wildlife.

The open grassland is rich with flowers and herbs such as thyme, stem-less thistle and rock rose. Butterflies include both small pearl-bordered and dark-green fritillary, as well as brown argus. Pockets of heathland occur over leached soil, and here the plants differ from the limestone grassland with bell heather, heather, tormentil and heath bedstraw. The craggy outcrops support some delightful ferns, including the maidenhair spleenwort. Glow-worm beetles prey on the abundant snail population.

Among the woodlands are an unusual pocket of yew on Cross Plain, and signs of a long history of land use within King's Wood, a notable ancient woodland site, such as old pollards, boundary banks and a characteristic association of plants and invertebrates. There are some magnificent small-leaved lime trees and an exceptionally rich ground flora, including toothwort, sanicle, yellow archangel, woodruff, bluebell, ransom and dog's mercury. Birds such as the green woodpecker, buzzard, blackcap, chiffchaff and cuckoo can also be seen.

[†] Footpaths; bridleways; West Mendip Way crosses site.

[P] Small car park at Kingswood and limited parking along Webbington Road.

[★] Local facilities; leaflet; interpretation panels.

[▲] 293.5 ha (725 acres) 10ml SW of Weston-super-Mare, off A38 on minor roads.   [182:ST422561]

Montacute   Somerset

This manorial estate is dominated by a grand Elizabethan house built of warm yellow stone. The historic parkland surrounding the well-documented house and formal gardens includes St Michael's Hill (the 'pointed hill' or *mons acutus* that gave the house and village its name) with the gatehouse of a former twelfth-century priory at its foot (not owned by the Trust) and an eighteenth-century 'pepperpot' tower on its summit, the remains of a mill, a copse and some post-medieval field patterns which have now been modified by modern agricultural practices. Old fish ponds can be seen near Abbey Farm.

There are ancient woodlands around St Michael's Hill, and interesting lichens on the parkland trees.

[†] Park and St Michael's Hill open all year; house open seasonally; walks in park and to St Michael's Hill; Ladies' Walk; nearest stations at Yeovil Pen Mill, Yeovil Junction and Crewkerne.

[P] Car park.

[★] Facilities at house; WCs (including disabled); leaflet; dogs allowed in park on leads.

[▲] 123 ha (303 acres) 4ml W of Yeovil, S of A3088, 3ml E of A303.
                                          [183 and 193:ST498170]

Pepperbox Hill   Wiltshire

Located at Brickworth Down, a chalk ridge above the River Avon, this hill is named after the seventeenth-century folly on its summit. The curious Jacobean tower was possibly built to provide ladies with a viewpoint from which to follow the progress of falconry and the hunt. The hill commands spectacular views across to Hampshire and the Isle of Wight.

It is one of the few downs where juniper thrives (attracting some special insect fauna such as the juniper shield bug), and is of much wildlife interest in the mixture of wood, scrub and grassland. In addition to juniper there is much whitebeam, dogwood, hawthorn, wayfaring tree, yew, guelder rose and wild privet. White and broadleaved helleborines are found in the areas of beech.

Seven species of orchid grow on the chalk grassland, with greater knapweed, dropwort, field fleawort and chalk milkwort, and the large numbers of butterflies and moths include the chalkhill blue and brown argus. Corn bunting, quail and nightingale may be seen or heard, along with other summer migrants such as chiffchaff, blackcap and garden warbler. Dormice occur.

There are remains of Celtic field systems, with downland banks and lynchets.

[🏃] By track.

[P] Car park.

[★] Information panel; view finder.

[⛰] 29 ha (72 acres) 5ml SE of Salisbury, N of A36.   [184:SU212248]

Plym Bridge Woods   Devon

These luxuriant oak woodlands border the River Plym and contain fascinating industrial archaeological remains to the north of Plym Bridge, many dating from the seventeenth century when the area was exploited for tons of slate cut from the exposed rock. Quarries, spoil heaps and the remnants of now disused modes of transport (including stone sleepers which are evidence of early tramways) litter the woods, creating new habitats for wildlife but hidden dangers for visitors.

The present bridge over the Plym was built in the eighteenth century over the remains of an earlier one damaged by flood, but there is known to have been a bridge here – for centuries the lowest crossing point of the river – since 1238. A disused railway line, now used as a cycleway, runs from Plymouth to Tavistock, and there is a weir on the river.

The woods are at their best in spring when a carpet of flowers covers the ground before the dense canopy casts its shade. Wood anemone, bluebell, wild garlic and primrose are common. Foxglove flourish in openings where the disturbance of quarrying has created ideal growing conditions, and mosses, woodrush, lady and male ferns, St John's wort, red campion and toadflax also occur. The clean atmosphere and continuity of woodland here encourage the growth of rare lichens. In the lush vegetation mammals and birds thrive, with lesser spotted woodpecker, marsh tit, redstart, pied flycatcher, nuthatch and treecreeper. Heron, wagtail and dipper breed along the river, and the woods are known for moths and butterflies with fritillaries, hairstreak and peacock. Damselflies and dragonflies settle on the reeds and grasses along the riverside.

[🚶] Extensive network of paths, including cycle path.

[P] 2 car parks including one in former quarry.

[★] Waymarked trails; information board at southern entrances to property; bathing and picnics along river.

[✉] 77 ha (190 acres) 3½ml NE of Plymouth, via minor road between B3432 roundabout and B3416.   [201:SX522595]

Polzeath to Portquin Bay   Cornwall

This property covers six miles of the dramatic coastline between New Polzeath and Port Quin, incorporating the headlands of Pentire and the Rumps, and the smaller promontories of Com Head, Carnweather and Doyden Points, and overlooking Padstow Bay at the mouth of the Camel Estuary. Sheltered bays and coves provide access to the foreshore with its rock pools and lichen-clad rocks. The small fields are bounded by characteristic Cornish hedges of herringbone-pattern stone filled with earth, and the lanes are bordered by primrose, bluebell, pink campion, stitchwort and hogweed. The precipitous cliffs provide ledges for nesting seabirds such as fulmar, gull and cormorant, and the short turf of the clifftops, kept smooth by grazing sheep recently reintroduced by the Trust, is studded with spring squill during May, followed by a carpet of sea thrift, sea campion, stonecrop, violet, thyme and kidney vetch.

The unmistakable outlines of elaborate Iron Age defensive earthworks span the neck of the Rumps, and old lead mines and waste tips near Pentireglaze bear witness to the later industrial exploitation of the area's mineral wealth. Lundy Bay is the site of the natural rock archway of Lundy Hole, one of the many distinctive features of the coast, and is bordered by thickets of hawthorn, blackthorn and gorse scrub which provide ideal nesting habitats for birds such as stonechat, linnet, wren, finch and thrush, and shelter for many butterflies, including green hairstreak and speckled wood.

There are many vernacular buildings in the area, some with slate-hung walls, as well as a Gothic tower on Doyden Point and a Bronze Age bowl barrow (burial mound) visible from the cliff path at Pentire Haven. Other barrows are on farmland and are protected from the plough.

⊞ Coastal footpath linked by network of paths across farmland, including good circular walks.

P Car parks at New Polzeath, Pentireglaze lead mines, Pentire Farm (limited), Port Quin and Lundy Bay.

★ Local facilities at Polzeath; leaflet; information board; viewpoints along coast.

⊞ 293 ha (723 acres) 6ml NW of Wadebridge, off A39.   [200:SW968805]

The Quantocks: Beacon Hill and Bicknoller Hill
Somerset

These hills form an area of open moorland, rising from 150 metres to 300 metres at the northern end of the Quantock Hills AONB. The land is dissected by three major east-west running combes: Long Combe, Bicknoller Combe and Weacombe Combe, the last two with small streams and adjacent wet flushes. The hill slopes have a covering of bracken with scattered hawthorns and other woody species. The open summits are heath-dominated, either by vigorous dwarf shrub heath or grass heath.

The whole property lies within the Quantock Hills SSSI. It is a fine example of semi-natural landscape supporting a community of four characteristic dwarf shrubs (heather, bell heather, bilberry and western gorse) together with associated plants such as dodder and green-ribbed sedge. Red deer are common, with upland birds such as meadow pipit, stonechat and raven.

This magnificent walking country offers splendid views over the Bristol Channel, the Vale of Taunton Deane, the Brendon Hills and Exmoor. A fairly rich scattering of archaeological sites includes Bronze Age bowl barrows on Beacon Hill and an Iron Age enclosed camp at Trendle Ring.

☒ Open access.

🅿 Car park at Staple Plain.

★ Information panel; other local facilities.

🏢 291 ha (720 acres) ½ml S of West Quantoxhead, off A39. [181:ST116411]

The Roseland Peninsula   Cornwall

Curving round St Mawes Harbour and overlooking the historic town of Falmouth, the Roseland Peninsula is a delightful blend of beaches, cliffs, creeks, woods and farmland, and ideal for circular walks. The former strategic importance of St Anthony Head is apparent from the numerous military associations and remains. The Armada was sighted from here, and the headland was fortified during the Napoleonic Wars. St Anthony Battery was the site of a late nineteenth-century gun emplacement, later to be used during both World Wars. After 1945 this area had become overgrown with impenetrable scrub, but following major restoration work in 1997 a new walk and wheelchair path have been created in the 'rock-cut-ditch', giving access to the wartime observation post and a newly constructed bird hide.

Seabirds nest along the craggier cliffs, and towards the cliffline the grasslands are at their most colourful in May and June with sea thrift, sea campion and other maritime species. The stretch of coast south of St Just-in-Roseland as far as Newton Cliffs is included in the Candidate SAC which protects some unusual calcareous seaweed known as maërl. Footpaths skirt the sinuous creeks of the picturesque Percuil River, some of which were exploited in the Middle Ages as tide mills. The cliffs of Porthmellin Head, on the seaward side of the indented headland, are bordered by the beaches of Towan and Porthbeor.

☒ Network of footpaths; foot ferry from St Mawes to Place (1ml); path to St Anthony Head with access for wheelchairs; path to viewfinder; observation post; birdwatcher's hide.

🅿 Car parks at Portscatho, Porth, St Anthony Head, St Mawes, Castle Point, Percuil and St Just.

★ WCs at Portscatho, Porth, St Anthony Head, St Mawes Castle and St Just; leaflet; viewfinder; picnics.

🏢 243 ha (600 acres) 10ml SW of Tregony (by road), 2½ml E of Falmouth (by ferry).   [204:SW8632]

St Agnes and Chapel Porth   Cornwall

From St Agnes Beacon, a heather-covered ridge between the coast and the village of St Agnes, there are spectacular views along the coastline. The tall chimneys, miners' trackways and remains of engine houses at the head of tin and copper mine shafts bear witness to the centuries of industrial exploitation of the area. The remains of Great Wheal Charlotte, Wheal Coates and the engine house of Towanroath stand proud against the cliffline, and the rocks, home of basking adders and lizards, are pitted with a honeycomb of mine shafts.

The scarred landscape is now softened by the purple, green and brown hues of the heath, which is of very great wildlife importance, with herbs and flowers such as the pale dog violet, spring squill and bloody crane's bill flourishing near the cliff edge. Grey seal and basking shark can be seen around the coastline, and birds such as fulmar, razorbill, guillemot and gannet nest in the cliffs. Rare and localised plants can be seen at Chapel Porth (where the remains of the eleventh-century chapel still exist), with lime-loving plants such as cowslip at Mulgram Hill.

A number of heathery mounds on St Agnes Beacon are Bronze Age burial mounds, and the remains of a small Iron Age cliff castle adorns the promontory of Tubby's Head. Traditionally, bonfires were lit on the Beacon for celebrations or as a warning signal. South of Chapel Porth, ancient field patterns are masked by heather and taller vegetation inland. Chapel Coombe, a sheltered valley with willow, gorse and elder, attracts birds and butterflies (clouded yellow, painted lady and common blue).

[🚶] Network of paths; South-West Coast Path.

[P] Car parks at Chapel Porth, St Agnes Beacon and Head.

[★] Seasonal refreshments and WCs at Chapel Porth; viewpoint from St Agnes Beacon; leaflet; information boards at Chapel Porth and Wheal Coates.

[⬛] 173 ha (428 acres) W and NW of St Agnes.   [203:SW710504]

Salcombe (East): Mill Bay to Prawle and Woodcombe Point   Devon

Overlooking the picturesque harbour of Salcombe, the coastline to the east of the Kingsbridge Estuary extends from Mill Bay round a dramatic series of points to Prawle Point, the southernmost tip of Devon and used as a coastal lookout.

To the west, Maceley and Elender coves are shielded by the rocky headland of Gammon Head, which commands superb and unspoilt views along this Heritage Coastline. The jagged cliffs, the rocks encrusted with orange, black and yellow lichens, are ideal for birdwatching, with seabirds such as fulmar, kittiwake and gull nesting along the undisturbed stretches. (The stepped appearance of this part of the coast is the result of the lowering of the sea level, with the 'steps' being the ancient clifflines and the level land raised beaches.)

The cliff edges beyond the bounds of cultivation support a mosaic of herb-rich grasslands, heath, gorse and thorn scrub, with sea thrift, campion, rock samphire, bloody crane's bill, spring and autumn squills, rock spurrey, stonecrop and kidney vetch. Prawle Point is an extremely important landfall site for migrating birds, and is very popular with ornithologists. The rare cirl bunting breeds in the area. Butterflies include the dark-green and small pearl-bordered fritillaries.

Of interest is a Bronze Age wreck (classified a historic wreck) which has been identified off the coast. A circular whitewashed stone lookout hut stands on Gara Rock, and ancient field boundaries, defined by upright slabs of rock, can still be seen. Rickham Common Entrenchments are defensive earthworks with the remains of a gun battery.

[†] Network of paths and lanes for circular walks.

[P] Car parks at East Portlemouth, Rickham Common, Gara Rock Hotel, Prawle Point and East Prawle.

[★] WCs at East Prawle; leaflet; swimming at Mill Bay and Sunny Bay off Limebury Point.

[⚓] 243 ha (600 acres), access via minor roads from Kingsbridge or by ferry from Salcombe.   [202:SX740375]

Salcombe (West): Bolt Head to Hope Cove   Devon

To the west of Salcombe, at the mouth of the Kingsbridge Estuary, the Trust owns six miles of rugged coastline consisting of a series of headlands and coves extending to Hope Cove.

The maritime history of the area is reflected in the local names, and over forty vessels have been wrecked along the coastline, including a four-masted Finnish barque, which struck the Ham Stone and which can sometimes be seen in the sands of Starehole Bay.

Sharp Tor is succeeded by the more prominent Bolt Head, an important location for seabirds such as fulmar, kittiwake and gulls. Bolt Head and the Warren are rich in butterflies, including colonies of silver-studded blue. A path leads inland along the sheltered Starehole Bottom, where damp hollows harbour plants which include hemlock water dropwort, hemp agrimony, angelica, marsh St John's wort, marsh pennywort and lesser spearwort. At Bolberry Down, ancient field patterns are defined by slabs of rock containing plates of mica. The path continues to Bolt Tail, a spectacular headland complementing Bolt Head and the site of Bolt Tail Camp, an Iron Age promontory fort. Another site of interest is a mound of earth and stone, known as Grant's Grave since the eighteenth century.

On the cliffs the rocks and scree are important for rare lichens, and the coastal heath habitat supports a variety of plants such as sea thrift, sea campion, rock samphire, bloody crane's bill, spring and autumn squills and kidney vetch, as well as many ants, grasshoppers and beetles. Butterflies flourish, and skylark, great spotted woodpecker, willow warbler, chaffinch, stonechat, linnet and whitethroat are seen.

🚶 South Devon Way along coast linked to inland paths; circular routes around Bolt Head and Starehole Bay.

🅿 Car parks at Overbecks Museum, Soar Mill Cove Hotel and Outer Hope.

★ Local facilities at Salcombe; NT shop, refreshments and displays about local natural history at Overbecks (seasonal opening); leaflets; viewpoints from headlands; path suitable for wheelchairs from Bolberry Down.

📧 427 ha (1055 acres), 7ml S of Kingsbridge, off A381, access on minor roads.   [202:SX725360 to 668397]

Saltram Park   Devon

A welcome green island in Plymouth's grey sprawl, this estate provides a vital open space for visitor and local alike. It comprises almost 200 hectares of parkland surrounding a prestigious eighteenth-century mansion and garden, located near the tidal creek of the Plym Estuary.

The estuary is a regionally important site for its winter population of waders, which include black-tailed godwit and the occasional avocet, along with large flocks of dunlin, curlew and redshank. These and many other species can also be seen on Blaxton Meadow saltmarsh project at the northern end of the estate. The amphitheatre, a relic of the opulent Georgian past, is located along the riverbank with Saltram Wood as magnificent backdrop. Blaxton Quay is also of historical interest.

Dotted around the rest of the park are various habitat types from ponds to butterfly meadows, including mixed woodlands. Mature oak and sycamore in the parkland carry a rich lichen flora.

[🏃] Network of footpaths; cycle track starts at Saltram and leads up the Plym Valley to the southern reaches of Dartmoor; house open seasonally; no public right of way; local bus service from Plymouth.

[P] Car park.

[★] NT shop, restaurant and other facilities in house; dog restrictions in some areas (dog waste bins also installed).

[▦] 190 ha (470 acres) 2ml W of Plympton, 3½ml E of Plymouth between A38 and A379.   [201:SX520557]

Southdown Cliffs, Coleton Fishacre, Dartmouth and the Dart Estuary   Devon

The Trust acquired these properties as a result of the Dart and Start Bay Appeal and Enterprise Neptune, in order to protect the valuable coastline on either side of the Dart Estuary.

To the west of the ancient town of Brixham, a series of promontories shelter sandy bays, and the unstable cliffs of Southdown and Woodhuish are covered with scrubby vegetation, ideal for small migratory birds. Plants include sea campion, thrift, rock samphire, heather and autumn squill.

The garden of Coleton Fishacre, sheltered in Pudcombe Bay, is run by the Trust and open to the public, and the Trust also owns a string of woodland properties along the east side of the estuary, including Long Wood, a typical Devon oak woodland with evidence of traditional coppicing, once used for the tanning industry and the production of charcoal. Bluebell, dog's mercury, ramson and ferns flourish, and several of the woods contain active badger setts. The hedgerows around Brownstone and Coleton are rich in flowers such as primrose, red campion, cow parsley and honeysuckle.

There are some disused lime kilns in the area, as well as remains from the Second World War.

Scabbacombe Head, with its more jagged rocks, attracts large numbers of seabirds with fulmar, gull, shag and cormorant nesting on the ledges where the outcropping rocks are covered with lichens, including some rarities. The dramatic headlands of Outer and Inner Froward Points overlook Mew Stone, another haven for seabirds and seals. The Trust has introduced pony grazing to the clifftop grasslands at Froward Point, which has greatly enhanced the nature conservation interest by countering the invasion of rank vegetation.

Overlooking the east bank of the Dart Estuary, the Trust also owns much of the coastline along the western approach to Dartmouth. Dyer's Hill is a steep wooded rise where an old rope walk (with remains of the rope works) passes through the dense sycamores. Gallant Bower is also a wooded mound with good views of the Britannia Royal Naval College and crossed by a network of paths. On the summit can be seen the earthworks of a Royalist fort built in 1645. The surrounding woodlands are varied and include some mature oak, sycamore and ash. The ground flora includes bluebell, ramson and dog's mercury.

Dartmouth Castle (English Heritage) defends the restricted harbour entrance, and on Blackstone Point, now the site of the coastguard lookout, is a seventeenth-century gun battery.

A path leads along the Little Dartmouth cliffs from Blackstone Point around Compass Cove to Warren Point, and visitors may notice the stone gate-posts, a characteristic feature of the south Devon landscape.

🚶 By foot from car park at Sharkham Point (not NT); network of definitive and permitted paths along coastline, estuary and inland; network of paths linking properties to Warren Point; footbridge across deep gully at Compass Cove.

🅿 Car parks at Coleton Barton, Woodhuish, Sharkham Point (not NT), Dartmouth and Little Dartmouth.

★ Local facilities; NT shop in Dartmouth; WCs at Dartmouth Castle; leaflets; viewpoints.

❗ Informal parking causes congestion so please use car parks.

▣ 531 ha (1313 acres) $\frac{1}{2}$ml S of Brixham, N of Dart Estuary, 3ml S of Dartmouth, E of Little Dartmouth.

[202:SX927540 and 878506 to 880490]

Stonehenge Down   Wiltshire

The famous and well-chronicled circle of ritual standing stones, owned by the State and under the guardianship of English Heritage, is the focal point of the surrounding open downland. A substantial part is owned by the Trust and forms part of a designated World Heritage Site. Over a period of time, the Trust intends to return arable fields to pasture, as a more appropriate setting for the many prehistoric monuments.

The area is an internationally important prehistoric landscape, containing monuments such as the Cursus and the Stonehenge Avenue, neolithic long barrows and large numbers of Bronze Age barrows – many in distinct groups.

At present just over half of the estate is under cultivation; there are some relics of chalk grassland in the enclosures around the barrows which support a variety of wild flowers such as clustered bellflower, rock-rose, small scabious, stemless thistle and cowslip. The seventy acres of nineteenth-century woodland plantations provide useful habitats for resident birds, including the sparrowhawk, a local speciality, as well as badger and roe deer.

[🚶] 8 miles of permitted paths; bus service from Salisbury to Stonehenge.

[P] Car park.

[★] English Heritage shop; refreshments; WCs (including disabled); archaeological walks leaflet available from information point in car park and NT shop in Salisbury; 12 information panels.

[⛭] 582 ha (1438 acres) 1–3ml W of Amesbury, at junction of A303 and A360.   [184:SU123425]

Stourhead   Wiltshire

Situated below the escarpment of the Wessex chalk plateau, Stourhead is famed for its fine house and classic eighteenth-century parkland and garden, with many beautiful features including lakes, bridges and temples.

Although much of the planting dates from the eighteenth century, there are some remnants of the medieval 'Forest of Selwood' and wood pasture, part of the old manorial estate, which are particularly important for the diversity of their plants, birds, invertebrates and lichens. Wood-cock, green and great spotted woodpeckers, jay, nuthatch, treecreeper and chiffchaff are common.

The lakes and ponds, lying on a natural springline, create valuable wetland habitats, attracting birds such as great crested grebe, coot, tufted duck and mute swan. The upper pond is good for dragonflies.

The formal landscape, an AONB, merges with the wooded ridges and valleys, many with ancient woodland sites and rich in wildlife. Overlooking the estate, White Sheet Down and Hill (now in part a nature reserve, SSSI and the site of a neolithic causewayed camp, Bronze Age barrows and Iron Age hill fort) are important tracts of chalk grassland which harbour many notable snails, butterflies and grasshoppers. The southern and south-western slopes have the most interesting flowers, with cowslip, clustered bellflower, thyme, ox-eye daisy and several orchid species. Butterflies include marbled white, and chalkhill and adonis blues.

Other points of interest are an Iron Age hill fort in Park Hill Woods, some Celtic and medieval field patterns with strip lynchets and pillow mounds, and Pen Pits, small quarries once used for grindstones and whetstones.

[i] House open seasonally; garden open all year during daylight hours; local stations at Gillingham and Bruton and bus service from Gillingham.

[P] Car park.

[★] NT shop; inn and restaurant; WCs (including disabled); garden accessible to wheelchairs and path round lake (very steep in places); Wiltshire Trust for Nature Conservation leaflet, general leaflet and guided walks leaflet; guidebook available at information centre; base camp.

[▣] 1070 ha (2645 acres) at Stourton, off B3092, 3ml NW of Mere on A303.
[183:ST779340]

Tintagel   Cornwall

Tintagel stands on a dramatic coastline of headlands and cliffs, with castles, ancient field systems and relics of a former slate-quarrying industry. Tintagel Castle has a literary association with the Arthurian legends and is a popular place for holidaymakers. There is a Norman church at Glebe Cliff.

To the north, the neck of Willapark is backed by the defensive ditch and rampart of an Iron Age cliff castle, and there is also an old lime kiln. The outlines of ancient field patterns or lynchets can be traced at Bossiney Common to the east. Barras Nose, a headland overlooking Tintagel Castle, was bought by the Trust in 1897 after a local appeal instigated by the plans to build the massive King Arthur's Castle Hotel nearby. Remains from the Dark Ages on Tintagel Island, still owned by the Duchy, are under the guardianship of English Heritage.

Impressive rock fissures can be seen along the Glebe cliffline, where there is evidence of old slate quarrying in which the rocks were cut by men lowered precariously over the cliff edge. The quarried stone was used locally to build cottages with traditional slate walls, or 'hedges', constructed in a chevron design or 'curzyway'. The relics of this once industrial landscape are now colonised by a rich variety of wildlife, including coastal grass and heathlands with thrift, sea campion, rock samphire, dyer's greenweed, kidney vetch, wild carrot, betony and many other species. Grey seal breed along the rocky shore, and seabirds include shag, guillemot, fulmar and razorbill.

⚡ Coastal footpaths and connecting paths; bus service from Bodmin, Bude and Wadebridge.

P Car parks at Bossiney, Tintagel Church and Trebarwith Strand.

★ Youth hostel; local facilities at Tintagel, Bossiney and Trebarwith Strand; leaflet; information boards at Glebe Cliff and Trebarwith Strand; viewpoints.

⬛ 81 ha (200 acres) off B3263, S of Tintagel village.   [200:SX056884]

Trelissick   Cornwall

Trelissick is famous for its large garden with many rare sub-tropical plants, but beyond the bounds of the formal garden are parklands and areas of broadleaved woodlands covering the steep banks and shores overlooking the creeks of the Fal Estuary and Falmouth Harbour. Evidence of oak coppicing is common throughout the woods (the bark was used for tanning leather and the wood for charcoal). The dead wood, glades, clearings and small wetlands make a rich and diverse habitat. The lichens and invertebrates associated with the older oaks are particularly important and provide evidence of continuity of ancient woodland and wood pasture. Wet ground in the Lambsclose Plantation includes royal fern, a characteristic plant of wet woodland, heath and flushes.

As well as oak, other trees such as ash, pedunculate oak (a sessile oak), hazel, holly, beech and hawthorn can be seen. Birds include the great spotted woodpecker, nuthatch, jay, chaffinch and treecreeper. Pipistrelle and brown long-eared bats roost and feed in Lodge Plantation, and the plants of Namphillow Wood include primrose, lesser celandine and bluebell. South Wood is rich in a variety of woodland plants (bluebell, herb bennet, cow wheat and ferns) as well as remnant heathland plants. Soft shield fern grow at the head of Lamouth Creek.

The estate is bounded by Lamouth Creek to the north and Channels Creek to the south, estuarine habitats which add to the ecological interest of the area. The wooded edges of the creeks provide ideal platforms for kingfisher feeding on small fish, and curlew, redshank, greenshank, oystercatcher and shelduck feed on the mudflats exposed at low tide. Historical and ecological records reveal evidence of ancient woodland, fragments of which have been modified by later planting of conifers. Also of historic interest is the well-preserved promontory fort of Roundwood at the junction of Cowlands and Lamouth Creeks.

⚡ Garden closed in winter, but walks in park and woodland accessible throughout the year; circular walks; stations at Truro and Perranwell, and bus service from Truro.

P Car park.

✖ NT shop (with plant sales) and restaurant; WCs (including disabled); batricar; leaflets; exhibition gallery; programme of theatrical and musical events (details from Property Manager or regional office).

🚈 162 ha (400 acres) 5ml S of Truro, on both sides of B3289, above King Harry Ferry.   [204:SW837396]

Wembury Bay and the Yealm Estuary   Devon

The secluded Yealm Estuary lies to the east of Plymouth and round the headland of Heybrook, sheltering the villages of Newton Ferrers and Noss Mayo. The mouth of the estuary is protected by the Trust, but Great Mew Stone, within Wembury Bay (one of the first voluntary marine nature reserves) is now owned by the Ministry of Defence.

To the west, a path leads from Wembury along the High Cliffs to Warren Point, commanding beautiful views of the estuarine landscape which includes wooded slopes, open farmland, sheltered creeks, cliffs and rocky coves. To the east, the Warren, as its name indicates, was once associated with the breeding of rabbits for fur and meat (the Warren Wall and Warren Cottage can still be seen). The Revelstoke Drive (built a century ago) follows the coastline through woodlands and along the clifftops from Noss Mayo round Gara Point to Stoke Point.

Points of interest include Wembury Mill, now converted to a café, the miller's house which is let as holiday accommodation, and Gunrow Signal Station, situated on the scenic cliffs above Revelstoke Drive.

The estuaries, where the river waters meet the sea, are rich habitats for wildlife, with waders such as redshank and greenshank sheltering and feeding along the tidal coves. Winter visitors include great northern diver. The woodlands, extending from Noss Mayo to Mouthstone Point, are also of interest, dominated by mature oak, sweet chestnut and beech. The clifftops include grasslands where autumn squill, kidney vetch, rock rose and thyme flourish. Cirl bunting can sometimes be seen. The Warren abounds with butterflies, including dark-green fritillary and grayling.

Wheatear occur, with stonechat and other small birds frequenting the gorse and scrub.

[†] Coastal path linked to inland routes (easy walking with few steep sections); circular routes from Noss Mayo; foot ferry across the estuary in summer.

[P] Car parks at Wembury, Stoke Point and Warren (Noss Mayo).

[★] Shop at Wembury; WCs and refreshments at Wembury Beach and Noss Mayo; leaflet.

[!] Dogs restricted on Wembury Beach from May to September.

[▣] 370 ha (915 acres) 5–6ml E of Plymouth, access to W of estuary from Wembury village, E via Noss Mayo.   [201:SX530480]

The West Dorset Hill Forts: Pilsdon Pen, Lambert's Castle and Coney's Castle   Dorset

West Dorset is renowned for the series of Iron Age hill forts which dominate its steep greensand hills. Pilsdon Pen (the highest point in Dorset), Lambert's Castle and Coney's Castle all provide superb views over the Marshwood Vale to the sea, and the three hills are covered with a mixture of heath, scrub, grassland, woodland and wet flushes which create a diverse landscape rich in wildlife.

At Pilsdon Pen the wet flushes, typical of the greensand, contain bog asphodel, bog pimpernel and heath spotted orchid among the many damp-loving plants. Within the ramparts of the Iron Age hill fort are the banks of medieval pillow mounds (rabbit warrens).

At Lambert's Castle a mixture of woodland, heath, scrub, hedgebanks and flushes provides a variety of habitats. Wood warbler, nuthatch and redstart are among the many birds that nest in the woodland. Medieval field systems can be seen, as well as the site of a post-medieval fair and a telegraph station.

Damp-loving plants also thrive in springs and flushes at the foot of Coney's Castle.

[†] Network of footpaths.

[P] Car parks at all 3 sites.

[★] Local facilities; interpretation panels at all 3 sites.

[▣] 120 ha (297 acres) 3ml SW of Broadwindsor and 5ml E of Axminster.
          [193:SY414012, 366988 and 372975]

West Exmoor Coast: The Heddon Valley, Woody Bay and the Hangman Hills   Devon

On the western extremity of Exmoor National Park, this property contains some of the most beautiful features of the North Devon landscape, with heather moorland, cliffs, deep wooded combes, narrow lanes and isolated hamlets. The precipitous cliffs, designated Heritage Coast, are the highest in England and are the classic example of 'hog's back' cliffs. Guillemot, kittiwake, fulmar, razorbill, jackdaw and raven inhabit the cliffs.

The Little Hangman and Great Hangman, Holdstone Down and Trentishoe Down together form an extensive and important tract of coastal heath. In late summer these hills are transformed by the colours of the flowering heathers and gorse. Stonechat, linnet, tree pipit, wheatear and whinchat thrive on the heaths. Miners' tracks can be seen crossing the Great Hangman, where manganese, silver, iron and copper were once extracted. There is also an old iron mine (and two prehistoric hut circles) on Holdstone Down. Trentishoe Barrows are two prehistoric burial mounds.

The hanging oak woods (with old ash pollards) and meadows of the deep Heddon Valley are a pleasant surprise for those walking the South West Coast Path. Important ferns, mosses and lichens flourish in the woods, which harbour many birds such as redstart, pied flycatcher, wood warbler, and lesser spotted and green woodpeckers. Buzzard are often seen circling overhead. The meadows along the bottom of the valley are important for wetland flowers, and are home to a multitude of butterflies, including Britain's three large fritillaries, the silver-washed, dark-green and the rare high-brown.

The cove of Heddonsmouth is flanked by screes, a remnant of the last Ice Age, and to the east, beyond the waterfall of Hollowbrook and Highveer Point, secretive Woody Bay is clothed with oaks. Disused post-medieval lime kilns can be seen at Woody Bay and Heddonsmouth, and there is a path leading from Woody Bay to the Roman signal station on the knoll above Martinhoe. Thanks to the Enterprise Neptune appeal, the Trust now owns over forty per cent of the coastline in Devon. Woody Bay was one of the first of these acquisitions in 1967.

[⚐] Network of paths along coast and valleys; circular walks of varying lengths from Hunter's Inn; South West Coast Path.

[P] Car parks at Combe Martin, Holdstone Down, Hunter's Inn, Trentishoe Down, Martinhoe and Woody Bay.

★ Local facilities; WCs opposite car park at Hunter's Inn; leaflet;
information centre and shop in Heddon Valley; viewpoints from Highveer
Point to Woody Bay (good views across to South Wales); dogs to be
kept on leads at all times.

▣ 460 ha (1136 acres) on N Devon coast between Ilfracombe and Lynton,
access from A399 and from narrow minor roads N from A399 and A39.
[180:SS565477 to 675487]

West Penwith: Botallack to Penberth   Cornwall

This is one of the most exposed and windswept areas of the Cornish coast,
where cliffs, headlands and secluded coves overlook the Atlantic Ocean to
the west and are backed by a historic landscape of lanes, fields and scattered hamlets to the south.

From the prominent rocky headland of Kenidjack, north-east of Cape
Cornwall (donated in 1987 by H. J. Heinz Ltd in association with the
World Wildlife Fund), the Trust owns a number of separate properties of
great archaeological and ecological interest. Coastal grasslands and
coastal and inland heaths provide much of the latter. The strongly
maritime heath shows interesting 'waved' formations, due to constant
exposure to the prevailing winds, and provides a base for plants such as
heather, bell heather, western gorse, tormentil, common milkwort, heath
bedstraw, gorse, spring squill, heath spotted orchid, sedges and grasses.
On the seaward slopes sea campion, thrift, scurvy grass, buck's horn
plantain, rock samphire and sea beet can be seen.

The coastline is also important for seabirds, with kittiwake, guillemot,
razorbill, fulmar, shag, cormorant and oystercatcher present. Buzzard,
peregrine and kestrel can be seen hunting, and lapwing, corn bunting
and the scarce nightjar are also present.

The well-preserved engine houses scattered over the landscape date
back to the region's more recent tin-mining history (the Levant engine
house is a notable example). Beneath the ground there is a maze of
tunnels, galleries and chambers. The sheltered Priest's Cove has been a
landing place for centuries. Chapel Carn Brea, the first and last hill in
England, is clad with heath and many archaeological remains. At Carn
Gloose is the entrance to a Bronze Age grave. Pedn-mên-du is a historical
coastguard look-out and signalling headland. Maen Castle is thought to
be the earliest Iron Age cliff castle in West Penwith.

Further to the south, the granite cliffs east of Pedn-mên-an-mere have been eroded to an unusual block-shaped formation. Treen Cliff rises above the beautiful sandy cove of Pedn-vounder Beach, and Penberth Cove has been a productive fishing harbour for centuries. The slopes of the Penberth valley are covered with minute meadows or 'quillets', many now overgrown with scrub, which were once used for growing violets and daffodils for market.

[⚡] Network of footpaths along coastline.

[P] Car parks at Botallack, Cape Cornwall, Chapel Carn Brea, Sennen, Treen and Porthcurno.

[★] WCs at Sennen, Porthcurno and Treen; leaflet; information points at Botallack Count House and at Mayon Cliff lookout, above Sennen.

[♨] 486 ha (1200 acres), access via St Just on B3071 or Land's End on A30.
[203:SW351319]

West Penwith: St Ives to Pendeen   Cornwall

This is a remote and unspoilt coastline of coves, headlands and rocky cliffs and plateaux towards the western extremity of Cornwall. The stunning ancient landscape of prehistoric field systems has seen relatively little change over the centuries. Its archaeological and wildlife value is now protected, not just by the Trust but also by the designation of West Penwith as an Environmentally Sensitive Area, in which farmers are encouraged to conserve historic features and farm in traditional ways.

Prehistoric cliff castles can be seen at Gurnard's Head and Bosigran. Tin-mine engine houses, such as the one at Carn Galver, and other industrial remains in the Porthmeor Valley punctuate the farmland. Unimproved cliff and commonland provide habitats for a wide variety of wildlife. Grey seal inhabit the coastline, and manx shearwater, gannet, guillemot and kittiwake can be seen along the cliffs.

There are rich bogs, mires, stream sides and small wooded valleys of great ecological importance, such as the lower Treveal Valley, where dense scrub provides resting cover for migrating birds, as well as nesting sites. Many plants of interest are found, with purple moor grass, rushes such as the black bog rush, St John's wort, southern marsh orchid and royal fern (in damp areas). Large Cornish 'hedges' or walls border the small, irregular fields, and headlands are capped by rocky granite tors. Zennor Head, a prominent granite point, is reached from the village of Zennor and is bordered by the characteristic ancient field patterns. From the summit of Carn Galver there are splendid views of the ancient landscape of small fields, narrow lanes, scattered farms and isolated cottages. Below Carn Galver the field patterns of Rosemergy provide an excellent example of an Iron Age radial field system.

🚶 Network of footpaths along coastline.

🅿 Car parks at Wicca, Zennor and Carn Galver.

★ Viewpoints; leaflet; information centre at the Wayside Museum in Zennor.

🏞 890 ha (2200 acres) N of B3306, W of St Ives.

[203:SW498411 to 415365]

Abinger Roughs, Piney Copse and Netley Park
Surrey

These three North Downs properties, which include a farm and some cottages, are part of the Surrey Hills AONB and characterised by sloping wooded ridges overlooking valleys to the north.

Abinger Roughs, above the hamlet of Abinger, is an area of woodland with scrub, grassland and plantings of beech and conifers. The oak, birch, beech and pine woods, with several fine old trees, provide habitats for many birds including great and lesser spotted woodpeckers, nuthatch, treecreeper and wood warbler.

Netley is made up of grazed parkland, pasture and woodland, while Piney Copse is a mixed wood. Netley Park contains small areas of unimproved grassland and some fragments of ancient beech woodland along the chalk ridge which support a ground flora of spurge laurel, wood melick, wood sedge and nettle-leaved bellflower.

- 🚶 Network of footpaths.
- 🅿 Car park at Abinger Roughs.
- ★ Local facilities; information boards; nature trail.
- ⊞ 219 ha (541 acres) 7ml W of Dorking, and 11ml W of Dorking, off A25.
[187:TO111480]

Bembridge and Culver Downs
Isle of Wight

Located at the eastern end of the beautiful Isle of Wight, these downs (an SSSI and AONB) are dominated by the chalk ridge which runs across the island from east to west. The sheer cliffs rising out of the English Channel are used by nesting birds, and are of great geological interest.

The remainder of the property includes areas of chalk grassland on the slopes and ridges of Bembridge and Culver downs, and areas of agricultural land. A mile to the north is Bembridge Windmill (also owned by the Trust), the only one on the island and an example of a tower mill, and also of interest is the nineteenth-century Bembridge Fort, commissioned by Lord Palmerston's government as part of the south-coast defence system (not open to visitors), and two late nineteenth-century gun emplacements at Culver Down. There is also the impressive stone column of the Yarborough Monument (not owned by the Trust).

The flora is varied and the downs support both chalk and natural grassland communities, although some areas of downland have been agriculturally improved. The high exposure factor ensures that many plants occur only in stunted form. None the less, a wide range of chalk specialists is found, such as yellow-wort, horseshoe vetch, squinancy-wort and lady's bedstraw. The insect fauna is restricted by the windswept conditions, but includes the chalkhill blue butterfly and various uncommon beetles. Scrub pockets provide a useful breeding habitat for several species of small bird. The coastal landslip known as Redcliff is home to the rare Glanville fritillary and burrowing bee wolf.

⊞ Open access to downs; coastal path; local station at Brading; no access to fort.

P Car park at Bembridge and Culver downs.

✦ NT shop at Bembridge Windmill (seasonal opening); leaflet; display.

⊞ 42 ha (104 acres) 2ml E of Brading, off B3395.   [196:SZ624860]

Black Cap   East Sussex

This property straddles one of the most important sections of the South Downs AONB and from the 'Cap' plantation on the top of the ridge there are magnificent views across the Wealden Basin and over the undulating slopes and combes behind Brighton. To the south-east, the Ouse river valley can be seen as it winds down to the sea.

An ancient bostal (downland track) leads up the characteristic north-facing scarp slope of herb-rich chalk grassland and scattered scrub. In spring and summer the tussocky sward supports a varied community of plants, including musk and fragrant orchids, field scabious, round-headed rampion, marjoram and various species of vetch. The mixed scrub is alive with birds such as goldfinch, song thrush, corn bunting and, in autumn and winter, redwing.

The gentle south-facing dip slopes, once ploughed, are now grazed by cattle and sheep in order to maintain the conditions under which the local flora best thrives. A dew pond was restored as part of the National Trust's centenary project and has been naturally colonised by an interesting array of insects, including many dragonflies and damselflies. This new environment also provides an excellent bathing and feeding ground for birds such as chaffinch and yellowhammer. Of historical interest are the Bronze Age burial mounds that are scattered on the brow of the hill.

Hidden behind the scarp slope is Ashcombe Bottom, a secluded and peaceful woodland containing ancient oaks and coppiced hazel. Clumps of dog violet, bluebell and early purple orchid can be seen in spring, before the bracken fronds grow tall. A network of rides and footpaths leads through the woodland to hidden grassy glades, home to butterflies and other insects.

[†] Open access; footpaths from Lewes and B2116; South Downs Way runs adjacent to property.

[P] Very limited roadside parking on B2116.

[★] Local facilities in Lewes.

[⚓] 252 ha (623 acres) 2½ml NE of Lewes off B2116 Offham to Plumpton road, East Sussex. [198:TQ374125]

Black Down and Marley Common   West Sussex

Part of the greensand ridge of the north Weald, at 280 metres Black Down is the highest point in Sussex, forming a prominent landmark for miles around and commanding good views across the well-wooded landscape of the Weald. The plateau was once an extensive heath created by grazing and managed as common pasture with bracken cut for bedding and fuel collected from the woodland fringe (which contains some old wood pasture). Marley Common lies below Black Down and is a mixture of wood and heath. Pine and birch scrub is currently being restored to heathland to benefit specialised wildlife.

The Victorian Poet Laureate Lord Tennyson was inspired by the landscape and built his house on the shoulder of the down.

The main summit area and other relict areas of heathland are dominated by heather and bell heather, with wetland plants such as cross-leaved heath, round-leaved sundew and common and hare's tail cotton grasses. The old woodlands include Quellwood Common in the south, part of an ancient wood pasture, with oak, beech and holly woods to the south-east. Pine woodland dominates the remainder of Black Down, with rowan, birch, gorse, bramble and bilberry.

Birds include nuthatch, woodcock, nightjar, crossbill, meadow pipit, linnet, yellowhammer and green, great and lesser spotted woodpeckers. There is a strong invertebrate interest, centred on the bogs, dry heathland and older woodland areas. On its north side, the open meadows and parkland of Valewood Park, with its pattern of small fields, trackways and banks, offer a contrast to the woods of Black Down.

Of historic interest are old chert (local sandstone) quarries on Black Down, and some hammerponds at Shottermill, used for milling corn. Woodland coppices produced charcoal to supply the ironworks.

⊞ Network of footpaths and bridleways.

🅿 Car park off Tennyson Lane; informal parking.

★ Local facilities.

▣ 391 ha (965 acres) 1ml SE of Haslemere.   [186 and 197:SU922308]

Bookham and Bank's Common   Surrey

This large area of wooded commonland is linked by a network of ancient routes, footpaths and bridleways, and covered by extensive patches of mature woodland. Its history dates back to at least AD666, when the manor is known to have been owned by Chertsey Abbey, and the commons are listed in the Domesday Book as providing pannage (the right to graze pigs on acorns) for the monks.

The woodland contains many very fine ancient oaks, and a varied range of other trees with shrubs as younger 'infill'. Rich grasslands, a series of ancient ponds and a fragment of heath also occurs. Common grazing ceased in the 1940s, but has recently been re introduced to part of the property.

It is renowned for its insect life, which has been well studied and includes many national rarities, especially beetles and flies. Insects new to Britain have been discovered here. Many notable butterflies, including purple emperor and white admiral, can be seen in the semi-natural woodland, with birds such as nightingale, great spotted woodpecker, great, long-tailed and marsh tits, treecreeper and nuthatch.

The ancient ponds, once used by the monks of Chertsey Abbey for storing fish, are an important habitat for palmate, great crested and smooth newts, with many frogs and toads. Ditches and streams support wetland plants such as water mint, bur reed, horsetail, water figwort, gipsywort, meadowsweet, great hairy willowherb and marsh woundwort, and purple moor grass and heather grow on a pocket of heathland near the ponds. Some of the grassland is dominated by rushes and bracken.

⊞ Network of footpaths and bridleways; station at Bookham.

🅿 4 car parks.

★ Leaflet; information boards.

▣ 183 ha (452 acres) 3ml W of Leatherhead, just N of Bookham station.
[187:TQ130557]

Box Hill Surrey

Located on a prominent chalk scarp overlooking the River Mole, this important SSSI (and proposed SAC) is cut by a number of dry combes to make up the attractive 'karst' or limestone scenery, a rare feature in southern Britain. The hill is named for the box trees, native to the site, and the prolific yew is also distinctive, especially on the steep slopes of the scarp. Much of the high beech wood was destroyed in the storms of 1987 and 1990, but natural regeneration and the programme of replanting will ensure the continuity and richness of the associated wildlife.

The chalk grasslands contain many characteristic plants and invertebrates, including several scarce species. Over a dozen species of orchid have been recorded, and at least 400 species of other plants. More than two-thirds of the current species of British butterflies are found on the hill, relying on key larval plants such as horseshoe vetch, bird's-foot trefoil, hairy violet and sheep's fescue.

The areas of box harbour the rare Box Hill bug, and the pockets of juniper attract the juniper shield bug. The many species of molluscs and beetles, some listed as rare or endangered, are indicators of the antiquity of parts of the woodland. Scrubby areas of dogwood, wayfaring tree, yew, ash, birch, box and spindle create ideal nesting sites for many smaller birds, and there are many birds of prey such as sparrowhawk, kestrel and tawny and little owls. Kingfisher and grey wagtail can be seen near the river. Mammals include badger, roe deer, fox, yellow-necked mouse, weasel and the ubiquitous rabbit.

The hill has been a centre for field study since Victorian times, and now has the Juniper Hall Centre on the site. It also has literary associations, with visitors from John Evelyn and Celia Fiennes to John Keats, Jane Austen and George Meredith, and provided a hiding-place for refugees from the French Revolution. The recent purchases of nearby Chapel Farm and Box Hill Farm have added a much-needed landscape 'buffer zone' and important extra wildlife interest.

Also of interest are some prehistoric tumuli, field systems, the Roman road of Stane Street and the Box Hill fort, built in 1899.

- [🚶] Network of footpaths; North Downs Way crosses property; stations at Boxhill & Westhumble and Dorking, and bus service from Leatherhead.
- [P] Car parks.
- [★] NT shop; WCs (including disabled); leaflets for self-guided walks; information centre; maps in car parks; guidebook; North Downs

countryside pack; educational pack; viewpoint; level walk from car park to viewpoint and beyond for disabled.

⬛ 386 ha (954 acres) 1ml NE of Dorking, 1½ml S of Leatherhead, E of A24.

[187:TQ1751]

Bramshaw Commons   Hampshire

This very extensive network of manorial wastes and commons within the boundaries of the New Forest includes Cadnam and Stocks Cross greens, and Bramshaw, Cadnam, Furzley, Half Moon, Penn and Plaitford commons. The New Forest, a Royal Forest established in the eleventh century by William the Conqueror, evolved with its own charter for enclosure, cultivation, hunting, grazing and commoners' rights.

Of interest are two Bronze Age cairns on Plaitford Common, and a twin-bowl barrow on Furzley Common.

The manorial wastes, usually heathland, provided the commoners with timber, fuel and other useful commodities. Today they represent the best surviving example of lowland heath and mire in Europe, still managed by the common grazing of ponies, pigs, donkeys, cattle and sheep.

The Bramshaw heaths and mires are among the most important in the New Forest. The flora is very rich, and includes large populations of penny royal and small fleabane; long-leaved sundew, marsh St John's wort and bog asphodel occur in the mires. The dry heaths are particularly good for Dartford warbler and woodlark. The invertebrate fauna is extremely rich: the rare fairy shrimp occurs in a seasonal pool; there is an impressive list of solitary bees and wasps; there are some scarce dead-wood beetles along the wood pasture fringes; and standard heathland butterflies such as grayling, green hairstreak and silver-studded blue occur. The commons also provide a habitat for the scarce blue-tailed damselfly, raft spider and grasshoppers.

🚶 Open access; station at Southampton Parkway.

🅿 Car park at Black Hill.

★ Information boards in car park and at the main cross roads.

⬛ 568 ha (1404 acres) between Bramshaw, Cadnam and Plaitford, on N edge of New Forest, just S of A36, 10ml W of Southampton.

[184 and 185:SU297178]

Chyngton Farm
East Sussex

Located on the west side of the Cuckmere estuary to the east of the old Cinque port of Seaford, this property is important for its exceptional wetland habitats, which include wet pasture meadows and relict saltmarsh. Plans to partially breach the sea defences at the river mouth will improve the flood plains on the valley floor and encourage the regeneration of the saltmarsh and associated wildlife. The farm also contains areas of improved pasture and arable reversion, and lies within the Seaford to Beachy Head sssi. It is also part of the Seaford Head local nature reserve.

In winter the invertebrate-rich wet meadows support hundreds of lapwing, wigeon and teal, which can be seen feeding alongside waders such as ringed and grey plovers, redshank and curlew. In spring and autumn, whimbrel and little egret can also be seen here. Birds of prey hunt over the area and include peregrine falcon, sparrowhawk and kestrel, whilst along the river kingfisher are often seen. Clumps of thick scrub support large numbers of small birds, including yellowhammer and, in summer, several species of warbler.

The ditches and 'innings' (what?) which throng the farm provide excellent conditions for dragonflies, including black-tailed skimmer and emperor, whilst the saltmarsh supports a valuable community of interesting plants, including glasswort, sea lavender and sea purslane. On the seaward side the shingle bank and beach are home to yellow-horned poppy, teasel and sea kale.

- [🚶] Public footpath from adjacent Seven Sisters Country Park.
- [P] Car park in country park.
- [★] WCs and refreshments in country park visitor centre (not NT); local facilities.
- [⛴] 118 ha (290 acres) between Cuckmere Haven and Seaford.

[199:TV510990]

Cissbury Ring
West Sussex

Set on a chalk promontory on the South Downs, with good views across to Beachy Head and the west Isle of Wight, and part of the Sussex Downs AONB, this Iron Age hill fort with its ditch and ramparts encompasses about sixty-five acres. It is the second largest in England and an SAM. Archaeological evidence shows that this strategic site was also important for flint production during the neolithic period, and was later cultivated during Celtic and Roman times (some strip lynchets can still be seen).

Also valued as an SSSI, the chalk grassland covering the earthworks supports a wide range of downland plants such as horseshoe vetch, cowslip, stemless thistle and several species of orchid (including pyramidal and common spotted). Butterflies include chalkhill blue and dark-green fritillary.

A dry combe or steep-sided valley cuts into the chalk plateau, and is also rich in lime-loving flowers and grasses such as rock-rose, horseshoe vetch, quaking grass and ploughman's spikenard.

[🚶] Open access on foot only (no bicycles); network of footpaths; station at Worthing.

[P] Car park in Findon Valley.

[★] Information board in car park; walks guide (in Sussex Downs leaflet pack).

[♿] 50 ha (123 acres) 1½ml E of Findon on A24, 3ml N of Worthing.

[198:TQ130078]

Devil's Dyke Estate   West Sussex

This magnificent ridge of chalk downland lies within the Sussex Downs AONB and runs for seven miles from Wolstonbury Hill through Newtimber Hill, Saddlescombe Farm and the Fulking Escarpment. It includes the spectacular Devil's Dyke, the largest chalkland dry combe in Britain and home to many associated plants and butterflies. From the summit there are dramatic views north towards the Weald and south over the sea. The archaeological and ecological diversity of this ancient landscape is such that it has been designated an ESA.

Sensitive management of the open grassland has helped ensure that plants such as lady's bedstraw, ribwort plantain, burnet saxifrage, round-headed rampion and common knapweed thrive here. An impressive range of orchids includes common spotted, bee, frog and twayblade, and butterflies such as adonis and chalkhill blues, grayling, brown argus and green hairstreak can be seen in season. Breeding birds include skylark, willow warbler, meadow pipit and corn bunting.

Of historical interest are the remains of a Norman motte and bailey castle (an SAM), the site of a deserted medieval village, Bronze Age burial mounds and old lime kilns. Devil's Dyke also has evidence of its Victorian heyday, with the relics of a steep grade railway and of a cablecar which once crossed the valley.

On the slopes of adjacent Newtimber Hill there are stands of juniper scrub, and the open grassland contains a number of scarce plants, most notably the red star thistle, restricted to the eastern South Downs. The ancient woodland contains old coppice stools among the oak, ash and beech, and birds such as green woodpecker, nuthatch and treecreeper can be seen. All three species of British newt (great crested, plamate and smooth) are present in the dew ponds.

🚶 Open access; South Downs Way; stations at Brighton and Hassocks; bus service from Brighton to Devil's Dyke (summer weekends).

🅿 Car parks at Devil's Dyke and Summer Down Road.

★ Viewpoint and public house (not NT) at Devil's Dyke; information/recruitment point (seasonal); education visits; leaflet.

⬛ 646 ha (1600 acres) 5ml NW of Brighton.   [198:TQ258110]

Ditchling Beacon   East Sussex

Located on the South Downs Way, this high point on the Downs commands extensive views over the Sussex Weald, the mouth of the River Ouse and out to the English Channel. The escarpment is an SSSI, and the whole area falls within the Sussex Downs AONB. The steep slope of the escarpment includes a fine example of quality downland. The site has slight traces of the rampart and ditch of an Iron Age hill fort.

Used traditionally by local graziers as a sheep walk, the chalk grass-lands on the South Downs ridge are rich in wild flowers, with marjoram, salad burnet, devil's bit scabious, carline thistle and common spotted orchid all frequent locally. There are numerous mounds of the yellow meadow ant, indicating ancient turf (see *Harting Down* for a more detailed explanation).

🚶 Open during daylight hours; South Downs Way; footpaths and a bridleway cross the site; circular walks.

🅿 Car parks at top and bottom of ridge.

★ Information board with maps; wheelchair access to South Downs Way and Beacon from car park.

⬛ 25 ha (61 acres) 6ml N of Brighton, off unclassified Brighton to Ditchling road.   [198:TQ333130]

Drovers Estate
West Sussex

This large traditional mixed estate is part of a patchwork of agricultural land dominated by large stands of woodland, some of which are the remains of an ancient hunting preserve of the Earls of Arundel. Many of these woods are a blend of old coppice and mixed plantations, and some of the former coppiced areas are to be restored to improve their value to wildlife.

Woodland flowers are particularly notable here and include species such as celandine, wood anemone and primrose. In spring nightingales can be heard singing in the coppice and buzzards, a scarce bird in southern England, often soar overhead.

[i] Open access; footpaths (some permitted); bus services from Midhurst and Chichester.

[P] No formal car park.

[★] Walks guide (in Sussex Downs leaflet pack).

[▨] 485 ha (1200 acres) just N of Singleton, straddling the A286.

[197:SU874147]

Figsbury Ring
Wiltshire

These distinctive earthbanks are the remains of a well-preserved Iron Age hill fort located on a chalk promontory overlooking the Vale of Salisbury. The fort consists of a single circular bank and outer ditch breached by two openings, with an internal quarry ditch forming a second ring. A continuous programme of management, together with cattle-grazing, keeps the site free from encroaching scrub and maintains its botanical interest.

The warm south-facing slopes of the banks are well suited to chalk-loving plants such as pyramidal, fragrant, bee, common spotted and frog orchids, harebell, thyme and small scabious. Twenty species of butterfly have been recorded, including adonis and chalkhill blues and brown argus, and among other invertebrates of note is the large population of the spectacular giant robberfly *Asilus crabroniformis*, a harmless – if frightening – yellow and black fly which can be seen during late summer.

[i] From car park (RADAR lock for disabled access); station at Salisbury.

[P] Car park.

[★] Information panel.

[▨] 11 ha (27 acres) 4ml NE of Salisbury, ½ml N of A30 London road.

[184:SU193338]

Frensham Common   Surrey

This fine example of open Surrey heathland, one of the largest expanses in the Weald and designated an sssi and spa, consists of dry and wet heath, some woodland, scrub and ponds. It is of great importance for heathland insects, reptiles and birds, such as nightjar, stonechat and whinchat.

The common and Great Pond are leased to Waverley Borough Council which manages the area. The Great Pond was excavated in the thirteenth century on the site of a smaller pond, and used to supply fish to the Bishop of Winchester's Court when visiting Farnham Castle.

The Little Pond is also man-made and was formed when a dam was built in 1246. It has some important fen habitats, with fringes of yellow iris, sweet flag and common reeds, and alder and willow carr. Marsh cinquefoil, bur marigold, water mint and angelica are also found, along with many species of damselfly and dragonfly. The pond is managed partly as a bird sanctuary, and supports reed bunting, reed and sedge warbler, snipe, redshank, great crested grebe and water rail.

Both ponds were drained during the Second World War to remove distinctive identification features in the landscape, and were used for tank exercises until being refilled in 1949.

On the heathland are plants such as bell heather, ling, gorse (including dwarf gorse) and bracken in the drier areas, with mosses, sedges, common and cotton grasses and round-leaved sundew on wet ground. Sand lizards occur, along with heathland insects such as silver-studded blue butterfly, and numerous mining bees and digger wasps. The spider fauna is also rich.

[🚶] Network of footpaths and bridleways.

[P] Car parks.

[★] WCs (including disabled); information room at Great Pond.

[!] There is a great risk of accidental fires.

[▣] 373 ha (922 acres) 10ml S of Farnham, both sides of A287.

[186:SU859419]

Frog Firle Farm   East Sussex

Part of the South Downs aonb and including an sssi, this spectacular property offers classic South Downs country rich in natural and cultural history. From the ancient downland river cliff of High & Over there are outstanding panoramic views of the valley and of the meandering River Cuckmere running down to the sea.

As well as natural beauty, this area illustrates the influence of land use on the downs through the herb-rich sward which has developed. Within easy reach of the High & Over car park is the famous white horse carving, as well as a Bronze Age burial mound. From here the path leads down an ancient bostal towards the farm, an eighteenth-century flint and tile barn, and the site of a medieval farmstead.

Sweeping down to the alluvial valley, the herb-rich grassland, often dotted with sheep, is dominated by creeping fescue and brome grass. The nationally rare red star thistle grows in abundance in the disturbed earth of the farm tracks. In early summer the slope of the northern combe is dotted with pyramidal and burnt orchids, and also supports important colonies of butterflies, including chalkhill blue and marbled white.

On the valley floor the ditches, lined with rushes, provide a valuable winter habitat for teal, snipe and wigeon. Dragonflies recorded here include the ruddy darter, emperor and emerald damselfly. The ponds were restored in 1998 and provide a valuable wildlife habitat and educational resource. They are now home to redshank, heron, Canada goose, moorhen and kingfisher.

🚶 Footpaths across farm from car park and from Seaford, Alfriston and Littlington; station at Seaford.

🅿 Car park at High & Over.

★ Local facilities in Seaford and Littlington.

🏠 187 ha (461 acres) off B2108 Alfriston to Seaford road.   [199:TQ517012]

Hackhurst Down and Little King's Wood   Surrey

On the North Downs escarpment, with views across the valley of Tillingbourne, these two properties lie within the Surrey Hills AONB. Part of Hackhurst Down, overlying a chalk ridge, is included in a local nature reserve because of the rich diversity of its insects and plants.

Also of interest are some historic field boundaries and evidence of old coppicing. The North Downs Way runs through the properties.

The grassland supports a variety of plants such as salad burnet, wild basil and marjoram, hairy violet and bird's foot trefoil. This in turn supports a rich butterfly fauna. There is a notable stand of juniper at Hackhurst Down, which harbours the scarce juniper shield bug. There are also thickets of such typical native species as wayfaring tree, whitebeam, privet, dogwood, hazel, yew and ash; and Little King's Wood has some mature oak and beech trees.

[🚶] By footpath from Abinger Hammer; North Downs Way; stations at Dorking, Gomshall and Shere.

[P] Car parks at Abinger Roughs and Ranmore, and on local council parking areas.

[★] Local facilities.

[🚌] 30 ha (73 acres) ½ml NE of Gomshall and Shere stations; 4ml W of Dorking, on A25 above Gomshall.   [187:TQ092486 and 090492]

Hale Purlieu   Hampshire

Situated on the northern side of the historic royal hunting ground of the New Forest, this former manorial waste is still grazed under the traditional commoners' rights, and is made up of dry and wet heath and mires.

Heathland plants include dwarf gorse, purple moor grass and bog asphodel, with two types of sundews, marsh St John's wort, meadow thistle and two species of cotton grass occurring in the wet heath. Birds such as Dartford warbler, nightjar, snipe, stonechat and curlew can be seen, and many insects, including the red damselfly, inhabit the ponds and streams.

Millersford Plantation, leased to the Forestry Commission, includes Corsican and Scots pines, and there are some mixed woodlands of oak, holly, birch and beech. Great spotted woodpecker and woodcock can be seen.

Of historical interest are some old boiling pits (for heating stones to warm food or for saunas) and some prehistoric barrows.

[🚶] Network of footpaths.

[P] Car park at Lady's Mile.

[★] Local facilities.

[!] There is a great risk of accidental fires.

[🚌] 207 ha (512 acres) 3ml N of Fordingbridge, off B3080.   [184:SU200180]

Harewoods   Surrey

This agricultural estate in an unspoilt part of the Surrey countryside contains a variety of landscape features, such as ancient woodland, unimproved meadows, hedges, marl pit ponds and streams, which makes it of considerable conservation interest.

The semi-natural oak and ash woodlands, which also contain hazel and wild service tree (an indicator of their antiquity), have a rich ground flora with wood spurge, yellow archangel, spurge laurel and a spectacular display of bluebells in spring. Outwood Common, long ungrazed, has important ancient trees and is reverting to a broadleaved woodland of oak, ash and hornbeam.

[🏃] Network of footpaths and bridleways.

[P] Informal parking at Outwood Common, Branslands Wood and Horne Court.

[★] Local facilities; information boards.

[🚆] 823 ha (2034 acres) 3ml SE of Redhill, E of A22.   [187:TQ327456]

Harting Down   West Sussex

One of the largest areas of ancient chalk downland owned by the Trust, this local nature reserve and sssi has traditionally been grazed by sheep and continued grazing is vital to maintain the range of species. Small hummocky mounds, the nests of yellow meadow ants, are a sign that the grassland has not been ploughed for a long time, if ever, and those areas of downland that were ploughed in the early 1970s are now reverting to pasture. The area is part of the South Downs ESA.

The sward on the steep slopes is dominated by rather rank upright brome grass, and rarities, such as chalk milkwort and musk orchid, are restricted to the skeletal soil areas. There is an area of chalk heath and an excellent juniper stand. Invertebrates include Duke of Burgundy fritillary and grizzled skipper butterflies, the exquisite blue carpenter bee and the rare cheese snail.

Of historical interest are an Iron Age hill fort (an SAM), some earthworks and cross-ridge dykes, formally part of the Uppark estate.

[🏃] Open access; crossed by the South Downs Way.

[P] Car park.

[★] Tea-room at Uppark; picnic area; walks guide (in Sussex Downs leaflet pack).

[🚆] 210 ha (520 acres) 4ml SE of Petersfield, off B2146.   [197:SU790180]

Headley Heath   Surrey

Lying within the Surrey Hills AONB and part of the Mole Valley to Reigate SSSI, this property contains the largest remaining area of acid heathland on the North Downs. This includes a significant tract of rare chalk heath habitat, where acid- and chalk-loving plants mix. Extensive conservation work has been carried out with the objective of restoring the open heathland vegetation of heather and gorse. As part of the management process, the heath is grazed by Highland cattle.

Headley supports many threatened species, including unusual invertebrates that are dependent on this very rare habitat. Common lizards and slow worms may be seen, and birds include stonechat, linnet and woodlark. The occasional Dartford warbler is present. The many ponds support interesting aquatic communities, including great crested newt and several types of dragonfly.

[⚥] Network of footpaths and bridleways.

[P] 2 car parks.

[★] Catering caravan (open most days); information boards; leaflets.

[⬛] 214 ha (500 acres) 4ml S of Epsom, 2½ml SE of Leatherhead astride B2033.   [197:TQ205538]

Highdown Hill   West Sussex

On this ancient chalk knoll bounded by Worthing, the sea and the South Downs, archaeological remains have revealed evidence of the successive civilisations that have occupied the site. The ditch and rampart of an Iron Age fort is obvious, but the remains of an earlier Bronze Age settlement, a Romano-British settlement and a Anglo-Saxon cemetery also exist here. A 4.5-metre high raised beach, created as a result of a fall in the sea level, forms the southern boundary.

The grassland includes some important wildlife habitats, and plants associated with the old chalk grassland include cowslip, common spotted orchid, kidney vetch, vervain, rock-rose and chalk milkwort. The carthusian snail, a rare mollusc associated with fine unimproved grassland, has been found, and there are many birds such as whitethroat, linnet, goldfinch and willow warbler which nest in thickets in the old chalk pits.

[⚥] Open access; network of footpaths and bridleways; station at Worthing.

[P] Car park (not NT).

★ Local facilities.

⬛ 21 ha (52 acres) 1ml N of Ferring, 3ml NW of Worthing.

[197 and 198:TQ099042]

Hindhead   Surrey

Hindhead Commons comprise some of the most extensive areas of lowland heath in an AONB of importance for its large expanses of undeveloped countryside. The slopes of the Devil's Punch Bowl, a large natural amphitheatre, are covered with heath, small streams and areas of woodland.

The Punch Bowl was formed by springs cutting down and back into the soft rock, and is the largest spring-formed feature in Britain. The process can still be seen occurring around the springs in the bottom of the bowl.

Until the First World War, the bowl was inhabited by 'brom squires', who made brooms from the surrounding birch trees.

Gibbet Hill, a sandstone hill with views across the Weald, marks the site where three footpads (highwaymen on foot) were hung after murdering a sailor on the then wild wastelands of Hindhead Common – the Sailor's Stone commemorates the event.

Grazing of the heathland by commoners ceased around 1940, which allowed the spread of birch, pine and bracken over the heather, but this encroachment is now being reversed by a programme of active reclamation. Exmoor ponies and cattle are now helping to restore and maintain these areas.

The heath is dominated by heather, bell heather, cross-leaved heath and dwarf gorse, with bracken and common gorse and grasses such as purple moor grass. Older woods and wood pastures of oak, holly, ash and beech coppice occur in places, as in Highcombe Copse, and alder, willow and bog bean grow along the stream at Highcombe Bottom, with a series of small mires. Green, great and lesser spotted woodpeckers can be seen in the woods, with nightjar, stonechat and woodlark on the heath. The valley bottom supports a rich insect fauna, including rare craneflies.

🚶 Network of footpaths and bridleways.

🅿 Car park.

★ Café; information board; leaflet for self-guided walks.

⬛ 647.5 ha (1600 acres) NW of Haslemere, E of A3 and A287 junction.

[186:SU891358]

Holmwood Common   Surrey

This large area of ungrazed commonland is crossed by a network of paths and rides which are popular with walkers. Its ownership can be traced back to Edith, widow of Edward the Confessor, from whom it passed to William the Conqueror. There is a history of squatters, smugglers, sheep stealers and highwaymen. The first road through the area was a toll road along the western edge, built in 1755 on the Horsham-London route.

The Trust is actively encouraging the present balance of open grassland, scrub, bracken and pockets of old woodland, which attract a wide range of birds and insects, including numerous moths and some unusual species of butterfly such as purple and brown hairstreaks and white admiral. The streams are bordered by water mint, lady fern, yellow flag, water figwort and fleabane, and feed the many ponds.

[🚶] Network of footpaths and bridleways; station at Dorking.

[P] 5 car parks around the common.

[★] Local facilities; viewpoint with panorama of the North Downs; information boards.

[▦] 263 ha (650 acres) 1ml S of Dorking, both sides of A24. [187:TQ184454]

Hydon's Ball and Heath   Surrey

This area of heath, within the Surrey Hills AONB, with a steep, wooded south-facing slope commanding fine views across the Surrey landscape, is a memorial to Octavia Hill, one of the founders of the National Trust.

The woodland is a mixture of planted species with natural regeneration, and includes oak, rowan, holly, birch, pine and chestnut. Bilberry and bracken grow on the common. Amelanchier and Gaultheria, two non-native shrubs, were planted by Gertrude Jekyll as an embellishment to the woodland.

The remaining area of heath on the summit is fairly small, but the diversity of woodland, scrub and open grassland is ideal for a range of birds such as nightingale, sparrowhawk, and lesser, great spotted and green woodpeckers. Redpoll, siskin and brambling visit the common in winter.

[🚶] Network of permitted paths and bridleways.

[P] Car park.

[★] Local facilities.

[▦] 51 ha (126 acres) 3ml S of Godalming, 1½ml W of B2130. [186:SU978396]

Leith Hill   Surrey

The highest point in the south-east of England, this hill is covered by woodland on its slopes, and remnant heathland on Coldharbour Common and Dukes Warren. Many of the woodlands have been replanted, but there are still interesting semi-natural oak, hazel and alder woods, and some actively worked hazel coppice.

A fortified folly built in 1765 dominates the hilltop, and commands magnificent views across the North and South Downs. On the southern slopes of the hill is the Rhododendron Wood, a mass of colour in spring and early summer.

Many of the woodlands contain plants which indicate their antiquity, particularly parts of Mosses Wood and Frank's Wood. The oak and hazel conceal a ground flora of typical woodland herbs such as yellow archangel, wood spurge and sweet woodruff. The elusive white admiral butterfly can be seen. In spring, both Mosses and Frank's Woods have a fine display of bluebells. Woodland birds include nuthatch, treecreeper and wood warbler, and the open heathland is home to tree pipits and reptiles such as the common lizard and adder.

🚶 Network of paths and bridleways; 2 waymarked circular walks; guide (£1, from machine); station at Dorking.

🅿 6 car parks (3 NT, 3 County Council).

★ Refreshments and information room in tower; telescope and fine panoramic views from the top; information boards; nature trail.

🚩 348 ha (860 acres) 4ml SW of Dorking, NW of A29.   [187:TQ139432]

Limpsfield Common   Surrey

Lying on the greensand ridge on the Kent border, Limpsfield Common is part of the Surrey Hills AONB. The common, dominated by woodland, includes the Chart, Moor House Bank and Common, Scearn Bank, West Heath and Little Heath. This is a popular venue for walking, and includes a network of paths and rides and the course of a Roman road.

The woodland of oak, birch and sycamore has largely colonised the former open heathland, although small areas of heathland remain, with pine plantations and holly and hazel in pockets of ancient oak and beech woods. Woodland birds such as woodcock and green woodpecker can be seen.

🚶 Network of footpaths and bridleways across (unconnected) sites.

P Lay-bys.

★ Local facilities; information boards.

⊞ 138 ha (340 acres) 15ml E of Reigate, 2ml SE of Oxted, off B269.

[187:TQ090492]

Ludshott Common and Waggoners' Wells Hampshire

One of the largest remaining areas of lowland greensand heath in the western Weald, and part of the East Hampshire AONB, Ludshott Common was first recorded in the Domesday Book. For centuries it was exploited by local commoners for peat, thatch, gorse and grazing, and since the nineteenth century it has been a valuable open space in the area. A severe accidental summer fire in 1980 affected more than 400 acres of the common and eliminated much of the invading Scots pine. Although the heather is beginning to recover, the gorse is again very vigorous and invasive.

Waggoners' Wells consist of a series of man-made ponds fed by a stream, which were originally hammerponds serving an iron foundry known as Wakeners' Wells, on the site. They are of great wildlife interest and contain a variety of fish.

Heather, bell heather, dwarf and European gorse, and the bristle-leaved bent characterise the heathland. The scrubby vegetation provides a habitat for linnet, stonechat, woodlark, nightjar, visiting great grey shrike and the scarce Dartford warbler; there are a great many spiders and butterflies (including silver-studded blue, grayling and green hairstreak).

Pockets of semi-natural sessile oak woodland occur along the valley sides, and the mature trees lining the ponds to the east of the property harbour fascinating lichen communities with other plants characteristic of an ancient site. Nightingale, redpoll, woodcock, spotted flycatcher and tawny owl use the marginal scrub, and kingfisher, coot and other wildfowl inhabit the ponds.

⊀ Network of footpaths and bridleways.

P Car park.

★ Leaflets; nature trails.

⚠ Accidental fires are a hazard.

⊞ 285 ha (705 acres) 1½ml W of Hindhead, S of B3002.   [186:SU855350]

Oldbury Hill and Styant's Wood   Kent

On the summit of Oldbury Hill, commanding a powerfully defensive position, is one of the finest Iron Age hill forts in the Medway, with substantial earth ramparts two miles in length. Ancient woodland, scrub and relic heathland, typical of the prominent greensand ridge, disguise its complete outline.

The woodlands support oak, birch and Scots pine (the pine originally planted but now reseeding naturally in appropriate areas), with a variety of fungi and plants colonising from the former heathland, including heather and bilberry. Sizeable areas of oak coppice are systematically being recoppiced, making this one of the few Kentish woods where this traditional Wealden management is being practised.

The hill and woods are a Greensand Ridge Special Landscape Area, and part of the Metropolitan Green Belt, managed by the Kent County Council. The small caves and shallow rock shelters in the sandstone ridge were probably used by paleolithic man.

- 🚶 Open access from road; footpaths and bridleways; stations at Borough Green and Wrotham, and local bus service from Sevenoaks and Tunbridge Wells.
- 🅿 Car park.
- ★ Information panel and map; picnic area in car park; caravan and camp site.
- 📷 62 ha (153 acres) N of A25, NW of Ightham, 3ml SW of Wrotham.

[188:TQ582561]

One Tree Hill   Kent

The storms of 1987 badly damaged the wooded plateau of this Special Landscape Area of the Greensand Ridge, which lies within the North Downs AONB. Located on the crest of a sandstone escarpment with panoramic views across the Weald, it is part of the One Tree Hill and Bitchet Common SSSI, containing the remnants of a former more extensive ancient woodland. (The name of One Tree Hill originally referred to a large beech tree that grew near the summit until 1924, since replaced with a copper beech.)

Only the scarp slope is truly ancient woodland, however, since there is evidence that the plateau area was put to agricultural use during the eighteenth and nineteenth centuries. The intention of the Trust's foresters and ecologists is to leave the damaged areas of woodland to regenerate naturally, although there has been some token planting and the changing ecology will be closely recorded. The extensive storm damage of 1987 would have been a common occurrence in the larger primeval woods, with the glades rejuvenating themselves and thus continuing the woodland cycle.

The northern part of the property consists of a developing secondary oak and birch woodland. Oaks are locally frequent, with stands of sweet chestnut and a dense band of blackthorn scrub. Ash coppice is evident on the steep scarp slope (originally this would have been a wych-elm and ash woodland), with a good shrub layer and a range of ground flora species characteristic of the base-rich soils. The woods support a varied bird population, with lesser and great spotted woodpecker, blackcap, chif-fchaff, nuthatch and treecreeper.

On the summit is the supposed site of a Roman cemetery, and an old Anglo-Saxon woodland boundary bank can be seen.

[⚹] Footpaths across plateau and bottom of escarpment; Greensand Way crosses property; one permitted bridleway (fenced); station at Sevenoaks.

[P] Car park.

[★] Viewpoint; informal picnic areas; path (steep) to main viewing area passable by wheelchairs.

[▦] 14 ha (34 acres) 2ml SE of Sevenoaks, between Underriver and Bitchet Common.   [188:TQ560532]

Oxted Downs   Surrey

This distinctive Surrey chalk landscape of rounded hills, steep valleys and 'hanging' beech woodlands (Gangers Hill, Whistler's Steep, Hanging Wood and South Hawke) on the slopes of the North Downs, is part of the Surrey Hills AONB.

Although storm damage has taken its toll of the magnificent mature trees, the woodlands are now gradually regenerating, and the ground flora of bluebell, dog's mercury and sanicle is flourishing. There are some important areas of chalk downland and scrub on the slopes, with many downland plants such as cowslip, violet, autumn gentian, ploughman's spikenard, basil thyme, harebell and dwarf thistle. The grassland slopes support typical downland butterflies and grasshoppers.

[⚹] North Downs Way.

P Small car park above South Hawke on ridge at Woldingham.

★ Local facilities.

⛭ 27.5 ha (68 acres) 1ml NW of Oxted.   [187:TG374538]

Petts Wood and Hawkwood   Kent

This assemblage of ancient woodland, copses, hedgerows, streams and farmland provides much-valued countryside on the edge of London. The woodlands have played a significant part in the region's economy, with the sound timbers used for shipbuilding until the nineteenth century, when a fire destroyed the oaks which were replaced with exotic trees. These give the area a unique quality; among the crowned oak are birch, rowan, alder, ash, Scots pine, European larch, hornbeam and sweet chestnut. The uncommon wild service tree grows in the old hedgerows.

Petts Wood includes one of the few remaining areas of ancient woodland in London, with evidence of old earthwork boundaries (between the wood and St Paul's Common), and plants such as lily-of-the-valley (rare in the region) and wood anemone. Many birds make their home here, including lesser spotted woodpecker, tawny owl, treecreeper and jay. The river banks, rich in wildlife, are bordered by old willows, although the storm damage of 1987 destroyed large numbers of these trees.

A point of interest in Petts Wood is the monument to William Willett, the inventor of British Summer Time.

A number of ponds, two of which (in Pond Wood and Flusher's Wood on the Hawkwood Estate) are man-made, provide a habitat for newts and frogs.

🚶 Open access to Petts Wood off A208; permitted paths cross both estates; no public access to farmland or woods on Hawkwood Farm.

P Informal parking.

★ Horse riding only permitted on the public bridleways; way-marking only on bridleways; short section only of path suitable for wheelchairs (slopes and uneven surfaces).

⛭ 137 ha (338 acres) between Chislehurst and Orpington, W of A208.
                                                    [177:TQ450687]

Polesden Lacey, Ranmore Common, Denbies Hillside and White Downs
Surrey

Lying mainly to the south of the nineteenth-century Regency villa of Polesden Lacey is a beautiful and varied landscape of mature woodlands, beech walks, wooded commons, chalk downland and chalk scrub. The parkland around the house has been influenced by the tastes of various owners over the years, and from the lawns and terrace there are fine views across the valley to Ranmore, a wooded common on the slopes of the North Downs which can be reached from the house by numerous paths.

The scarp slopes of Denbies Hillside and White Downs are an sssi and part of the Surrey Hills AONB. They contain some of the richest chalk grassland in Britain, separated by blocks of woodland, including yew. The grassland flora is highlighted by rarities such as man orchid and species indicative of quality old downland, such as basil thyme, clustered bell-flower and round-headed rampion. Nearly every British chalk grassland butterfly occurs, including colonies of adonis blue and silver-spotted skipper. Exmoor ponies and Soay sheep are used to maintain the rare habitat by grazing. There are also rare moths, notably the straw belle, a North Downs speciality, and the orange-tailed clearwing, whose larvae bore into the stems of wayfaring trees. The invertebrate interest extends to micro moths, beetles, bees and snails.

The property contains several blocks of ancient woodland which hold characteristic plants such as columbine, nettle-leaved bellflower and early dog violet. Secondary woodland of beech, oak and ash has been colonising both the clay plateau heath and downland for the last century, with a flora of white helleborine, bluebell, foxglove and wood anemone. Butterflies, including purple hairstreak, white admiral and silver-washed fritillary, can be seen in the rides and clearings, and birds include sparrowhawk and green, lesser and great spotted woodpeckers.

🚶 From Westhumble; minor road N of railway line from Dorking; network of footpaths at Ranmore Common; walks round Polesden Lacey grounds and gardens; house open seasonally; station at Boxhill & Westhumble (2½ml walk from Polesden Lacey) and bus service from Guildford.

P Car parks at Polesden Lacey, Denbies Hillside and south of Ranmore Common.

[★] NT shop and tea-room; WCs (including disabled); information board; leaflet machine; nature trail; summer events programme (contact house); picnic sites; youth hostel.

[▣] 160 ha (395 acres) 1ml W of Dorking.   [187:TQ145503]

Reigate and Gatton Park   Surrey

Rising steeply to the north of Reigate is the chalk downland that comprises Colley and Reigate hills. The area, in the Surrey Hills AONB, is a mixture of open grassland and woodland, and has excellent views over the neighbouring countryside. Part of its historical interest is a late nineteenth-century 'mobilisation centre', known as the Fort, and some old firestone and hearthstone mines.

Gatton Park lies to the east. The land was originally used as a park in 1449, and was one of the first to be landscaped by 'Capability' Brown. It is only partially owned by the Trust, with the eastern section belonging to the school set up by Sir Jeremiah Colman, the former owner.

One of the original owners was Leofwin Godwinson, brother of King Harold II, and the estate was later given to Anne of Cleves by Henry VIII as part of their divorce settlement. It was described by William Cobbett in his *Rural Rides* as the third most rotten borough in England.

Both properties are an important part of the Mole Gap to Reigate SSSI, of which the scarp slope here is of national importance for its chalk downland habitat of short turf with associated wildlife species. Grassland plants include stemless thistle, harebell, orchids, thyme and salad burnet, with butterflies such as brown argus, green hairstreak and chalkhill blue. Gatton has a small but valuable area of long chalk sward and scrub.

Margery Wood, now separated from the escarpment by the M25, was named by the Anglo-Saxons and is almost certainly ancient woodland, as are Great Buck Wood and Nut Wood in Gatton Park, with beech, elm, yew, Midland hawthorn, broad-leaved helleborine, common spotted orchid, bluebell, primrose and wood spurge.

[⋏] 8 access points to both sites; footpaths; station at Reigate.

[P] Car parks at Wray Lane (off A217) and at Margery Wood.

[★] Kiosk and WCs at Wray Lane; guided walks and talks; information boards.

[▣] 138 ha (340 acres) between Reigate Hill and Banstead Heath; and 1½ml NE of Reigate, just N of A242 on W side of Gatton Park.

[187:TQ250520 and 265522]

Runnymede
Surrey

These historic meads on the banks of the Thames are the site of the signing of the Magna Carta, the great charter of English liberties, by King John in June 1215. A network of footpaths links the Magna Carta memorial with the memorials to John F. Kennedy and the Royal Air Force on neighbouring land. Further paths lead through the meadows and agricultural land, up the wooded slopes of Cooper's Hill, to Langham Pond and along the river.

A wide range of plants grow in the rich swards of the meadows and pastures, such as pepper saxifrage, cowslip, common knapweed, great burnet, betony, sneezewort and devil's bit scabious. There are mature oaks in the old boundary banks on Cooper's Hill, some fine old hornbeams and huge wild cherry trees.

Langham's Pond includes fen, wet grassland and open water habitats, and is notable for the variety of invertebrates, with many damselflies, dragonflies and water beetles. Aquatic and fen plants include frogbit, fine-leaved water dropwort and flowering rush. Brown-eared, pipistrelle and noctule bats can be seen feeding over the ponds in the evenings, and the wetland habitats attract many birds such as redshank, mallard, coot, lapwing, pied wagtail, and sedge and reed warblers.

- 🏃 Network of footpaths; Thames National Trail along river; station at Egham.
- 🅿 Riverside car park; hardstanding car park at tea-room (all year).
- ✴ Tea-room (seasonal); WCs; information board; boat trips; fishing (daily permits available from Warden).
- ⛺ 74 ha (183 acres) 1½ml above Runnymede Bridge on River Thames, between Windsor and Staines, S of A308.   [176:TQ007720]

St Catherine's
Isle of Wight

St Catherine's Point, the most southerly point of the island, is surrounded by the agricultural land of Knowles Farm, a geological sssi. The strange, tumbled landscape, the western extremity of the Isle of Wight undercliff, extends from St Catherine's to Bonchurch, and is the result of the blue lias clay slumping under the weight of the chalk and sandstone above.

A variety of unusual plants thrive on the point, occupying the wide range of habitats from landslip and cliffs to grassland and scrub. Of special note are milk vetch, tufted centaury, subterranean clover and hoary stock. There are also many rare lichens. The invertebrate fauna includes species which are on the northern edge of their European range. There are a number of rare beetles, weevils, bees, wasps and ants, and a renowned colony of the glanville fritillary butterfly, an Isle of Wight specialist which is virtually restricted to National Trust property.

The ridge of St Catherine's Down, a mile inland from the point, rises in a steep west-facing escarpment of greensand to the chalk knoll of St Catherine's Hill, with the fine fourteenth-century lanterned lighthouse (in the care of English Heritage), originally part of an oratory and possibly the oldest in the country apart from the Pharos at Dover. From the summit there are spectacular views of the rest of the island. At the other end of the down is the Hoy Monument (not owned by the Trust), erected in memory of a visit by Tsar Nicholas I in 1814.

🏃 Open access to St Catherine's Hill and Down (not accessible from Knowles Farm); network of footpaths on St Catherine's Down.

P Car parks at Blackgang viewpoint and Windy Gap.

★ Viewpoint on St Catherine's Hill.

🗺 109 ha (270 acres) 2ml W of Niton, off A3055.   [196:SZ495755]

Scotney Castle Estate   Kent

This romantic ruin of a fourteenth-century moated castle, surrounded by charming gardens and parkland, lies on the River Bewl. The remains of the old manor are hidden among the ancient woodlands and old parkland trees, within the High Weald AONB. Various features of medieval life in the park and woodland have been identified, such as banks, ditches, lynchets (the strips between two pieces of ploughed land), and ridge and furrow farming. There are some quarries, and the sites of possible old iron workings.

The mature trees within the parkland and remnant woodland pasture, the ancient and more recently planted woodlands, and coppices of sweet chestnut all provide a network of valuable wildlife habitats. The estate is an SSSI because of its considerable importance for lichens and unim-proved grassland. Insects associated with dead wood are also of particular interest here.

An area of pasture woodland is partly enclosed by old boundaries. Ponds in some old marl pits have now been colonised by wetland plants and hold good populations of dragonflies and damselflies, including the rare brilliant emerald dragonfly. The River Bewl, which crosses the property, and the River Teise to the north, flow through areas of unimproved meadows rich in flowers. Brown long-eared bats roost in the old buildings.

[⚲] Castle and garden open seasonally; several public footpaths cross estate; 2 circular walks from car park (5ml or ¾ml); local station at Wadhurst and bus service from Tunbridge Wells.

[P] Car park at castle.

[★] WCs open as garden; estate walks leaflet (from NT shop or Regional Office); information board and map in car park near entrance to garden; benches at scenic points along circular walks.

[⛴] 312 ha (770 acres) 1ml S of Lamberhurst, on E of A21, 8ml SE of Tunbridge Wells. [188:TQ688353]

Selborne Hill   Hampshire

Encompassing some fine examples of beech 'hanger' woodlands on the chalk escarpments of east Hampshire, designated an sssi and within the East Hants AONB, these fragments of ancient landscape around Selborne are of great ecological importance. The observations of the Rev. Gilbert White, pastor and naturalist, published in *The Natural History and Antiquities of Selborne* in 1788, are an invaluable record, with lists and locations of individual scarce plants, of the ancient hangers, the Short and Long Lythes along the Oakhanger valley, the historic wood pasture, chalk grassland and mixed woodland of Selborne Hill and Common. White's famous zig-zag path to the top of the beech hanger on Selborne Hill is still in use.

Although the storms of 1987 and 1990 severely damaged the mature trees, new vistas have been opened up, with glades encouraging the regeneration of the natural vegetation.

The well-drained soils on the chalk substrate, ideal for beech with some maple and ash along the lower slopes, also support a distinct range of flowers such as woodruff, yellow archangel, wood spurge, wood anemone and bird's nest orchid. Above the hangers, mixed woodlands of oak and ash grow on the clay plateau of Selborne Hill, with wood sorrel, broad buckler fern and enchanter's nightshade. The woods harbour many rare invertebrates and molluscs associated with dead wood and pollards, including the ash black slug, which is characteristic of ancient woodland sites, and five species of Ctenophora cranefly (large, spectacular creatures with feathered antennae). Beech pollards stand on old wood pasture, grazed until the mid-nineteenth century.

The woodland glades provide feeding grounds for many butterflies, including the silver-washed fritillary, green and purple hairstreaks and the occasional white admiral and purple emperor. Nightingale regularly breed.

🚶 Via Selborne village; network of paths.

🅿 Car park.

★ Shops, museum, pubs and tea-room in village; WCs (including disabled) in car park; leaflets and guidebooks.

📷 101 ha (250 acres) 4ml S of Alton, W of B3006.　　　　[186:SU735333]

The Seven Sisters: Crowlink and Birling Gap

East Sussex

Crowlink and Birling Gap lie within the famous Seven Sisters, where sweeping downland meets sheer chalk cliffs. The properties form part of the East Sussex Heritage Coast and fall within the Seaford to Beachy Head SSSI. As part of the South Downs AONB, they are a nationally important landscape and are managed in a sensitive and traditional manner, with extensive stock grazing to maintain the characteristic short flower-rich turf.

The grassland along the coastline supports a rich variety of plants, including salad burnett, wild thyme, viper's bugloss, horseshoe and kidney vetches, and dropwort. Butterflies include silver-washed fritillary, chalkhill blue and marbled white. The mixed scrub provides excellent shelter for insects and birds such as stonechat, linnet, whitethroat and the occasional Dartford warbler. In summer skylarks can be heard singing high overhead and wheatears display in the combes.

Areas of acid chalk heath can be found where silty soils overlie the chalk at Birling Gap, with its purple flush of heather contrasting with the vibrant yellow of tormentil. The narrow strip of foreshore at the base of the cliffs supports a range of marine wildlife in the rock pools and amongst the shingle, whilst fulmars and kittiwakes nest along the cliffs.

Settlements have existed here for thousands of years – the remains of a Beaker settlement can be seen at Birling Gap, and an Iron Age rampart encircles the hill. A number of Bronze Age barrows can be found across Crowlink, one of which was excavated by English Heritage in the summer of 1997.

⟦🏃⟧ Footpaths and bridleways; South Down Way along coast; stations at Eastbourne and Seaford; bus service through East Dean and Friston.

⟦P⟧ Car parks on road to Crowlink, south of Friston Church and at Birling Gap.

⟦★⟧ Refreshments at Birling Gap; WCs (including disabled); information boards at Crowlink and Birling Gap; access for disabled from Crowlink car park to Flagstaff Point (only in dry weather).

⟦▣⟧ 286.5 ha (708 acres) 5ml W of Eastbourne, S of Friston, via East Dean to Beachy Head road linking A259 and B2103. [199:TV545974 and 554960]

Shoreham Gap and Southwick Hill   West Sussex

Overlooking Brighton and Shoreham, this ancient chalk downland landscape is located on the dip slope of the South Downs, and part of an AONB. A large dry combe cuts the rise, and there is just visible evidence of a prehistoric field system.

The Brighton by-pass has been diverted through a tunnel under the hill, to avoid damaging the landscape.

Areas of ancient unimproved chalk grassland contain good downland plants such as horseshoe and kidney vetches, rock-rose and dropwort. Butterflies such as small blue and chalkhill blue occur.

⟦🏃⟧ Open access; South Downs Way crosses property.

⟦P⟧ Car park near South Downs Way at Upper Beeding and Kingstone lane.

⟦★⟧ Local facilities.

⟦▣⟧ 241 ha (596 acres) 2ml NE of Shoreham.   [198:TQ208097]

The Slindon Estate   West Sussex

This property consists of a large expanse of sweeping downland dissected by dry valleys, with hanging beech woods on the scarp and old wood pasture on the dip slopes, much of which was damaged in the storms of 1987 and 1990. The estate includes Bignor and Coldharbour hills, and Glatting Beacon, from which there are spectacular views of the South Downs and the coastline. The famous Bignor Roman villa is nearby.

Other points of historical interest include a neolithic causewayed enclosure at Barkhale, several Bronze Age round barrows, some cross-ridge dykes, the medieval deer bank surrounding Slindon Park and a folly overlooking Court Hill Farm.

Much of the original downland on the more gentle slopes has been under arable cultivation in recent years, but large areas at Gumber Farm have now been put back to permanent pasture. There is an area of chalk heath and scrub on the plateau above the scarp.

Encompassing most of the village of Slindon with its flint and brick cottages, the estate is also crossed by the largest remaining section of the Roman road, Stane Street. There is evidence of the pitched chalk and flint surface with ditches on either side.

In Slindon Wood is a preserved shingle beach, showing that the sea level was once 40 metres higher than it is today. The old Slindon Park on the southern part of the estate still has the impressive bank and ditch of its medieval park pale.

Much of the woodland is on ancient woodland and wood pasture sites, including the fine beech woods on the steep scarp slope. The storm-damaged woods are regenerating, with saplings and woodland plants flourishing in the lighter glades caused by the storms; ash and yew are also common. Typical ground plants of the beech woods include bluebell, dog's mercury, wild garlic, wood anemone, wood sedge, greater butterfly orchid, butcher's broom, nettle-leaved bellflower, twayblade and over sixty-five species of moss and liverwort. White admiral and silver-washed fritillary butterflies occur.

The grassland supports stemless thistle, small scabious, rock-rose, cowslip, and early purple and common spotted orchids.

The North Wood plantation is leased to the Forestry Commission.

[🏃] Extensive network of footpaths and bridleways; South Downs Way; Slindon Park open daily; stations at Barnham, Arundel and Chichester; bus to Slindon Common.

[P] Car parks at Dukes Road, Park Lane, Slindon and Bignor Hill.

[★] Car park information boards; walks leaflet from Fontwell TIC; camping and accommodation at Gumber Bothy.

[⛺] 1425 ha (3520 acres) 6ml N of Bognor Regis, on A29.   [197:SU9608]

Stockbridge Down   Hampshire

This ancient chalk downland, designated an AONB and SSSI, has a long history of common grazing rights. These historic manorial customs are still maintained by the Trust, Lord of the Manor since 1946, which is now grazing its own flocks of sheep in order to maintain the rich grassland and to control the further invasion of scrub. A major scrub-reduction programme is currently in operation.

Distinctive plants of the chalk grassland include cowslip, thyme, harebell, horseshoe vetch, greater knapweed, yarrow and violet. There are many downland butterfly species, including chalkhill blue, and some scarce moths. The scrub of hawthorn, blackthorn, dogwood, privet and juniper provides valuable nesting sites for birds such as blackcap, yellowhammer, nightingale, and garden and willow warblers.

Of historical interest are some Bronze Age barrows, and the very important Iron Age camp of Woolbury Ring at the north-east corner of the property.

[⚥] Network of footpaths.

[P] 2 car parks.

[★] Information boards in main car park; limited access for disabled.

[🚍] 65 ha (165 acres) 12ml E of Salisbury.   [185:SU379349]

Toys Hill   Kent

Former heathland and wood pasture, and part of the historic commons of Brasted Chart, Toys Hill is one of the most important tracts of ancient woodland in Kent. Standing on the greensand ridge south of the North Downs, within an AONB, the woodlands are a prominent feature in the landscape.

In the past this historic landscape was where peasants grazed pigs and cattle, beech and oak trees were pollarded to provide firewood and food for grazing stock, and charcoal was produced for the Wealden iron industry and for hop-drying. The old banks and sunken tracks which can be seen thoughout the woods resulted from these activities.

Only a few of the old beech pollards survived the storm of 1987. Birch is regenerating strongly throughout the damaged areas, and holly, rowan and Scots pine are also frequent in places. The plateau supports one of the largest native stands of sessile oak in the Weald, and there is an interesting transition to pedunculate oak downslope. A large area of Scords Wood is designated a 'non-intervention area', where natural regeneration can gradually come through the devastated native beech woodland. Ash and wych elm woodland occurs along the undamaged lower slopes.

The woods hold valuable pockets of lowland heath, which the Trust is endeavouring to conserve and enlarge. Many woodland birds are found and fungi are plentiful, including poisonous species such as death cap and apricot yellow chanterelle. There are some unimproved meadows outside the woodland, and a redundant water tower is now serving as a site for roosting bats.

⟨⟩ Circular walk linking Emmetts Garden, Ide Hill and Chartwell; green and red waymarked trails; circular bridleway.

[P] Car park.

[★] Leaflet; guide for Chartwell (the home of Sir Winston Churchill) includes waymarked Weardale walk; information panels; viewpoints; non-intervention zone for scientific monitoring; picnic area; circular route for wheelchairs; base camp available for volunteer group bookings.

▣ 149 ha (368 acres) 5ml SW of Sevenoaks, 2½ml S of Brasted, 1ml W of Ide Hill.   [188:TQ465517]

Ventnor
Isle of Wight

The southernmost chalk downs in the country, designated an AONB and SSSI, this property lies inland from the town of Ventnor. The crest of St Boniface, the highest point on the Isle of Wight, rises to 240 metres. St Boniface Down, the first Trust acquisition on the island, commands impressive views across to the mainland and is notable as one of the richest chalk grassland in Britain. Adding to this interest, on the acid soils on the top of Luccombe Down is one of only two remaining areas of heathland on the island.

The Trust is currently involved in a programme of heathland restoration, using New Forest ponies for grazing. The downland is being managed by cattle-grazing, aided by feral goats and a continuous programme of clearing the invasive scrub, particularly the alien holm oak. Heathland plants include bell heather, ling, dwarf gorse and bilberry. The grassland supports a very wide range of plant species such as horseshoe vetch, rock-rose, autumn gentian, slender centaury and a variety of orchids. The property is also very important entomologically, with an interesting colony of adonis blue butterfly.

Woodlands such as the semi-natural Luccombe Copse include mature field maples and evidence of some old coppice stools.

Luccombe Down is the site of a Civil Aviation Authority radar station, which was originally one of the first radar stations established to defend the English Channel. There are also eight Bronze Age burial mounds. Luccombe Farm, (the buildings are not owned by the Trust), is made up of a traditional pattern of meadows, downland, beach and cliffs.

⟨⟩ Off Down Lane in Upper Ventnor, E off Newport road; network of footpaths.

[P] Car park off private road from Ventnor Dairy.

[★] Local facilities and information in Ventnor.

[⊞] 231 ha (570 acres) on SE coast off A3055 or B3327.   [196:SZ570782]

West Wight: Headon Warren, the Needles and Tennyson Down
Isle of Wight

The Needles headland, at the western extremity of the chalk backbone of the Isle of Wight, is part of the impressive Heritage Coast west of Brightstone. Between the Needles and Tennyson Down (named after the Poet Laureate who lived at Farringford in the 1870s) is West High Down, and these properties, with Afton, Compton and Brook downs, form a distinctive ridge of chalk downland from which there are spectacular views of the island and across to the mainland.

The ridge originally extended across Christchurch Bay to Dorset, where the chalk of Ballard Down can be seen in the distance. The ancient grassland has changed little over the centuries, and forms one of the most important downland sites in Britain. There are many archaeological remains along the prehistoric ridgeway. Alum Bay (not owned by the Trust) is a popular tourist spot renowned for its multi-coloured sands, and backed by steep sandstone cliffs. The clifftop is dominated by heathland and the scrub of Headon Warren where the occasional Dartford warbler can be seen.

Some of the richest chalk grassland in Britain can be found on the West Wight ridge, with a remarkable variety of plants and insects, including several maritime chalk species. The important heathland site supports bell heather, ling and dwarf gorse, and on the landslipped undercliffs there is a variety of habitats in the small cliffs, scrub and wet flushes.

On Tennyson Down there is an area of chalk heath where chalk plants coexist with acid-loving species such as heather. Cormorant, shag, guillemot, fulmar and razorbill nest along the cliffs.

Of historical interest on Headon Warren and the chalk downs are a number of notable Bronze Age and neolithic burial mounds and enclosures. On the Needles headland is the Old Battery, a Palmerstonian fort built in the 1860s with impressive views of the Needles and Christchurch Bay; the New Battery was built in 1891. There is also a rocket-testing site, built in 1960.

[⊼] Downland accessible from Alum Bay, High Down car park and Freshwater Bay; Isle of Wight coastal path; Tennyson Way; waymarked paths; network of footpaths across downs; Battery open seasonally.

P NT car parks at Afton and High downs; parking at Needles Pleasure Park in Alum Bay.

★ Tea-room in coastguard look-out at Battery; WCs and small kiosk at the Needles; guidebook to the Needles Battery; information boards in main car parks; bus service to Alum Bay.

▣ 186 ha (459 acres) SW of Totland, off B3322.   [196:SZ310851]

West Wittering: East Head   West Sussex

This narrow spit of sand and shingle dunes is located at the mouth of Chichester Harbour, an important natural tidal inlet. Designated an sssi, East Head and Chichester Harbour form one of the most important sites in western Europe for populations of overwintering waders and wildfowl.

Along the shingle, occasional little tern and ringed plover can be seen. The large numbers of wintering waders and wildfowl include sanderling, shelduck, Brent goose, wigeon, pochard, teal, mallard, golden-eye, merganser, redshank, curlew, grey plover, and bar-tailed and black-tailed godwits.

The shape and position of the dynamic sandy promontory has fluctuated over the years, as has the build-up of saltmarsh communities sheltered by the spit. The protection that East Head gives to the tidal inlet is also important in sheltering the harbour, and for the development of the series of estuarine creeks, mudflats, saltmarshes and reedbeds.

Erosion of the dunes has caused great instability, which could lead to more sand 'blow-outs' and to the eventual breach of the spit by the sea; an appeal has therefore been launched for money to repair such breaches. Visitors are asked to keep to the paths to avoid further erosion.

Over a hundred species of flowering plants are found among the coastal dune habitats around East Head, including thrift, sea heath, sea bindweed, golden samphire and evening primrose. On the sand and shingle sea holly, salt wort, sea heath, sea rocket and yellow-horned poppy can be seen, with a rich assemblage of plants such as glasswort, sea lavender and sea spurrey in the saltmarsh. East Head is entomologically very rich, especially for moths, mining bees and digger wasps.

🚶 By foot only; regular buses from Chichester to West Wittering village.

P Car parks (not NT).

▣ 45 ha (110 acres) E of entrance to Chichester Harbour, via A286 and B2179.   [197:SU765985]

The Wey and Godalming Navigations   Surrey

This stretch of navigation or canalised river is a historic link from Surrey to the main thoroughfare of the Thames and the 2000-mile inland water-way network. Pleasure craft have now replaced the horse-drawn barges which used to negotiate the sixteen locks from Godalming to the Thames. Today it is an important 'wildlife corridor' in a heavily popu-lated area. On the banks of the waterway are pollarded willows, and the tranquil backwaters support a great abundance of waterside flora and fauna. There is also a disused railway line which is now a pleasant walk bordering meadows owned by the Trust, some of which are SSSIs.

The river was opened for navigation in 1653, connecting London to Guildford, and was extended to Godalming in 1760. It is now used by leisure, rather than commercial, craft. Dapdune Wharf in Guildford, the site where the Wey's wooden barges were built, is open to the public and has some interesting displays. The Worsfold Gates at Send still have the original hand sluice paddles.

⟦🏃⟧ Open access to towpath from all bridges; boat access from Thames at Weybridge, or slipways at Stoke Lock or Pyrford Marina; stations close to navigation at Addleston, Byfleet, New Haw, Guildford, Farncombe and Godalming.

⟦P⟧ Several car parks.

⟦★⟧ Leaflet and maps; free mooring for visitors; 4 boat hire centres; boat trips from Guildford and Godalming; navigation office at Dapdune Wharf. Navigational licences are required for all craft.

⟦🗺⟧ 20ml of navigation and towpaths from Godalming to the River Thames at Weybridge, through Guildford.   [176:TQ073655 to 186:SU997489]

The White Cliffs of Dover   Kent

This string of properties along the famous Dover chalk cliffline is situated where the North Downs meet the English Channel and includes St Margaret's Bay, Bockhill Farm, Langdon Cliffs and Great Farthingloe. Arable farmland, tourism and industrial development, in particular around the mouth of the Channel Tunnel, have given greater importance to the Trust's role in protecting these clifftops, chalk grasslands and stretches of white rock.

The remaining fragments of ancient grassland on the clifftops support an exceptionally rich flora, including burnt, pyramidal, bee and fragrant orchids, meadow clary, ivy-leaved broomrape, chalk milkwort, knapweed, ox-eye daisy and rock-rose. Fulmar, kittiwake, house martin and peregrine inhabit the cliffs, and flocks of migrant birds use them as a point of arrival or departure for their journeys. The shrubby thickets are also important staging posts for migrant warblers, thrushes and finches in spring and autumn. The chalk is famed for its collection of fossils such as echidnoids. Butterflies are plentiful, including chalkhill and adonis blues.

St Margaret's Bay includes a number of properties of clifftop grassland and farmland. To the east, Kingsdown Leas covers a mile of clifftop, and Bockhill Farm, 111 hectares of farmland abutting the clifftop, is crossed by numerous footpaths. South Foreland Point, a small area of downland with a nineteenth-century lighthouse, lies to the east of Langdon Cliffs and Langdon Hole, properties with particularly valuable grasslands which attract many orchids. Great Farthingloe, to the west of Dover, covers a mile of exposed clifftop with flower-rich grasslands backed by farmland. Many of these clifftop grasslands are neglected and in need of sensitive grazing.

The area is peppered with wartime relics (fortification and heavy-gun sites, and a subterranean radar complex), and the Trust land surrounds the nationally important granite obelisk of the Dover Patrol Memorial.

[↟] System of maintained paths along coast and across farmland; the Saxon Shore Way coastal path; statutory path waymarked by the Countryside Commission.

[P] Car park at Gateway Visitor Centre at Langdon Cliffs.

[★] Visitor centre at Langdon Cliffs, with coffee shop, WCs (including disabled) and interpretative displays; viewpoints from Langdon Cliffs over Port of Dover; wheelchair access on paths from car park and roads, and to viewpoints on the Leas and Bockhill; no horse riding or mountain biking on any part of property.

[⛺] 131 ha (323 acres) between Capel-le-Ferne and NE Dover.
          [179:TR370451, 366437, 370455, 335422 and 290393]

Wickham Manor Farm   East Sussex

The Trust owns the surrounding SAM of Winchelsea, plus a 4½-mile stretch of the Royal Military Canal, built at the beginning of the nineteenth century as a defensive measure against the perceived threat of invasion by Napoleon.

A mile to the south-west of the village, on the road to Pett, is Wickham Manor Farm, a working Sussex farm. This property is of great nature conservation interest, and commands extensive views across open arable farmland towards the sea. A large variety of birds can be seen, including kestrel, green woodpecker and mistle thrush. Pett Level and Pewis Marsh provide an ideal habitat for the native marsh frog, and mute swan can be found on the canal.

The broadleaved woodland of Wickham Farm contains English elm, sweet chestnut, ash and sycamore, and has a marvellous ground flora of red campion, yellow archangel and cowslip. There is a rookery in the southern end. The much-altered fifteenth-century farmhouse (not open to the public) once belonged to William Penn, the founder of Pennsylvania in 1672.

[🕆] Pedestrians only on footpath across farm and leading to village; access to canal footpath at Appledore; station at Winchelsea.

[P] Limited roadside parking in Winchelsea.

[★] Tea-rooms, shops and WCs in Winchelsea.

[⛺] 160 ha (394 acres) 1ml SW of Winchelsea, 2ml W of Rye, 9ml E of Hastings on A259. [189:TQ898165]

Witley and Milford Commons   Surrey

Designated an SPA, Witley and Milford Commons are good examples of Surrey heathland and scrub, with woodland fringes. Like most Surrey heaths, the commons were central to the local communities until early this century, when they were used for grazing, turf-cutting and other enterprises.

The Trust is reclaiming heathland from pine woodland and bracken, managing different areas for different species, and also managing the scrub at Milford to encourage breeding birds, especially nightingale. The varying water-table levels lead to areas of both wet and dry heath, with heather, bell heather and bilberry in the drier parts, and in wet places common cotton-grass and mosses. Nightjar, siskin and many warblers are among the birds to be found, and the bushes of dwarf gorse are an important food source for a number of scarce insects. Heathland butterflies such as green hairstreak and silver-studded blue occur, and purple emperor can be found in the woodland.

The birch, oak and pine woods provide some shelter and habitat variety, although some areas are being cleared in the programme of heath reclamation. Reptiles such as common lizard and adder can be seen, as well as roe deer on the common.

Of historical interest are some Bronze Age burial mounds, and iron workings from the sixteenth and seventeenth centuries. The commons were used as army camps during both World Wars.

🏃 Footpaths.

🅿 3 car parks.

★ Information at the Witley Centre; leaflet; WCs; waymarked nature trails (yellow routes accessible to wheelchairs in dry weather); dogs permitted on leads.

▰ 153 ha (377 acres) 5ml W of Godalming, 1ml SW of Milford.

[186:SU932407]

Woolbeding   West Sussex

This large estate, part of the Sussex Downs AONB, encompasses an Anglo-Saxon settlement with farmland, woods, hedges and commons of great conservation value. To the north near Redford, Woolbeding and Pound Commons (sssi) are registered commonland consisting of heathland and ancient wood pasture. Woolbeding Wood is a characteristic 'hanging wood' above the River Rother, and a number of other woodlands containing a rich diversity of wildlife are thought to be on ancient sites. There are a few old pollarded trees.

Heather, cross-leaved heath, bell heather, dwarf gorse, gorse, bristle bent, bilberry, bracken and purple moor grass can be seen on the open expanses of heath, which are being enlarged by clearance of the birch wood and dense bracken.

On summer evenings nightjar can be heard, and other birds include redstart, lesser spotted woodpecker, wood warbler and tawny owl, with grey wagtail and kingfisher along the river banks. The open heath is important for bees and wasps.

🏃 Access to commons and part of woodlands only; restricted to rights of way over farmland.

🅿 4 small informal car parks.

▰ 446 ha (1102 acres) 2ml NW of Midhurst.   [197:SU869261]

Ankerwycke
Berkshire

A pastoral landscape, comprising 17th-century parkland with medieval ponds and waterways. The superb collection of large and unusual trees includes black walnut, London plane, lime and sessile oak, some of which support large growths of mistletoe. Rich in wildlife, the parkland and ponds provide ideal habitat for several species of bat, and the ponds are also home to the nationally rare water vole, as well as great crested newt, club-tailed dragonfly and white-legged damselfly. Birdlife is particularly notable here, with little and tawny owls present alongside a large population of the dramatic and noisy ring-necked parakeet, an Asian species which escaped from captivity some years ago and now lives ferally in the area.

The park surrounds an SAM containing the 2,000-year old Ankerwycke yew (currently 11.8 metres in circumference) and the ruins of the 12th-century Priory of St Mary Magdalene. This area is rich in archaeological earthworks dating from the Neolithic to early Iron Age periods, and there are impressive displays of snowdrop and wild daffodil in spring.

- 🚶 Main access from Magna Carta Lane and Wraysbury church.
- 🅿 Small car park off Magna Carta Lane.
- ★ Guided walks and talks; information board in car park.
- 🚻 60 ha (148 acres) on the north bank of the river Thames, opposite Runnymede and near Wraysbury.   [176:TW006731]

Ashdown Park and the Uffington White Horse
Oxfordshire

Situated among the rolling Berkshire Downs, these properties are of great archaeological interest. Uffington White Horse, a famous landmark for miles around, dates from the late Bronze Age. A hill fort of similar age crowns the hill, with burial mounds located between the two features. Below the horse lies the flat-topped mound of Dragon's Hill, the supposed site where St George slew the dragon; and at the foot of the hill is the dramatic dry valley known as the 'Manger'. The downland, both here and at Ashdown, is grazed by sheep as part of a management programme aimed at improving biological diversity.

The parkland around the charming seventeenth-century Ashdown House is surrounded in turn by woodland and farmland, including the remains of a medieval deer park and a field of sarsen stones supporting rare lichens. Since National Trust acquisition in 1983, a programme of woodland restoration has been undertaken, involving the planting of oak, ash and beech. Adjoining the woodland is Alfred's Castle, a defended settlement with evidence of Iron Age and Roman occupation.

[🚶] Guided tours only to house; woods closed on Fri; open access to White Horse Hill.

[P] Small car park near house.

[★] Access difficult for wheelchairs; dogs on leads in woodlands only.

[♿] Ashdown Park 95 ha (235 acres) 2½ml S of Ashbury, 3½ml N of Lambourn, W of B4000, and White Horse Hill 202 ha (499 acres) 6ml W of Wantage, 2ml S of Uffington, S of B4507.

[174:SU284823 and 293866]

The Ashridge Estate and Ivinghoe Beacon
Hertfordshire and Buckinghamshire

Stretching along the north-eastern edge of the Chiltern escarpment on the Hertfordshire and Buckinghamshire border from Berkhamsted to Ivinghoe Beacon, this huge estate includes a varied landscape of commons, heath, ancient semi-natural and secondary woodland, farmland and downland. Ashridge Commons and Woods, and Ivinghoe Hills, have been designated sssis.

This property is rich in archaeological remains. Bronze Age barrows exist around Ivinghoe Beacon and an impressive Bronze Age hill fort at the top of the Beacon. The landscape is characterised by a surprising number of enclosures and settlement sites, with lynchets, sunken droveways and occasional dykes.

The highlights of the estate are woodlands on the chalk scarp and combe; wooded commons with giant old pollards, most notably at Frithsden Beeches; lawns and rides of the medieval Ashridge Park; and downland and scrub at Ivinghoe Beacon.

In the woods bluebell, sanicle and sweet woodruff grow among the beech and oak trees, with ash and hornbeam also present. Woodland birds include redstart, woodcock, wood warbler, lesser spotted woodpeckers, tawny owl, firecrest, sparrowhawk, tree pipit and hawfinch. Fallow and muntjac deer can be seen.

Ashridge Commons hold pockets of relict heathland, an unusual habitat in the north Chilterns, and huge old beech pollards, which support a number of rare beetles and other specialist dead-wood invertebrates. The spectacular downland slopes at the northern end of the property are important for calcareous grassland flowers and insects, especially those associated with rough downland. Following the demise of sheep-grazing in the 1930s, and the subsequent loss of grazing rabbits affected by myxomatosis in the 1950s, the hills became increasingly covered by hawthorn scrub and choked by coarse grass. The Trust has reduced the scrub volume and implemented a suitable sheep-grazing regime. The slopes hold one of the strongest colonies of the Duke of Burgundy fritillary butterfly in the country, as well as many other scarce downland insects and a range of downland flowers.

🚶 Network of footpaths; stations at Berkhamsted and Tring.

🅿 Several car parks, including Steps Hill for Ivinghoe Hills, and at Bridgewater Monument; special parking for disabled by visitor centre.

★ Monument, shop, refreshment kiosk and exhibition room open seasonally; WCs (including disabled); leaflet; disabled facilities in visitor centre; batricars. Dogs must be kept on leads.

🏠 1821 ha (4500 acres) 3ml N of Berkhamsted, at Northchurch, between A41 and B489, both sides of B4506.   [165:SP970131]

Bradenham   Buckinghamshire

This is a large estate surrounding the manor and village of Bradenham in Buckinghamshire (the Trust owns many of the village houses), with farmland and woodland including Bradenham Woods, an extensive area of ancient beech wood which is considered among the best in the Chilterns, containing valuable evidence of medieval landscape and woodland management. There are also some old field enclosures. Park Wood is another area of characteristic beech woodland on an ancient site, and Grimm's Ditch, running through the north-east corner of the wood, is also of historical interest.

Although beech has been the predominant species on this property for many years, the woodlands are now being managed to encourage other trees typical to the Chilterns, with oak, whitebeam, wild cherry and ash.

The woodland floor is covered in flowers such as dog's mercury, primrose, sweet woodruff, wood anemone and bluebell. The ash-black slug, a scarce species of ancient forests, occurs.

There are some small but extremely valuable pockets of chalk grassland along the south-facing slope below the woodland edge. Some scarce plants grow here, including juniper and fragrant, bee and fly orchids.

There is also a rich butterfly fauna, notably small blue and Duke of Burgundy. The Trust has recently taken several thin soil fields along the valley side out of cultivation and is allowing them to develop a natural sward. Early results are highly encouraging.

⚹ Network of footpaths; open access to main areas of woodland; paths through Coppice and Park Woods; stations at High Wycombe and Princes Risborough.

Ⓟ Small car park next to youth hostel (not NT).

★ Local facilities.

⚏ 449.5 ha (1111 acres) 4ml NW of High Wycombe, 4½ml S of Princes Risborough, E of A4010.   [165:SU825970]

The Buscot and Coleshill Estates   Oxfordshire

These two large properties are situated in the fertile Thames Valley on the eastern edge of the Cotswolds. They include the attractive villages of Buscot and Coleshill, with the surrounding woodland and farmland. The Cotswold stone cottages in Coleshill village, with the Home Farm buildings, are an integral part of a well-planned nineteenth-century model farm. Also of interest is the Great Coxwell tithe barn, and Buscot's deserted village to the west of Weir Field.

Old pollarded trees line the River Thames at Buscot, and the River Cole, which runs through the Coleshill Estate, has recently been restored to its original course. Along both the Cole and the Thames there are fragments of old hay meadows, once very extensive in the Thames Valley, where there are some small reedbeds and marshes. Curlews and lapwings feed on the meadows, and kingfishers can be seen along the rivers.

On Badbury Hill, the highest point in the area, is an unexcavated Iron Age hill fort.

Evidence of traditional woodland management can be detected in a number of woods, although many of the old coppice stools of oak and ash were replaced by conifers at the turn of the century. There are good hedgerows throughout the estate which support a wide range of wildlife.

⚹ Footpaths; circular walks.

Ⓟ Car parks at Badbury Hill and Buscot village.

★ Local facilities; popular picnic site (not NT) at Buscot Weir, including shop, tea-room and WCs.

⚏ 3035 ha (7500 acres) on A417 Faringdon to Lechlade road, and B4019 Faringdon to Highworth road.   [163:SU266942 and 237972]

Coombe Hill and Low Scrubs   Buckinghamshire

This stretch of chalk downland, designated an sssi, is the highest point in the Chilterns with views across the Vale of Aylesbury, the Berkshire Downs and the Cotswolds. On the summit stands a monument (not owned by the Trust) dedicated to the men who fell in the Boer War.

The Trust has recently introduced its own flock of sheep to control scrub invasion and to encourage the rich grass sward of the downland. The grassland on the steeper slopes contains many flowers typically found on chalk, with thyme, harebell, bird's-foot trefoil, horseshoe vetch, rock rose, dropwort and wild strawberry, which are used by a variety of downland butterflies and insects. Shrubs include juniper (which supports the juniper shield bug), wild privet and whitebeam.

On the plateau is some important relict heathland, and in the wooded areas oak and beech predominate. Many of these woods have been planted over the last few centuries, but evidence of coppicing and ancient pollards suggests a longer history of wood pasture commons in the area.

To the east lies Low Scrubs, an area of wooded common once used for gathering firewood. Woodland plants include helleborine, yellow archangel, broad buckler fern and enchanter's nightshade.

[🏃] Network of footpaths; Ridgeway and South Bucks Way long-distance footpaths; station at Princes Risborough.

[P] Car park at Coombe Hill, off Dunsmore road.

[★] Local facilities at Princes Risborough; limited disabled access to plateau area.

[⛺] 86 ha (213 acres) $1\frac{1}{2}$ml W of Wendover, $3\frac{1}{2}$ml SE of Princes Risborough, S of B4010.   [165:SP849066]

Finchampstead Ridges and Simon's Wood   Berkshire

Finchampstead Ridges lies on the south-facing scarp of the Blackwater Valley, with impressive views to the neighbouring counties of Hampshire and Surrey. The upper slopes are heather clad with pine clumps, while on the wetter lower slopes there are oak and holly. Simon's Wood lies close to the Ridges on the gentler northern slope and is crossed by the Roman road from London to Silchester, known locally as the Devil's Highway.

Both properties include fragments of the formerly extensive heaths of

Hampshire and Berkshire and these are now being recreated through a policy of active management. The dry heath supports a wide range of invertebrates and lichens. *Sphagnum* moss, purple moor grass and marsh pennywort occur in the wetter areas with lesser wintergreen and broad-leaved helleborine in the more wooded parts. Siskin and spotted fly-catcher are common migrants and the increasing area of heath has prompted the return of the woodlark to Simon's Wood.

Heath Pool, for which the Roman road forms the northern boundary, lies in the middle of Simon's Wood, with the smaller Spout Pond located at the bottom of the Ridges. Both provide a good habitat for populations of dragonfly, including the four-spotted chaser and the emerald and common azure damselflies.

[⚲] Open access; walk to Heath Pool; footpaths; marked bridleways; station at Crowthorne.

[P] Large car park at Simon's Wood; roadside parking on Ridges.

[★] Ridge plateau accessible by wheelchair.

[⬓] 24 ha (60 acres) ¾ml W of Crowthorne station on B3348, 4ml S of Wokingham.   [175 and 186:SU808634]

The Hughenden Estate   Buckinghamshire

Once owned by Benjamin Disraeli, Hughenden Manor is set on the rolling, east-facing slopes of the Hughenden Valley and contains many mementoes of the great statesman. Some of the trees in the park and woodland are relics of his planting schemes. The surrounding landscape, including Tinkers, Woodcock, Flagmore and Hanging Woods, lies within the Chilterns AONB and contains much of wildlife interest.

A number of the estate woods, such as Great and Little Tinkers Woods, are known to be on ancient woodland sites, and have a rich ground flora of primrose, bluebell and dog's mercury. Birds include tawny owl, green, great and lesser spotted woodpeckers, treecreeper and nuthatch. A winterbourne stream runs along the valley bottom.

A programme of new planting has been started in order to re-create the park as it was during its heyday in the 1870s. Green Farm, part of Disraeli's original estate, has recently been acquired.

[⚲] Open access to woodland walks and park; garden and house open seasonally; station at High Wycombe and bus service from Aylesbury to High Wycombe.

[P] Car park; special parking for disabled near house.

⊠ NT shop and tea-room; WCs (including disabled) in stableyard; dogs allowed on leads in park, woodland walks and car park only; dog rings and water in stableyard.

⊠ 270 ha (668 acres) 1½ml N of High Wycombe, W of A4128.

[165:SU866955 and 855957]

Lardon Chase, the Holies and Lough Down

Berkshire

This spur of downland lies to the west of Goring and Streatley, with good views overlooking the Thames Valley where the river divides the Chilterns from the North Wessex Downs. The slopes form one of the largest remaining areas of chalk grassland in the county and support a wide range of flowers and butterflies.

The area has a long history of ancient settlements and there are several Neolithic and Iron Age forts. It is crossed by the Ridgeway and other ancient routes used by the Romans.

The grassland is being managed by controlled grazing and by scrub clearance, to encourage the growth of chalk-loving plants such as autumn gentian, clustered bellflower, blue fleabane, vervain, common rock-rose, horseshoe vetch and a good population of orchids. There are some good chalk downland butterfly species, including chalkhill blue and grizzled and dingy skippers.

Mining bees, wasps and wolf spiders can be seen and a variety of birds nest and feed on the shrubs, with green woodpecker visiting the grassland anthills.

The Holies is a grassy coomb, which before acquisition by the Trust was used for motorbike scrambling and turf stripping. Now the natural recolonisation of the bare land by chalk-loving plant species is being carefully nurtured and monitored.

⋔ Open access; footpath from youth hostel at Streatley.

P Small car park at Lardon Chase.

⊠ Local facilities in village.

⊠ 27 ha (67 acres) just N of Streatley, W of A417.

[174:SU588809 and 588813]

Maidenhead Commons and Cock Marsh   Berkshire

Bought by local residents and given to the Trust in 1934, these properties include commonland and greens to the south of the River Thames. The sites include a variety of habitats, with woodland, scrub thickets, grassland, downland ponds, riverside and meadows, and are ideal for walking.

Cock Marsh is one of the best lowland wetland sites owned by the Trust, and is of great importance for its flora and for breeding waders, although it is a habitat much at risk from drainage and the abstraction of water on the adjacent land. Some Bronze Age bowl barrows can be seen here.

Maidenhead Thicket, mentioned in historic documents dating back to the seventeenth century and the site of a prehistoric Celtic farm enclosure, contains an impressive display of wild flowers in the spring.

The pond system and calcareous marsh are exceptionally rich, supporting a long list of rare and local plants, including greater bladderwort, flowering rush, water violet, needle spike-rush and two very rare water peppers. There is also an impressive aquatic invertebrate fauna, including scarce dragonflies such as the variable damselfly and numerous specialist flies such as soldier flies. All three species of newt occur, along with an assortment of wetland birds.

[🚶] Network of footpaths and bridleways.

[P] Several small car parks at Cookham Moor, Winter Hill, Maidenhead Thicket and Pinkney's Green.

[★] Local facilities.

[▦] 341 ha (843 acres) N and W of Maidenhead.   [175:SU850800 to 890870]

Morden Hall Park   London

The former parkland surrounding Morden Hall, on the banks of the River Wandle, forms an oasis of countryside in the London conurbation. Once the site of an historic deer park, the undisturbed river banks, mature trees, grassland, woodland and fen now create a haven for wildlife.

The unimproved grassland in the park supports a great variety of wildlife, including plants such as yarrow, sorrel, common knapweed and ox-eye daisy, and sedges and water plantain flourish in the meadows and fens. Holly blue, meadow brown, small skipper and green-veined white butterflies can be seen. Dragonflies, grey wagtail and kingfisher are also found on the river, and nuthatch, great spotted woodpecker and spotted flycatcher inhabit the scrub.

The river divides into a number of watercourses before passing the old Snuff Mill, which ceased working in 1927. The Mill is now managed as an environmental education centre for school children.

[🚶] Open access during daylight hours; footpaths and riverside walkways (accessible to wheelchairs); Morden underground station 500 metres away and regular local bus service (15 routes).

[P] Car park in walled garden (closes 6pm).

[★] NT shop; café; exhibition room; garden centre (not NT); city farm (not NT).

[♨] 50 ha (124 acres) E of A24 Morden road and A297 Morden Hall road.
[176:TQ259687]

Pulpit Wood   Buckinghamshire

This is an important area of what could be referred to as 'ancient secondary woodland'. It was once open farmland, but reverted to woodland long ago, and in recent centuries has been managed as beech woodland. Glades of earlier grassland survive on the slopes, with old juniper bushes (important here and elsewhere in the Chilterns). Rich chalk grassland with mixed scrub occurs at the western end of the property. Part of the wood is managed as a nature reserve by the Berkshire, Buckinghamshire and Oxfordshire Naturalists' Trust. The earthworks of an Iron Age hill fort can still be seen.

Ash and oak commonly occur among the beech trees, with wild privet, blackthorn, yew, guelder rose and the wayfaring tree forming a scrubby edge which is an important habitat for many birds. The woodland ground flora is dominated by dog's mercury, but other plants include sanicle, enchanter's nightshade, wood sorrel and sweet woodruff.

[🚶] Network of footpaths; Ridgeway long-distance footpath runs alongside the wood; station at Princes Risborough.

[P] Small car park.

[★] Local facilities.

[♨] 26 ha (65 acres) $\frac{1}{4}$ml NE of Princes Risborough, $2\frac{1}{2}$ml SW of Wendover, off A4010.   [165:SW832048]

Sharpenhoe Clappers, Smithcombe and Sundon Hills
Bedfordshire

The steep slopes of these properties have for many years consisted of undisturbed open downland, although recent changes in agricultural practices have led to the gradual encroachment of scrub. The remaining open areas of grassland have been fenced for grazing and so still support associated downland species of flora and fauna.

All three properties have areas of beech woodland. The Clappers Wood, crowning the ridge of Sharpenhoe, is a noted site for scarce species of beetle, and the ground flora here includes dog's mercury, wild garlic, anemones and wood sedge. Fly orchids can be found in Markham Woods at the eastern end of the Sundon Hills, whilst at Smithcombe hazel scrub provides ideal habitat for the common dormouse. Green woodpeckers nest in the woods and can be seen feeding on the grassland anthills. The site of an Iron Age hill fort is of historical interest.

[†] Open access; network of footpaths.

[P] Small car parks at Sharpenhoe and Sundon.

[★] Local facilities.

[▣] 122 ha (302 acres) 6ml N of Luton, between A6 (Barton-Le-Clay) and M1 (Harlington).   [166:TL065296 and 047285]

Watlington Hill
Oxfordshire

Rising to 213 metres above the beechwoods of Watlington Park in the Chilterns, this hill consists of skeletal soil chalk downland, scrub and beech copses and has impressive views over the surrounding countryside.

Together with neighbouring Pyrton Hill, it is designated an SSSI and is an excellent site for invertebrates, with over thirty species of butterflies and numerous other chalk grassland insects, especially those associated with heavily rabbit-grazed short turf. Typical flowers include horseshoe and kidney vetches, rock-rose, squinancywort, orchids and autumn and Chiltern gentians.

The beechwoods in Watlington Park are thought to be of ancient origin, although the trees have been felled and replanted several times. Woodland plants include common cow wheat and spurge laurel.

The marginal scrub of wayfaring tree, dogwood, whitebeam, privet and juniper provides a good habitat for scrub-nesting birds. The southern slopes are covered in yew woodland, a rare feature in the Chilterns.

[🚶] Open access; footpaths; Upper Icknield Way long-distance footpath (on prehistoric trade route).

[P] Small car park for both hill and woods off Watlington to North End road.

[★] Local facilities.

[♿] 45 ha (112 acres) 1ml SE of Watlington, E of B480.   [175:SU702935]

West Wycombe Hill   Buckinghamshire

Commanding grand views of West Wycombe Park, the River Wye and the surrounding countryside, the hill is crowned with a great golden ball on top of the church tower of St Lawrence, built for Sir Francis Dashwood, and infamous for its association with the eighteenth-century Hell Fire Club which is said to have met in the church and in a cave dug out of the hill.

Next to the church is a huge hexagonal mausoleum (not owned by the Trust) and the remains of an Iron Age hill fort. Nearby is the delightful village of West Wycombe which contains buildings of interest from medieval to Victorian times, many of which are owned by the Trust.

Chalk grassland, ancient woodland, scrub, old hazel coppice and mature trees planted as part of the grander landscape design of West Wycombe Park, add to the significance of this historic landscape.

The grassland supports many wild flowers and herbs, with lady's bedstraw, bird's foot trefoil, common rock-rose, wild basil, stemless thistle and hairy violet. Yew, blackthorn, juniper, whitebeam and wayfaring tree scrub merges into oak, ash and beech woods which contain evidence of traditional management in areas of old coppicing.

[🚶] Open access; footpaths; West Wycombe Park open seasonally; station at High Wycombe.

[P] Car park on top of hill.

[★] Local facilities in village.

[♿] 22 ha (55 acres) 2ml W of High Wycombe, W of West Wycombe, S of A40.   [175:SU828947]

Whipsnade and Dunstable Downs and Totternhoe Knolls   Bedfordshire

Commanding good views of the surrounding countryside, Whipsnade and Dunstable Downs are scarp slope ancient grasslands, the result of centuries of sheep grazing. The downs form the second largest area of chalk grassland in the county and, despite agricultural improvement of some of the original grassland and the encroachment of scrub, the steep slopes are rich in flora and associated fauna.

The areas of ancient grassland are fenced off, so that grazing can be used to maintain the high levels of conservation interest. Many chalk-loving plants and grasses are present, as well as scarce downland butterflies such as the chalkhill blue and Duke of Burgundy fritillary.

To the north west is Totternhoe Knolls, an area of woodland and chalk grassland, and also the site of a Norman castle.

[🚶] Network of footpaths.

[P] Car parks at Dunstable Downs Countryside Centre (B4541), Whipsnade Downs (B4540) and Totternhoe.

[★] NT shop, refreshment kiosk, interpretation area and WCs (including disabled) at Countryside Centre.

[▣] 178 ha (438 acres) SW of Dunstable, 4ml NE of Ashridge, between B4540 and B4541.   [165 and 166:TL000190]

The Blackwater Estuary: Copt Hall and Northey Island
Essex

A fingered pattern of drainage creeks, mudflats, bleak windswept salt-marshes and grazing lands, austere dykes and sea walls, tidal islands and fluctuating channels of water make up this estuarine coastline which is of international importance for its birds. The Trust owns a small part of the estuary; Ray Island is managed by the Essex Wildlife Trust.

At Copt Hall, in a combination of farmed land and estuarine habitats, grass has been sown on formerly arable fields to attract waders and geese, new copses planted and a new green lane created. There are old salt workings thought to date from Roman times, and known as Red Hills.

Northey Island is dissected by a maze of tidal creeks, with characteristic saltmarsh flora of sea plantain, sea lavender, sea spurrey and grasses. The many wading and overwintering birds include up to 5000 Brent geese mainly on specially managed farmland.

Somewhere around the island is the site of the celebrated Battle of Maldon in AD991, when the Anglo-Saxon Brihtnoth was defeated and killed by marauding Vikings.

[🏃] To Northey Island by appointment only from the Warden; saltmarsh path to Ray Island just before Strood Causeway to Mersea Island; public access to Copt Hall, circular walk around farm (keep to waymarked path).

[P] Small car park at Copt Hall.

[★] Northey Island nature trail; Copt Hall information board; access for wide-tyred wheelchairs.

[!] Do not walk along the top of the easily damaged sea wall at Copt Hall, to avoid disturbance of wildfowl.

[⛵] 405 ha (1000 acres) off B1025 S of Colchester; Northey Island reached by causeway at low tide; Copt Hall 8ml S of Colchester near Little Wigborough.   [168:TL872058, 007150 and 980147]

Blakeney Point and Morston & Stiffkey Marshes
Norfolk

Designated an NNR and SSSI, Blakeney Point is a spectacular example of a shingle spit and forms a constantly changing promontory, with shifting channels and anchorages. Seven miles in length, it holds a range of classic coastal habitats, with sand and pebble beach, saltmarsh and sand dunes. Common seals breed off the point of the spit and can be seen at close range from the boats. The mudflats and saltmarsh support plants such as marsh samphire, sea lavender, sea aster and sea purslane, and on the sand dunes grow sea bindweed, tree lupin and grasses. Sea campion, sea sandwort and yellow-horned poppy can be seen on the shingle.

Over 260 species of bird have been recorded, including many unusual migrants and large nesting colonies of common, Sandwich, Arctic and little terns. Ringed plover and oystercatcher are often seen.

Opposite Blakeney Point is Morston Marsh, a maze of creeks, mudflats and long-established saltings which continues into Stiffkey Marsh and contains some of the oldest saltmarshes along this historic coastline. Clinker-built boats with seaweed-strewn mooring ropes add to the character of this important wildlife site. The marshes support communities of maritime plants and in July are purple with sea lavender. The nutrient-rich tidal creeks attract many waders and wildfowl, including redshank, Brent geese, shelduck, wigeon and teal. In summer the marshes and pastures are frequented by snipe, lapwing and yellow wagtail, with reed bunting and bearded tit in the reedbeds. The drainage ditches, which are managed to ensure that the water levels benefit the large population of breeding birds, are also rich in insect life and wetland plants.

[↟] For Blakeney Point, access is either by ferry from Morston or Blakeney, or on foot along the shingle bank from Cley Beach (3ml); Morston & Stiffkey Marshes are served by coastal footpaths and a track to Morston Quay; North Norfolk Railway (at Wells, seasonal); otherwise, station at Sheringham with local bus service.

[P] Car parks at Morston, Stiffkey and further east at Salthouse, from where there are walks along the shingle bank and views over the marshes.

[★] Blakeney Point has shop and lifeboat house (seasonal); information centre at Morston Quay; leaflets; birdwatching hides; guided walks (groups by appointment).

[!] Visitors should note that bathing in the general area is dangerous.

[▦] 973 ha (2406 acres) between Wells and Blakeney, access from A149.
[133:TG0046, 132 and 133:TG010445/040447]

Blickling Park
Norfolk

This beautiful parkland surrounding a Jacobean mansion was landscaped during the eighteenth century. Concealed within the grander design are remnants of the earlier medieval manor, with approximately

240 hectares of woodland (some on sites of ancient and pasture woodland), 320 hectares of permanent pasture, a lake, many hedgerows and the River Bure.

The estate covers a wide range of wildlife habitats from river meadows (in an ESA) to the woodlands. The lake provides a habitat for many species of wildlife, including some locally rare insects and common water birds. Kingfishers can be seen on the river and lesser spotted woodpeckers nest in the woods.

[⚐] House open seasonally; park open all year; network of circular walks; Weavers Way long-distance footpath; station at North Walsham.

[P] Several car parks; special parking for disabled.

[★] NT shop and restaurant; tea-room with ramp for wheelchairs; WCs (including disabled); exhibition barn; leaflet with map; educational groups; plant centre in orchard; picnic area; coarse fishing in lake (permits available from warden).

[⛴] 1930 ha (4768 acres) 1½ml NW of Aylsham on A140, 15ml N of Norwich, 10ml S of Cromer each side of B1354.   [133:TG172800]

Brancaster   Norfolk

Over four miles in length, this property is a designated SSSI and covers an extensive area of saltmarsh, intertidal mud and sand flats, a wide beach-line and high dunes stabilised by marram grass inland. It also includes the site of the Roman shore fort of Branodunum. (The golf course, on former marshland, is not owned by the Trust.)

The rich variety of coastal habitats and its location opposite the Scolt Head Nature Reserve (leased by English Nature) contribute to the value of the area. A colony of little tern nests on the beach. Saltwort (known locally as samphire) grows on the younger saltmarsh, with thrift, sea lavender and sea aster covering the upper marshes. The sand and mudflats attract hordes of Brent geese, shelduck, oystercatchers, redshank and black-headed gulls. Sedge warblers and bearded tits breed in the reedbeds.

[⚐] 4 access points to the marshes; boardwalk to beach.

[P] Golf club car park at Brancaster Beach.

[★] Information boards at the harbour, Brancaster Staithe, and at Brancaster Beach; access for wheelchairs at harbour; ferry to Scolt Head, tides permitting, and boat-launching facilities (tel. 01485 210638); new Millennium Activity Centre at Brancaster Staithe (tel. 01485 210719).

1619 ha (4000 acres) between Wells and Hunstanton, off A149.

[132:TF800450]

Danbury and Lingwood Commons, Backwarden and Blake's Wood
Essex

This nature reserve and sssi consists of woodland and commons on a sandy ridge between the Crouch and Blackwater estuaries. Together the two commons form the second largest area of commonland in Essex after Epping Forest. The natural character of the land, combined with its exploitation by commoners for heather, grazing and woodcutting, has led to the development of a number of interesting wildlife habitats.

Danbury Common and the Backwarden (which is managed by the Essex Wildlife Trust), have an open character with expanses of heath invaded by bracken, broom, gorse, scrub and woodland of oak and birch. Recent clearance of the encroaching scrub has re-established more of the former heathland habitat with its associated wildlife of heather, common lizard and adder.

The area has strong links with the military past, with an earthwork on Danbury Common dating back to the Napoleonic Wars. Smugglers operating out of the estuaries also used the common to graze their ponies.

To the north, Lingwood Common is more heavily wooded with birch and oak where grassy glades are rich in butterflies and moths. Neolithic flints have been found on Beacon Hill, its highest point overlooking Danbury village. Blake's Wood is an area of sweet chestnut and hornbeam coppice, typical of the south-east, and is renowned for its bluebells and wood anemones. Oak, birch and hazel, coppiced in the past, are also common.

Open access; footpaths and bridleways; station at Chelmsford.

4 main car parks.

Leaflet; information boards; guided walks and talks.

130 ha (321 acres) 5ml E of Chelmsford, S of A414.

[167:TL7805 and 773068]

Darrow Wood
Norfolk

A small and isolated field of permanent pasture in a thinly-populated area surrounded by extensive arable farmland. The grassland is scattered with oak trees and features the remains of an 11th-century motte and bailey castle, as well as the earthworks of a Medieval consistory court.

[⚐] Public right of way enters the property at its south-western corner; station at Diss.

[P] No formal arrangements

[▦] 6 ha (15 acres) near the hamlet of Darrow Green, 7ml E of Bungay.

[155:TM265894]

Dunwich Heath and Minsmere Beach   Suffolk

On the coast, Dunwich Heath is an important remnant of the once extensive Sandlings Heaths, an area of lowland heath which used to cover this stretch of coastline. Now an sssi and very important for conservation, it was used as a sheep walk in medieval times. The heathland is covered in a blanket of heather, with heath bedstraw and three species of gorse (common, western and dwarf). Common lizard, grass snake, adder, glow worm, heather gossamer spider and heather beetle are some of the associated wildlife. Towards the sea, gnarled bell heather and clumps of gorse provide perches for stonechat and winchat. Nightjar breed here and many butterflies can be seen.

To the south-west, the heather gives way to birchwood, but a programme of cutting back this invasive scrub has reversed the decline of the heathland.

The continually eroding beach was once commonland to the thriving medieval town of Dunwich which gradually disappeared into the sea over the centuries as the cliffs were eroded. Later, the cliffs became the site of one of the first Second World War radar stations in England.

To the south lie the Minsmere reedbeds, separated by the flooded Docwra's Ditch, itself an interesting wildlife habitat. Minsmere Beach and its sandy cliffs run the full length of the eastern boundary.

[⚐] Network of footpaths; access to beach and coastal path.

[P] Car parks.

[★] NT shop and tea-room; WCs (including disabled); leaflets; information room; education base and officer; viewpoints; sea fishing on beach; picnic area; stair lift to information room and lookout; batricar; holiday flats.

[▦] 86.5 ha (214 acres) 2ml S of Dunwich on coast between Aldeburgh and Southwold, E of Yoxford, access signed on Westleton to Dunwich road.

[156:TM475683]

Felbrigg Park   Norfolk

Before the building of Felbrigg Hall in the seventeenth century, the park was a wild expanse of heathland exposed to the sea. The surrounding grounds were subsequently planted to screen the house from the open landscape of the north Norfolk coast. All that remains of the medieval village, which was burned to exterminate the plague, is a flint church within the estate. The village was relocated approximately a mile north of the original site. Earthworks give evidence of a Bronze Age barrow.

Some fine examples of ancient pollarded beech and oak trees are to be found in Felbrigg Great Wood, which was planted in the last few years of the seventeenth century. The owner, William Windham, was a keen tree-planter who set up his own nursery to supply the planting schemes, scattered across the estate. To the north of the house a wooded area is being restored to environmentally valuable wood pasture.

The mixed woodland consists of oak, sweet chestnut, beech, pine, rowan, birch, holly and hazel, and in the parkland some of the mature trees date back to 1581. A wide range of fungi can be seen, particularly on the decaying beech, along with a wide variety of woodland birds and wild flowers.

[*] House and garden open seasonally; parkland, woodland and lakeside walks open all year; free entry to woods and parkland; Weavers' Way long-distance footpath and other paths cross the estate; National Cycle Route 30 crosses park; station at Cromer.

[P] Several car parks on the estate.

[*] NT shop and catering; WCs (including disabled); leaflet and visitor information; wheelchair and Batricar (when house open and restricted to indicated routes).

[*] 687 ha (1697 acres) 2ml SW of Cromer off A148.   [133:TG197397]

Flatford   Suffolk

Located along the lower reaches of the River Stour in the Vale of Dedham, Flatford is a medley of classic timber-framed farmhouses and cottages now let to the Field Studies Council. Valley Farm, dating from the sixteenth century, is of particular note, and the famous seventeenth-century water-mill, the subject of John Constable's paintings, is now listed.

Judas Gap Marsh and Gibbonsgate Field and Pond, adjoining Willy

Lott's Cottage, add to the charm and wildlife interest of the area with its series of wetland and valley habitats.

Many insects, including damselflies and dragonflies, inhabit the ponds and marshes, and butterflies, moths and bees feed on purple loosestrife, water mint and water speedwell. Willows (some pollarded), reeds and bulrushes fringe the ponds and river.

[人] Via one-way traffic system; footpath along river to Dedham, Brantham or Manningtree; local station at Manningtree.

[P] Car park at top of hill (walk down); special parking facilities for disabled.

[★] NT shop, information and display at Bridge Cottage (limited opening); tea garden; WCs; birdwatchers' hide on Gibbonsgate Pond; information panel on Gibbonsgate Field circular walk.

[⛟] 26 ha (64 acres) on N bank of River Stour, 1ml S of East Bergholt.
[168:TM077332]

Hatfield Forest   Essex

A unique British historic landscape, Hatfield was first mentioned in the Domesday Book. Having escaped the widespread grubbing out of woodland over the centuries, it remains as a vestige of the once enormous Forest of Essex. The medieval core remains, and provides a record of the forest's evolution, with deer and cattle grazing among the coppiced and pollarded woods and trees. Increasing pressure is being placed on the ancient woodland and its rich wildlife by changes in the surrounding landscape, such as the expansion of neighbouring Stansted Airport.

A designated NNR, the forest is divided into sections separated by permanent woodbanks, with areas of grassland, glades, footpaths and wide grassy rides. Flowers such as water figwort, common fleabane, meadowsweet, hedge woundwort and wood speedwell flourish here and four hundred species of plants have been recorded. The woods contain thirty-six native species of tree and shrub with many plants characteristic of their ancient origins, such as herb Paris, oxlip and purple helleborine. The old hornbeam coppices are of particular interest since this tree is common only in the south. There are also more than 600 ancient pollards, of several different species and ranging in age from 400 to 650 years old.

A lake, created as part of an eighteenth-century landscape in 1746, is now one of the largest fen areas in Essex. Nightingales are among the many birds inhabiting the forest, with owls, great and lesser spotted woodpeckers, whitethroats and blackcaps. Fallow and muntjac deer can still be seen in great numbers.

Portingbury Hills are the remains of the earthwork of a late prehistoric settlement in Beggar's Hall Coppice, and there is an Iron Age hill fort underlying the rabbit warrens. Shell House, a rustic grotto, is worth visiting, and there is a medieval forest lodge (now tenanted) from which the affairs of the forest were conducted.

[⯅] Open access for pedestrians; seasonal vehicular access; footpaths along rides; station at Bishop's Stortford.

[P] Car park.

[★] Local facilities; refreshments; WCs (including disabled); leaflets; riding for members of Hatfield Forest Riding Association only; fishing by day permit during season; limited access for wheelchairs as some paths unsuitable and grass often wet; electric buggy available (tel. 01279 870678).

[▣] 405 ha (1000 acres) 3ml E of Bishop's Stortford, access from a side road leading S from A120 at Takeley Street.   [167:TL540200]

Horsey   Norfolk

Home to many rare birds, plants, animals and insects, the Horsey estate covers major areas of peatland and sites of national and international wildlife importance. The rich and varied habitats include fen, rough grazing marsh and open water, as well as an acid dune system. A drainage windmill, struck by lightning in 1943 but since restored (although not to working order), is a reminder of the way in which many of the Norfolk Broads were traditionally managed.

Horsey Mere covers almost 50 hectares and is one of the largest and best quality calcareous fens in the Broads. The breeding bird community is quite outstanding and includes such rare species as bittern, Cetti's warbler and bearded tit, as well as large populations of reed and sedge warblers and reed bunting. Marsh harriers can be seen quartering the reedbeds during the summer months. Barn owl and kingfisher are also present, and stonechats frequent the dune area. Winter brings large numbers of wildfowl, as well as the occasional short-eared owl. Resident mammals include water vole and the exotic Chinese water deer, best seen in the evening, with seals sometimes visible from the beach.

The fens and associated waterways support many scarce and characteristic Broadland species of plant and insect, including the spectacular swallowtail butterfly. The dune system is home to a population of natter-jack toad, as well as interesting plants such as sea holly and orchids. Current management practice at Horsey is focused on retaining the ecological balance of such fragile habitats within a mixed agricultural context, as well as on monitoring the extensive bird population.

[⅄] Access by public footpath and by circular walk from car park; access to beach at Horsey Gap; wheelchair access from Horsey Staithe to viewpoint over the mere; bus service from Great Yarmouth and Martham

[P] Car parks at windpump (pay-and-display) and at Horsey Gap

[★] Windpump (open seasonally) with small shop and light refreshments; information panels

[▦] 705 ha (1743 acres), 2½ml NE of Potter Heigham near B1159
[134:TG457223]

Ickworth Park   Suffolk

The park of the grandiose early nineteenth-century house at Ickworth was certainly influenced and possibly planted by the great landscape designer 'Capability' Brown. Clumps of imposing, ancient oak pollards, some more than 400 years old with encrusted bark supporting valuable communities of lichens, fungi and beetles, are scattered throughout the estate which is thought to be a former medieval wooded pasture and deer park.

The ancient woodlands are also of great interest, with mature oaks and hazel coppice dominating. Of particular note are Lownde Wood and Dairy Wood, which have old ditch and bank boundaries.

A chain of rich wetland habitats is created by the River Linnet, which runs through the estate, with the Fairy Lake, a series of ponds and a canal attracting numerous birds on the open water and reed fringes.

[⅄] Open all year (except 25 Dec) during daylight hours; footpaths; waymarked woodland and park walks; house open seasonally; station at Bury St Edmunds.

[P] Car park.

[★] NT shop and restaurant (seasonal, tel. 01284 735362 for times); WCs (including disabled); picnic area; children's playground; leaflets; guided walks.

[▦] 725 ha (1792 acres) at Horringer, 3ml SW of Bury St Edmunds W of A143.   [155:TL8161]

Orford Ness
Suffolk

At ten miles long, Orford Ness is the largest vegetated shingle spit in Europe and of exceptional nature conservation interest. The national and international importance of its geology and ecology is reflected in its many UK and European designations.

From 1913 until the mid-1980s the Ness was a secret military test site, during which period it witnessed many experiments in radar, defence systems, bombs and atomic weapons. Some of these activities affected the course of world history. This is a landscape of unusual character, its sheer scale perhaps its most surprising and memorable feature. It can be exposed, lonely, hostile and wild, and is characterised by contrasts: the man-made versus the natural, hard forms versus soft, and present stillness compared to the activity of the past.

There are a variety of habitats here, including shingle, grazing marsh, saltmarsh, mudflat and coastal brackish lagoons. Although the geomorphology is its greatest rarity, it has a highly specialised flora which includes the nationally scarce sea pea. The value of the Ness to birdlife is enhanced by its geographical location, at the extremity of eastern England. Undisturbed saltmarshes and mudflats constitute highly important feeding areas for resident and migrating waders and wildfowl. There are over forty species of breeding bird, including a number of Schedule One species such as avocet, little tern, barn owl and marsh harrier.

🚶 By boat from Orford Quay.

🅿 Car park on Quay Street, Orford (no parking on quay).

★ Trails and event, including guided walks; trail guide.

⛴ 744 ha (1838 acres) 12ml NE of Woodbridge (B1084), 10ml E of A12 (B1078, B1094), Suffolk.   [156:TM425495]

Sheringham Park
Norfolk

This parkland is important as one of the most complete and best-preserved landscapes designed by Humphry Repton, who brought up his family in the area. He described it as his favourite project, and in his 'Red Book' are views of the landscape before and after his work. Wooded hills frame the park and act as an important backdrop to the parkland.

The extensive woodland cover includes some impressive displays of rhododendron and azalea. The old oak and beech trees support interesting communities of lichens and beetles. A number of bats are attracted by the combination of old buildings and different wildlife habitats.

The estate extends to the coast and includes a section of the coastal path, where the cliffs contains some interesting geological deposits and provide nesting places for seabirds such as fulmars.

Of historical interest are Howe's Hill barrow, and some old sunken roadways. The folly, based on a suggestion in Repton's Red Book, was erected in 1976.

[⚲] Open all year round; waymarked walks; station at Sheringham.

[P] Car park; coaches to book.

[★] WCs (including disabled); leaflet; visitor information; boardwalk; gazebo/viewing tower overlooking park and coastline; two observation platforms overlooking azaleas and rhododendrons (May/June); raised boardwalk from car park; wheelchair and batricar available.

[▣] 312 ha (770 acres) 5ml NE of Holt, 2ml SW of Sheringham.

[133:TG135420]

The Suffolk Estuaries: Pin Mill and Kyson Hill

Suffolk

Characteristic of the deeply indented outline of the Deben, Orwell and Stour estuaries, this vulnerable stretch of mudflats, saltmarsh, cliffs and lowland woodland is rich in plants and birdlife.

On the south side of the River Orwell, Pin Mill (featured in Arthur Ransome's *We Didn't Mean to Go to Sea*) consists of a pocket of saltmarsh grading through cliffs to woodland. Sections of the woods were severely damaged in the 1987 gales, following which some areas were restored to open acid grass and heathland.

Kyson Hill (managed with the help of Suffolk Coastal District Council), has good views through wooded viewpoints over grazing meadows and the estuarine creeks of the River Deben.

[⚲] For Kyson Hill, footpaths along estuaries, from Broom Hill and along River Deben; for Pin Mill, circular walk around property with access up steps from Pin Mill Road.

[P] Car park on road to Pin Mill; car park at Broom Hill for Kyson Hill.

[★] Local facilities; information board at Pin Mill car park.

[▣] 5.5 ha (12 acres) 7ml SE of Ipswich off B1456, S of Woodbridge.

[169:TM206380 and 270477]

Sutton Hoo   Suffolk

The Sutton Hoo Estate sits along the estuary of the River Deben, opposite Woodbridge. From it came some of the most significant archaeological finds ever made on British soil, now displayed in the British Museum.

The estate contains areas of ancient Sandling heath, woodland, salting and tidal mudflat. The evocative burial mounds of the Anglo-Saxon burial ground, excavated in the 1930s, can still be seen.

Plans are underway to increase public access, improve nature conservation arrangements and provide enhanced interpretation of this complex but fascinating site.

[🚶] Access is currently by guided tour only; please contact the Visits & Guiding Secretary, The Sutton Hoo Society, Tailor's House, Bawdsey, Woodbridge, Suffolk IP12 3AJ.

[⛴] 93 ha (230 acres).   [169:TM288487]

West Runton   Norfolk

This property consists of a stretch of heathland and secondary woodland on the Cromer-Holt ridge, commanding good views along the north Norfolk coast. Deep, dry valleys dissect the ridge from north to south.

Known locally as the Roman Camp, it includes the highest point in Norfolk. There are also late Anglo-Saxon iron-working pits seen as circular hollows on the spurs of glacial ridges, excavated in 1964.

The woodlands support oak, ash, rowan, birch, sweet chestnut and beech. Birds include nightjar, fieldfare and redwing, and adder and slow worm are also found. Since the introduction of myxomatosis and the reduction of the rabbit population, scrub has encroached onto the site. Areas of heath are now being linked by the removal of trees.

[🚶] Free access all year; footpaths from Britons and Calves Well lanes; station at West Runton.

[P] Pay-and-display car park.

[★] Local facilities in West Runton; tea-rooms (not NT) opposite car park; information board.

[⛴] 43 ha (107 acres) between Sheringham and Cromer, 1ml S of West Runton station, off A149.   [133:TG177417]

Wicken Fen Cambridgeshire

Since Roman times East Anglia's Great Fen, a vast peaty wetland largely overlying gault clay, has systematically been drained by an extensive pattern of channels, dykes and sluices. Wicken Fen, a unique remnant of this ancient landscape, is made up of a series of wetland habitats, protected from drying out by the careful control of water levels and maintained by traditional reed and sedge harvesting techniques.

The Fen is the Trust's (and indeed the country's) oldest nature reserve, with the first part acquired in 1899, and it remains an island of natural life in the surrounding agricultural landscape. The water teems with countless aquatic invertebrates, among which are eighteen species of damselflies and dragonflies. Butterflies such as the brimstone, comma, wall brown, ringlet and Essex skipper flit over the open fields. Wigeon, shoveler, mallard, teal and tufted duck spend the winter here, and in spring the display of courting great crested grebe can be seen on the water, while snipe and woodcock display overhead. Marsh harrier, water rail, bearded tit, sparrowhawk and numerous warblers all breed, with many other species passing through on migration.

Ragged robin, yellow loosestrife, marsh pea, fen violet, milk parsley, comfrey and many other flowering plants and sedges line the ancient paths. Buckthorn, alder and guelder rose thrive in the damp ground, with birch, oak and ash dominating the developing woodland. Invading scrub is being removed in some areas to restore the traditional fen.

The area still shows signs of a long-established economy based on peat, reed and sedge-harvesting, and there are remains of old brickpits and a wind pump. Of further interest is Fen Cottage, and the Wicken Lode, a man-made waterway which may be of Roman origin.

[🕅] Open all year; Fen Cottage open seasonally or by appointment; station at Ely and local bus service.

[P] Car park near entrance; special parking for disabled.

[★] WCs (including disabled); William Thorpe building information room; school groups by appointment with Education Officer; birdwatchers' hides; boardwalk suitable for wheelchairs; tel. 01353 720274 for information and opening times.

[📧] 324 ha (800 acres) S of A1123, 4ml E of Stretham via A10, 3ml W of Soham via A142.   [154:TL563705]

Wimpole Park   Cambridgeshire

Matching the grandeur of the eighteenth-century house, the surrounding parkland, set in the Cambridgeshire countryside, has been strongly influenced by a number of famous landscape designers such as 'Capability' Brown and Humphry Repton. Axial avenues of trees, lakes, ponds, clumps and belts of trees provide a glorious example of a landscaped park. Beneath this, however, exists a manorial estate with a former deer park where aerial photographs have revealed old field systems with evidence of ridge and furrow farming. An eighteenth-century folly gives commanding views over the park, Hall and farm.

Traces of deserted medieval settlements have been found, with a moated manor house. A Roman settlement on Ermine Street has recently been excavated.

A 1½-mile-long avenue of lime trees, Bridgeman's South Avenue (formerly elms), has been replanted. The parkland is managed by the Trust and grazed by rare breeds of farm animals, including Longhorn and White Park cattle.

🏃 Rights of way and a series of waymarked walks; Hall open seasonally; stations at Shepreth and Biggleswade.

🅿 Car park at Hall.

🏛 NT shop and restaurant; WCs (including disabled); guide for Hall; Braille guide; events programme; children's corner; Wimpole Home Farm with prize-winning rare breed farm animals; shire horse trailer rides to Home Farm.

🚌 141.5 ha (350 acres) on N side of A603, 8ml SW of Cambridge, 6ml N of Royston.   [154:TL336510]

Alderley Edge
Cheshire

The majority of this estate was acquired in 1948, and the area is designated an SSSI for both biological and geological interest. To the east, the
sandstone escarpment or 'edge' forms a steep and wooded slope, the
result of faulting within the underlying rocks several million years ago.
Its close proximity to areas of extensive urban population, its predomi-
nately open space, woodlands, and the unsurpassed panorama over the
Cheshire plain make it a popular property to visit.

Enclosed grazing pastures and copse woodland lie to the west on the
more gentle slope. The area was formerly a mixture of heathland and
ancient woodland, and many trees in the mixed woodland have been
planted over several centuries, with the ancient woodlands of Waterfall
and Clockhouse woods dominated by oaks which harbour important
populations of invertebrates. The woods to the west are mainly beech,
with some birch, ash and Scots pine.

On the remnants of the former heathland can be found heather, purple
moor grass, bilberry, holly and birch, with a diverse associated moth,
butterfly and insect fauna. Birds seen in the area include redpoll, woodcock, green, great and lesser spotted woodpeckers, and tawny and little
owls.

The underlying rocks are rich in minerals, and the remains of old quarries, mine shafts and mineral workings (which can be a hazard for walkers) in the woodland are evidence that cobalt, lead and copper were once
mined in the area. A mythological wizard, reputedly Merlin, supposedly
guards the entrance to one of the caves, hence the nearby Wizard Inn
(now a restaurant). Some Bronze Age pottery and tools have been discovered, and the Armada Beacon has been used as a signalling point since
1588.

🚶 Part open access; network of footpaths, including link to Hare Hill Estate
(approximately 2ml, and return by same route); access to agricultural
land only along designated routes.

🅿 Main car park off B5087, next to Wizard Inn.

⭐ WCs (including disabled) in main car park; small information point in
stables next to Wizard Inn; horse riding permitted over certain routes in
good weather, some footpaths suitable for wheelchairs.

📧 92 ha (227 acres) both sides of B5087 Alderley to Macclesfield road.
[118:SJ860776]

Attingham
Shropshire

Originally part of a manorial estate, the parkland was designed in the late eighteenth century to complement the newly built and grand Hall. The famous landscape designer Humphry Repton modified an earlier layout by planting Scots pine, oak, elm and beech trees, which now stand as mature specimens throughout the estate and include some old beech pollards. (These trees are important for their associated colonies of insects and fungi.) A series of Repton's watercolours and his 'Red Book' have been used by the Trust as a guide in its efforts to restore the parkland.

The estate includes part of the Roman town of Viroconium, and covers the site of an Anglo-Saxon village. Small woods, hedgerows, ponds, an old canal and a disused railway line can be seen around the main parkland, but are not open to the public.

The former medieval deer park is now grazed by a herd of fallow deer. Despite agricultural improvements, a number of traditional farming features remain, and behind the grand landscape lie some valuable wildlife habitats. The Severn and Tern rivers have an interesting array of upland and lowland catchment qualities.

[🏠] House open seasonally; grounds open daily during daylight hours; permitted paths; restricted footpath and bridlepath; stations at Shrewsbury and Telford Central.

[P] Car park.

[★] NT shop; tea-room; WCs (including disabled); electric scooter for use in grounds; leaflet; guide to suggested walks; information centre; Mile Walk; guided walks; Braille guide.

[⛑] 1505 ha (3718 acres) 4ml SE of Shrewsbury, S of A5.   [126:SJ550099]

Brockhampton
Herefordshire

This extensive estate consists of gently undulating wooded slopes and parkland. The slopes are cut by small valley streams or 'dingles' with wooded banks, probably ancient woodland sites. Wild service trees are common and the woods include a typical flora of sweet woodruff, wood spurge, dog's mercury, yellow archangel and enchanter's nightshade. Woodpecker, pied flycatcher, redstart and great tit can be seen.

A number of mature oaks harbouring rare lichens have survived from the original woodland, although some unusual conifers such as redwood, pine and cedar have been planted for ornamentation in the parkland.

Birds of prey include buzzard, sparrowhawk and kestrel. The house outbuildings are a nationally important roost for the rare lesser horseshoe bat, which hunts over the park and lake.

[⊼] Paths, bridleways and waymarked walks through estate.

[P] Estate car park (charge) by chapel in top park.

[★] Tea-room (open weekends and Bank Hols) in estate car park; leaflet; information on walks in estate car park; waymarked parkland and woodland walks; woodland sculptures (accessed from A44 opposite Bringsty Forge); WCs.

[▦] 680 ha (1680 acres) 1½ml E of Bromyard, N of A44, off B4224.

[149:SO682546]

Calke Park   Derbyshire

Calke Park is a baroque mansion built on the site of a twelfth-century priory. The monks lived in a well-wooded landscape, since north of the house there were two woods and the wooded expanses of the Derby Hills. Remarkably, areas of this ancient wooded landscape survive today in what later became the Deer Park. The large numbers of very old oak, beech, ash and small-leaved lime trees, some of which date back to the fifteenth century, are one of the main glories of Calke Park, and provide a direct link with the primeval wildwood forest.

Consequently, Calke is one of the top ten sites in Britain, and Europe, for the specialist insect fauna associated with very old trees and woods which have never been cleared. There is also a chain of old ponds with curious names such as China House Pond, Betty's Pond and Thatch House Pond, and a large expanse of more recent eighteenth-century parkland, separated from the gardens by a sunken wall.

The outbuildings at the Abbey include stables, a brewhouse, bakehouse, smithy, dovecote and threshing barns. The church of St Giles is also notable.

[⊼] Permitted routes to estate; one-way system through park; park open daily during daylight hours; house open seasonally; timed tickets to house on busy days; stations at Derby and Burton-on-Trent.

[P] Car park.

[★] NT shop and restaurant; WCs; information room; carriage display in stable block; leaflets and educational material; play area; dogs on leads in park only.

[▦] 879 ha (2172 acres) 9ml S of Derby, on A514 at Ticknall. [128:SK356239]

Clent Hills
Worcestershire

This estate comprises three sandstone ridges rising to 304 metres (1000 feet) above the Midland plain, with panoramic views to the Severn Vale, Avon Vale and Welsh borders. Clent and Adams Hill form a backdrop to the landscape park at Hagley Hall, with large pollarded beeches and trademark clumps of Scots pine being the prominent features. The lower slopes are shrouded in scrub oak, beech, birch and bracken, with some remnants of the original acid grass heathland habitat. The whole area is interspersed with coniferous and mixed woodland plantings and includes an arboretum.

The hilltops are linked by a Trust-owned farm, High Harcourt, but the farm is let and not open to the public.

The hills are of county importance for breeding birds, and the larger trees harbour scarcer beetles, weevils and the notable solitary bee. Wet flushes, particularly on Walton Hill, are suitable for cuckoo flower and greater bird's-foot trefoil, the latter providing habitat for the longhorn moth.

⊠ Paths, bridleways; the North Worcestershire long distance trail crosses the hills; station at Hagley; bus services from Halesowen and Hagley.

🅿 NT car parks at Walton Hill, Uffmoor Green and Adams Hill; also Nimmings car park (run by Worcs CC, small charge).

★ Tea-bar and WCs (not NT) at Nimmings car park.

▣ 180 ha (443 acres) 3ml SE of Stourbridge, N of A491 and 8ml SW of Birmingham city centre.   [139:SO932803]

Clumber Park
Nottinghamshire

This property contains a unique mosaic of landscapes, with wet flushes abutting dry sandy heathlands and formal parkland standing next to both ancient and plantation woodlands. This rich diversity of habitat, and the extraordinary variety of plants and animals it supports, have resulted in the designation of over 400 hectares of the park as an SSSI.

The seat of the Dukes of Newcastle from the early eighteenth century until 1946, Clumber was originally part of Sherwood Forest. The house was demolished in 1938, but many features of the estate remain, including the traditional parkland landscape created by the 2nd Duke, who introduced exotic trees from around the world to add to the native oak and birch woods. The mature trees in the park are nationally important for rare deadwood beetles, and Clumber is home to seven species of bat and over 200 species of spider. The lowland heaths are nationally important and are of best regional examples of this habitat.

The serpentine lake covers 36 hectares and is home to a wide range of waterfowl, including breeding great crested and little grebes, and over-wintering gadwall and pochard. Recent subsidence in the park has created small areas of wetland which contribute to the diversity of birds found here.

[🚶] Daily during daylight hours; 13ml of tarmac roads; network of footpaths; 2 waymarked cycle routes; wheelchairs (can be booked in advance); local bus Mon-Sat; station at Worksop.

[P] Car park.

[★] NT shop, restaurant and tea-rooms; WCs (including disabled); information point; conservation centre; camping; caravan site; cycle hire.

[⬛] 1537 ha (3800 acres) $4\frac{1}{2}$ml SE of Workshop, $6\frac{1}{2}$ml SW of Retford, 1ml from A1/A57, 11ml from M1 (jct 30).

[120: SK645774 and 626746]

Croft Ambrey and Castle   Herefordshire

This historic landscape records centuries of working the land, battles, changes and fashions from prehistoric time through the medieval and Tudor periods to the nineteenth century. The hill is dominated by a spectacular Iron Age hill fort, with a triple ring of banks and ditches, offering stunning views across to the Welsh borders. Other earthworks remain from Iron Age and Roman building, and there are some pillow mounds or artificial rabbit warrens.

The extensive and varied estate of Croft Castle encompasses ancient pasture woodland and formal parkland, avenues of lime and sweet chestnut trees. Oak, ash and beech are among the mature trees, some of which are thought to be up to 350 years old. Ancient pollards are important for dead wood insects, molluscs and lichens, and the pasture woodland, used for centuries for grazing, fuel and cut wood, probably occupies an ancient site. A major new plan to reinstate pasture woodland is now being activated, in liaison with the Forestry Commission.

Fallow and muntjac deer can be seen in the woods of oak, ash, hornbeam, sweet chestnut, beech, hawthorn and elder, along with birds such as treecreeper, pied flycatcher and lesser spotted woodpecker. The uncommon hawfinch feeds on the seeds of hornbeam.

Hares, grey and red squirrels, fallow deer and weasels are found throughout the estate. The scarce Natterer's bat lives in the old buildings, relying on the surrounding varied habitats for its food. Buzzard are often seen overhead. Several species of butterflies, including the silver-washed fritillary, feed on the grasslands, and in the woodland rides and glades. Other scarce fritillaries are found on the hillside and on the bracken slopes.

⚑ Castle open seasonally; footpaths through estate; station at Leominster and local bus service from Birmingham and Hereford.

P Car park at Croft Castle (seasonal).

★ Refreshments available at Croft Castle; wheelchair access to parts of grounds; leaflet; information board in car park; picnics in parkland; dogs allowed on leads.

⬛ 561 ha (1385 acres) 6ml NW of Leominster, via B4361 from Leominster or B4362 from A49 Ludlow to Leominster road.   [137:SO455655]

Derwent and Howden Moors   Derbyshire

Rising eastwards and northwards from the famous Derwent and Lady-bower reservoirs, these moors contain some of the finest and most extensive stretches of heather moorland in the country. With Kinder Scout and the Snake Pass they form a very large and nationally important SSSI, mainly for the expanses of blanket peat and upland heath. These have some nine species of dwarf shrub (heather and its allies), including the unusual bearberry, rare outside northern Scotland. Wet heath and bog have cranberry, crowberry, cowberry, bilberry, cloudberry and cross-leaved heath, with cotton grasses and *Sphagnum* moss. The upland breeding birds are of great importance here, with red grouse, golden plover, dunlin, curlew, ring ouzel, peregrine, wheatear and even the unusual twite. The dramatic emperor, fox and oak eggar moths feed on the heather, and the area is a stronghold for the mountain hare.

Cloughs or steep valleys cut into the sides of the high plateaux, have important relicts of woodland, with oak, birch, aspen and ferns such as beech fern. Small springs, flushes and mires are also of interest, and the unusual ivy-leaved bellflower can be found here.

The blanket bogs have been badly affected by air pollution in parts of the High Peak (as outlined in the entries for Kinder Scout and Snake Pass) but the Derwent Moors are generally in good condition. Nevertheless, the Trust is monitoring the vegetation, and has undertaken a programme of regenerating the relict woodlands, mainly by natural means. These areas provide important habitats for many insects and birds, as well as increasing the natural woodland cover of the clough sides. Grey wagtail, dipper, woodcock and snipe can all be seen locally, with occasional sightings of short-eared owl, merlin, hen harrier and raven.

The area has some interesting archaeological remains, ranging from the mesolithic period through to the present day. Flint and chert artefacts found on the site suggest that prehistoric communities once used the area for hunting, and the barrow of Pike Low is a typical Bronze Age monument. Derwent has also been an important boundary marker throughout history – at one time part of the property formed the eastern boundary of the Royal Forest of the Peak.

[↟] Open access; network of footpaths and bridleways.

[P] Car parks around reservoirs (limited road access to upper part of valley at weekends).

[★] National Park/Severn Trent information centre and facilities south of Derwent Reservoir at Fairholmes; leaflets (including walks); new information shelter at Grindle Barn.

[⬛] 2618 ha (6468 acres) 13ml W of Sheffield, via A57 Sheffield to Manchester road.   [110:SK189885 (Grindle Barn)]

Dovedale   Derbyshire

Over thousands of years the River Dove has carved its way through this massive limestone plateau within the Trust's South Peak Estate, to create a deep, sinuous and spectacular gorge, long famous for its rock pinnacles, spires, arches and caves.

Dovedale is of great geological and physiographic interest for this striking karst scenery. It is also of great ecological interest for its limestone grasslands, crags and woodlands. There are some of the best calcareous ash woods in the country here, although only small parts of the extensive woody cover are ancient, now linked by much recent secondary growth. The Trust has cleared some of the secondary woodland, which has grown up since the early 1900s as a result of the decline in grazing, to reveal again the dramatic rock features. The ancient 'cores' have many unusual plants, such as angular Solomon's seal, lily-of-the-valley, herb Paris and small and large-leaved limes.

The limestone grasslands support many Derbyshire specialities, and both northern and southern limestone species mixed together, for example Nottingham catchfly, limestone bedstraw, stemless thistle, dropwort and greater burnet saxifrage. The crags, with their thinner soils and lack of grazing, harbour many more unusual plants such as Hutchinsia. All these habitats have specialist associated invertebrates, including glow worm and northern brown argus. Grey wagtail and dipper can be seen along the river.

There is evidence that the gorge was inhabited from early prehistoric periods. Surviving from later periods are some Bronze Age barrows, old lime kilns and post-medieval farm buildings. The names of the crags, such as Jacob's Ladder, Reynard's Cave and Lion Head Rock, originated with Victorian tourists, as did the famous 'Stepping Stones'.

[🚶] Footpath (accessible in parts by wheelchair).

[P] Car parks at Milldale and Stepping Stones end (not NT).

[★] NT information barn at Milldale; NT information centre/WCs at Ilam Park.

[♿] 651 ha (1607 acres) 4–7ml NW of Ashbourne, W of A515.

[119:SK148510]

Dover's Hill   Gloucestershire

This natural limestone amphitheatre (part of the Cotswold AONB) lies on the edge of the Cotswold escarpment, with impressive views across the Vale of Evesham. It is the site of the annual 'Cotswold Olympick Games', a tradition dating back to the seventeenth century, on the Spring Bank Holiday weekend.

There are numerous steep walks up the slope, passing through pasture, scrub, old pollarded trees, springs and woodland. In a number of places the limestone has fallen away, leaving an unusual landslip scenery.

Lynches Wood is an ancient woodland with bluebell, dog violet and wood sorrel. Tawny owl, great spotted woodpecker, treecreeper and blackcap are among the many birds to be found, and the large old ash, oak and field maple pollards support many specialist insects. The scrub of hawthorn, ash and sallow is ideal for whitethroat, garden warbler and yellow-hammer. Meadow saxifrage, a local rarity, can be found in the grassland along with a large number of snails which rely on the calcium content of the soil.

[🚶] Footpath to viewpoint; woodland trail; station at Moreton-in-Marsh.

[P] Large car park.

⊠ Leaflet; information board in car park; woodland trail through Lynches Wood; disabled access to topograph at viewpoint.

⊞ 74.5 ha (184 acres) north of B4035 between Chipping Campden and Weston-sub-Edge.   [151:SP137397]

Dunham Massey   Cheshire

Dunham Massey Hall stands in 25 hectares of parkland, which provides an ideal rural setting for the eighteenth-century mansion. It is also of increasing importance as a haven for wildlife, and a buffer against the threats of development and intensive agriculture which press up to its walls.

The estate consists of the house, garden, park and farmland, and was bequeathed to the Trust in 1976, but has been a popular recreational resort for the growing population of Manchester since the early nineteenth century. It is the medieval deer park (an SSSI) that is of prime importance to social historians and conservationists, since it embodies elements of the original forest or 'wildwood'. The current pattern of trees and woods dates from the landscape plantings designed in the eighteenth century (it is one of the last remaining unaltered formal English parklands), but these trees are now sufficiently old to have adopted the fauna which has lived in old trees on the site since the last Ice Age. A herd of fallow deer roams freely in the park.

The park also provides sites for hole-nesting birds, including all three species of woodpecker. An area of unimproved pasture and wetland is important for its range of plants, and there are a number of ancient ponds and water-filled marl pits which add to the range of habitats. An area of coarse grassland is an important source of nectar for the deadwood fauna.

⊠ Open access, except to areas designated as deer sanctuary; park open all year; house and garden open seasonally; local stations at Altrincham and Hale; bus from Altrincham stops at park gate.

P Large car park at entrance to property.

⊠ NT shop and restaurant in South Stables; WCs (including disabled) in North Stables; electric self-drive vehicle for use in grounds; information and park leaflet; guided walks.

⊞ 1284 ha (3172 acres) 3ml SW of Altrincham, off M56.   [109:SJ735874]

Edale
Derbyshire

The Trust owns a number of typical upland farms in the popular Derbyshire gritstone landscape of the High Peak Estate, lying south of the Kinder Scout massif and encircling the impressive conical form of Mam Tor and the head of the Vale of Edale. The open moorland merges with enclosed farmlands. A patchwork of gritstone walls surrounding improved pastures and the vernacular farm buildings dotted throughout the valley are an integral part of the character of the landscape.

Despite the majority of the meadows having been improved for agriculture, and thereby losing the variety of their flora, a number of herb-rich fields have survived, with plants such as adder's tongue fern, betony, yellow rattle and great burnet. Wooded cloughs, small woods and wooded river banks form an important part of the property and add to the wildlife interest. The Trust is actively conserving the remaining meadows, increasing the number of small woodlands and underplanting existing woods.

Beyond the field boundaries, moorlands – often with deep peat – have been heavily grazed and have lost some of their wildlife interest, requiring years of careful management to reverse the effects. Small streams, wet flushes and pockets of a former more extensive cover of heath, sedges, rushes, mosses, crowberry and cotton grass remain, and are being managed to enhance their wildlife value. The area is rich in upland and moorland birds, including red grouse, wheatear, golden plover and curlew.

Prehistoric burial practices on the ridge top are indicated by surviving barrows such as the Lord's Seat, a Bronze Age burial mound.

[⋏] Network of footpaths.

[P] Car park.

[★] National Park information centre at Fieldhead in Edale; leaflets; mountain rescue point; camping. NT information at Lee Barn, Dalehead, Edale End; camping at Upper Booth.

[⛍] 1012 ha (2500 acres) N of Hope Valley, off A625.   [110:SK100855]

Hamps and Manifold Valleys
Derbyshire

The river valleys of the Hamps and Manifold form part of the Trust's South Peak Estate and, like Dovedale, are distinctive for their limestone scenery, caves, rock cliffs, grasslands and woods.

The Manifold takes its name from the many deeply incised meanders which reflect the tortuous contours of the valley. The river meets its main tributary, the Hamps, at the great limestone cliff of Beeston Tor, before flowing on down to Ilam. During the summer months both rivers follow subterranean courses to emerge four to five miles downstream at the 'boil holes' in Ilam Country Park (see page 149). In the base of the valley runs the remains of the Leek & Manifold Light Railway track, which is now a metalled footpath and cycle track, popular with walkers and cyclists alike.

Both valleys contain a rich mosaic of grazed limestone grassland, small areas of meadow, scrub and woodland. The grassland supports many plant species such as rock-rose, thyme, melancholy thistle, cowslip, lady's mantle and occasionally grass of Parnassus. The naturally regenerating ash woodlands which cover the slopes of the valleys are rich with shrubs such as mountain currant and guelder rose, and parts have plants such as small-leaved lime indicative of the ancient origin of the woods. Wood vetch grows along the old railway track. Birds include wheatear, redstart and pied flycatcher. The valley sides contain some of the finest calcareous grasslands in Britain, which support many butterfly food plants, attracting species such as dark-green fritillary and the northern brown argus.

Grindon Moor consists of 9.5 hectares of heather moorland, containing cross-leaved heath, bell heather, cotton grass and bilberry. There is a good variety of upland birds, including curlew, lapwing, snipe and meadow pipit. A north-facing rock outcrop on the northern side of Ecton Hill has excellent examples of anticlines and sinklines, of interest to geologists.

Many hectares of woodland have been taken out of agricultural tenancy and fenced out to be managed for their high conservation value. In addition to property owned by the Trust, a further 506 hectares of the Throwley and Castern estates are protected by covenants.

[🚶] Free access to Wetton Hills; network of footpaths; Manifold Track.

[P] Car parks at Wetton Mill and Weags Bridge.

[★] Shop; café; WCs at Wetton Mill; Manifold Track suitable for wheelchairs.

[🏠] 442 ha (1091 acres) E of Grindon.   [119:SK095561]

Hardwick Park   Derbyshire

Hardwick Hall is a spectacular Elizabethan mansion built in the 1590s for Bess of Hardwick, a squire's daughter who became one of the richest landowners and most prodigious builders in England. The house is situated on a prominent limestone escarpment and surrounded by parkland which encloses remnants of a former medieval deer park, originally used by the manor for hunting. The ruins of Old Hardwick Hall, rebuilt by Bess shortly before embarking on her new hall, are under the guardianship of English Heritage.

Much of the surrounding estate is now a country park, with many paths and features of interest. There are two large ponds, Millers Pond and Great Pond, and five smaller ponds, built as fish ponds 400 years ago. Another chain of four ponds, the Carr Ponds, can be seen a little further afield in the eastern part of the estate. There is an old duck decoy, an ice-house, an old sandstone quarry and several acres of old, herb-rich grass-land with unusual plants such as adder's tongue fern. The ponds are of particular interest for wildlife, with birds such as great crested grebe, and many aquatic and marginal plants including branched bur reed, water plantain, marsh bedstraw, mare's tail, great reed-mace and many less common species. On Great Pond is an interesting area of alder and willow carr and fen.

A herd of longhorn cattle and a small flock of white-faced woodland sheep, both rare breeds, graze the parkland.

[†] Country park open daily during daylight hours; house and gardens open seasonally.

[P] Car parks in park and at hall.

[★] In park: leaflets; fishing permits; exhibition at information centre. At hall: NT shop; restaurant. WC (including disabled) at both park and hall; station at Chesterfield and local bus service from Chesterfield. Disabled access around Millers Pond.

[⬛] 805 ha (1990 acres) 6½ml NW of Mansfield, 9½ml SE of Chesterfield via A6175; approach from M1 (jct 29).   [120:SK463638]

Haresfield Beacon, Standish Wood, Stockend Wood and Maitland Wood   Gloucestershire

This series of properties, lying in the heart of the Cotswolds, has features typical of the scarp landscape: beech woodlands, limestone grassland, drystone walls and many archaeological remains. There are some disused quarries and old earthworks, with a dyke, a neolithic chambered long barrow and two round barrows on nearby Randwick Hill. A number of the woodlands are located on ancient sites, with evidence of historic land use, although some have been cleared and replanted.

Haresfield Beacon, designated a geological SSSI, is the site of a prehistoric hill fort, and gives impressive views across the Severn Estuary to the Welsh Hills. Remnants of old woodland pasture flank the hill.

Standish Wood, on the slopes of the escarpment, comprises several different woodlands containing a number of unusual plants associated with southern Britain. Among the stands of beech, ash, oak, birch and whitebeam grow bluebell, dog's mercury, wood anemone, sweet woodruff, wood spurge, and hart's tongue and hard shield ferns.

Stockend and Maitland Woods, on the shallower slopes, are thought to be part of an old pasture woodland and show signs of a traditional pastoral way of life. There is evidence of old coppicing, with some beech coppice stools. These woods contain an interesting flora which includes spurge laurel, wood melick and hart's tongue fern.

Woodland birds include blackcap, chiffchaff and great spotted woodpecker, and the limestone grassland, with its wide range of plants, supports many butterflies such as the brown argus, common blue and small copper.

The ridges are easily reached on foot from a number of neighbouring Cotswold villages; Pitchcombe, Painswick and Sheepscombe are particularly attractive and well worth visiting.

🚶 Footpaths cross the woodlands; the Cotswold Way follows the scarp line; stations at Stroud and Stonehouse.

🅿 One car park at Standish Wood; casual parking at other properties.

★ Information board in car park; topograph on Haresfield Beacon; camping area off Cotswold Way; Slimbridge Wildlife Trust on opposite side of M5 (about 10ml from Stonehouse).

🏞 146 ha (361 acres) 2–3ml NW of Stroud, between A419 and A46.
[162:SO820089 and 840087]

Ilam   Derbyshire

Ilam Country Park is situated in one of the most popular positions in the South Peak District, with magnificent views towards Thorpe Cloud and the entrance to Dovedale. From the terrace in front of the Hall, the garden and lawns slope down to the River Manifold and the village church. Within the park are 'boil holes', where the rivers Manifold and Hamps resurface after travelling underground, one of the largest resurgences in the country. A path leads from the boil holes along Paradise Walk, which is maintained as a landscaped promenade feature of the park.

From here one can view the ancient Hinkley Wood, of great interest to ecologists for its native populations of two rare trees, small- and large-leaved limes, and hybrids between them. Ash regeneration is now filling the many gaps left by the demise of the elm. Standing deadwood has been left where possible for insect and bird interest.

The river provides another important wildlife habitat, with birds such as kingfisher, dipper and grey wagtail commonly sighted along its banks.

Of historic interest are the remains of an Anglo-Saxon cross, and well-preserved remains of medieval ridge and furrow surviving in an area of permanent pasture.

- 🚶 Free access; network of footpaths; bus service from Derby.
- 🅿 Car park.
- ✪ NT shop and tea-rooms; WCs; information centre; education room for visiting groups; youth hostel; caravan site.
- ⬛ 34 ha (84 acres) 4½ml NW of Ashbourne.   [119:SK132507]

Kedleston Park   Derbyshire

Kedleston Park is a magnificent and classic eighteenth-century landscape. Robert Adam's masterpiece of Palladian architecture is set in extensive grazed parkland, with a series of lakes that includes the island lake, spanned by an arched Adam bridge; there are also remnants of earlier landscapes. The church dates from the twelfth century, the last survivor of the old village of Kedleston, which was moved in the early 1760s. The dense groves of old oaks in the north part of the park, beyond the island lake, are also medieval, surviving from an old deer park which once extended beyond the Trust's boundary to the north-east. On the slopes behind and west of the house, lines of old trees can be seen, representing hedges which were once part of an enclosed farmland landscape. The lakes were created by damming the Cutler Brook with six weirs.

The main wildlife interest of Kedleston is the invertebrate fauna associated with the ancient trees. The best area is in the northern part of the park, coinciding with the medieval park, but old trees elsewhere are also important, especially in the Long Walk woodlands along the southern edge of the property. The lakes have breeding water birds, although the huge flocks of Canada geese damage the quality of the habitat, and trample and enrich the lakeside grasslands. Areas of rough grassland and scrub, not attractive to the Canada geese, are also of value. Great spotted woodpecker and nuthatch can be seen in the woods.

⚹ House and park open seasonally; network of footpaths; stations at
Duffield and Derby.

P Car park.

★ NT shop and restaurant; WCs (including disabled); teacher's pack.

⊞ 331.5 ha (819 acres) 3ml NW of Derby off A52.   [128:SK312403]

Kinder Scout and Bleaklow   Derbyshire

The mass trespass of Kinder Scout in 1932 by ramblers from Manchester
and Sheffield and the beginning of the Pennine Way long-distance route
have put the magnificent massif of Kinder Scout among the most well-
known and popular moorlands in the Peak District. Kinder Downfall is an
impressive 30-metre high waterfall on the western edge of the plateau, in
the shape of an amphitheatre.

A thick blanket of peat, up to four metres deep, covers the plateau of
Kinder and Bleaklow. This ancient deposit, which began to develop over
6000 years ago, is now, in places, in an advanced state of degradation.
Erosion has been accelerated by the impact of man through air
pollution, accidental fire and overgrazing by sheep. The slopes below
Kinder Downfall were fragile and eroding too, mainly due to grazing,
and there was virtually no heather here when the Trust acquired
Kinder Scout in 1982. Since then, the Trust has initiated innovative
restoration measures on both the peat plateau and the slopes below.
Grazing levels have been dramatically reduced, with Trust wardens
actively shepherding sheep from the moor, and many methods of
revegetating the bare peat plateau are being undertaken. The slopes
now support good expanses of heather and bilberry, and some plants
are growing again on the eroded peat.

Kinder Scout has some fascinating historical associations. After the
Norman Conquest it was part of a Royal Forest, and in the Middle Ages
much of the land was owned by the Church who used it to breed horses,
then later sheep. Kinder links with Edale via Jacob's Ladder, a historic
packhorse route which has recently been resurfaced using traditional
techniques. Other historic features include Edale Cross and the remains of
a shooting refectory and shooting cabins dating from the late nineteenth
and early twentieth centuries.

⚹ Open access; network of paths and bridleways; Kinder Round Walk.

P Car parks at Edale and Bowden Bridge (1ml east of Hayfield).

☒ NT information point in Edale at Lee Barn; County Council information centre in Hayfield; information and camping at Bowden Bridge; Caravan Club caravans at Spray House; South Head information shelter; leaflets.

🏠 1332 ha (3291 acres) N of the Vale of Edale, S of A628(T). [110:SK0988]

Kinver Edge   Staffordshire

Kinver Edge is a prominent sandstone escarpment rising above the village of Kinver. Once all commonland, much of the area was taken into agriculture following enclosure in the eighteenth century, but has since reverted first to lowland heath and, more recently, to naturally regenerated birch, oak and pine woodland which encroaches on the heathland, although the Trust has now introduced a successful programme of control. Fragments of the historic Mercia Forest remain in the old woodlands.

The mixed woodlands include oak, birch, crab apple, hazel, spindle, guelder rose and aspen, with birds such as green woodpecker, wood warbler, tree pipit, sparrowhawk, redstart and woodcock. On the heath can be found heather, bell heather, wavy hair grass and bilberry, attracting butterflies, grasshoppers, mining bees and moths. The grassland includes a fascinating area of mobile sand with the rare dune grass *Corynephorus canescens*, and adders, slow worms and lizards inhabit the sandy slopes.

One of the earlier properties to be acquired by the Trust, it is noted for the unusual dwellings dug out of the sandstone, which were occupied as late as the 1960s by local workers, mainly from the foundries. Some of these have recently been restored and are open on selected days. There is also an Iron Age promontory fort.

🚶 Open access; footpaths.

P Car parks and parking along road.

☒ WCs; information boards; Kingsford Country Park nearby; limited wheelchair access.

🏠 114.5 ha (283 acres) 4ml W of Stourbridge, 4ml N of Kidderminster, 1½ml W of A449.   [138:SO835830]

The Long Mynd   Shropshire

With impressive views across to the Black Mountains and Cheshire, this great ridge, extending for ten miles, is one of several plateaux in the Shropshire Hills designated an AONB and SSSI.

The thin, acid upland soils support a cover of heather and fine, tussocky grassland on wild open moors which, with more sheltered incised valleys, are home to birds of prey, plants and insects of upland bogs, and a host of invertebrates in the streams which provide food for dipper and fish. Raven, buzzard and curlew are a common sight over the uplands, and other moorland birds include wheatear, ring ouzel, stonechat and red grouse. The woodlands in the lower valleys attract the pied flycatcher and tree pipit, and dipper and grey wagtail can be seen along the fast-flowing streams.

Bilberry grows among the heather, and moisture-loving plants such as the common spotted orchid, butterwort, round-leaved sundew, bog pimpernel and *Sphagnum* moss are found on the higher slopes around the springs and damp flushes. The fine, wiry moorland grasses are speckled with tormentil and heath bedstraw.

A scatter of archaeological remains from the Bronze Age, Iron Age and medieval times is evidence of centuries of man's habitation on the plateau, and sites of interest include a hill fort and earthworks, prehistoric tumuli, Bodbury Ring and the Port Way track, an old drove road.

⚹ Open access; roads; footpaths and bridleways cross the ridge; station at Church Stretton and Shrewsbury-Ludlow bus service, alight Church Stretton; shuttle bus to property at weekends and Bank Hols, April to Sept.

P Pay-and-display car parks at Carding Mill Valley.

★ Shop, restaurant and information centre at Carding Mill; WCs (including disabled); leaflet on walking routes; limited wheelchair access.

▣ 2367.5 ha (5850 acres) 15ml S of Shrewsbury, W of Church Stretton Valley and A49. [137:SO430940]

The Longshaw Estate   Derbyshire

This typical Pennine millstone grit landscape consists of low-lying moorland, the wooded banks of Burbage Brook, birch, rowan and oak woodland, enclosed farmland and old quarries where millstones were worked (numerous finished and half-finished stones can still be seen). Formerly a shooting estate, it is today extremely popular with walkers.

The woods of Padley Gorge are the most important areas of ancient oak woodland remaining in the Peak District. The trees and boulders on the woodland floor are covered with unusual lichens, and birds include pied flycatcher, sparrowhawk and tawny owl. For several years the woods have been fenced to exclude grazing stock, so that the ground layer of bilberry and other plant species is unusually luxuriant.

Other habitats on the estate include upland heath, open grazed woodland, acid grassland and meadows. The Fish Pond is a valuable habitat for dragonflies and other insects.

The estate is of great interest for its landuse history, with features ranging from the prehistoric period to medieval times. On Lawrence Field and Sheffield Plantation are enclosures dating from the Bronze Age but with evidence of re-use several centuries later. A network of ancient tracks, used for transporting lead, millstones, salt and corn cross the estate, and paved packhorse tracks can also be traced. A guidestone, dated 1709, in the middle of the estate marks the place where four roads met, providing clues to an early eighteenth-century road network. Other evidence of local industry includes a number of quarries which produced millstones and grindstones for use in the Sheffield tool and cutlery industries.

Near Eyam, famous for its self-imposed isolation during the plague of 1665, lie Riley Graves, now protected and managed by the Trust and where members of one of the families are buried.

⊞ Network of paths and trails; local station at Grindleford and bus service from Sheffield.

P Car park.

⊞ NT shop, tea-room and visitor centre; WCs (including disabled); Longshaw walks leaflet available from visitor centre (tel. 01433 631708).

⊞ 444 ha (1097 acres) 7½ml from Sheffield, 3ml SE of Hathersage, beside A625 Sheffield to Hathersage road.   [110 and 119:SK267801]

Lyme Park   Cheshire

A medieval deer park, Lyme includes extensive areas of parkland, woodland and moorland. Rather untypically, the ground rises quickly from around 210 metres at the main park gate to 396 metres at the top of Park Moor, thereby creating a dramatic setting for Lyme Hall, which lies at the centre of the park. The estate was given to the National Trust in 1946 and is a popular destination for the residents of Stockport and Manchester.

One of the main attractions of Lyme is its ancient quality, and it is possible to see how the landscape has evolved through the centuries from the surviving ancient wood pasture to the formal plantings of the seventeenth and eighteenth centuries. These provided vistas throughout the park, joining places of interest such as the The Cage, a restored hunting tower and prominent local landmark, with Paddock Cottage and the Lantern. During the nineteenth and twentieth centuries large areas of woodland were planted for commercial and sporting use, including the landscape planting along the present driveway.

Lyme is home to two herds of deer. The red deer are dsecendants of the important herd which populated the royal hunting forest of Macclesfield. The fallow deer are kept separate from the red and during the summer months can be found to the south of the house and gardens.

Two breeds of cattle are used for conservation grazing. Highland cattle graze the moorland so that the dominance of purple moor grass is reduced in favour of species such as heather and bilberry. Dexters are used to control rank grasses, thereby promoting the growth of wild flowers. Gritstone sheep are also grazed in the park, but are kept separate from the cattle.

The varied habitats at Lyme support a wide range of wildlife. Good numbers of skylark and snipe can be found on the moorland, with pied flycatcher in the lowland woods and grey wagtail along the valley streams. One new arrival is the raven, which has recently nested in the higher woods.

Some of the ponds scattered across the park have been given an SSSI rating because of their dragonfly populations. Probably the most important habitats are the open rough pasture and wood pasture, where specialised animal and plant communities have evolved to live with the onging presence of the red deer and their grazing habits.

[i] Park open 8am–8.30pm in summer, 8am to 6pm in winter; fallow deer sanctuary and calves' croft open 1 April to 30 Sept; network of footpaths, including lakeside path suitable for buggies and wheelchairs; Gritstone Trail and Pemberley Trail both start at main car park; station at Disley; bus services from Buxton and Stockport, with free minibus from entrance point to hall (seasonal, tel. 01663 762023 for details).

[P] Two car parks. Disabled parking at restaurant and hall.

[★] Two NT shops, restaurant, tea-room and information centre. Hall and gardens, Paddock Cottage and The Cage (all seasonal, tel. for opening times).

[▣] 557 ha (1377 acres) 6½ ml SE of Stockport and 9ml NW of Buxton, main entrance on A6.   [109:SJ965825]

May Hill and May Hill Common   Gloucestershire

This isolated conical hill with spectacular views over the Severn plain is designated an AONB. Formerly heathland, the hill was cultivated during the Second World War for barley and potatoes but has now reverted to a typical upland vegetation of coarse grass, gorse scrub, bracken and heather.

Pockets of wet flushes support mosses and damp-loving plants such as marsh pennywort, bog stitchwort, round-leaved crowfoot and bog pimpernel, and a number of ponds (a diminishing habitat in the county) add to the diversity of the wildlife with great crested newt, damselfly and pond skater.

A network of paths leads up the hill through attractive woodland to an SSSI on the summit, which is covered in gorse, bilberry and heather. Tree pipit are present here in summer, and yellowhammer are common among the gorse and heather. Butterflies include the small copper and green-veined white.

🚶 Open access to Common; 2 footpaths; network of paths through woods.

🅿 Small parking areas; no parking on road.

✪ Local facilities.

📌 53 ha (131 acres) 9ml W of Gloucester, towards Ross-on-Wye, N of A40.
[162:SO695215]

Minchinhampton and Rodborough Commons
Gloucestershire

Stretches of Jurassic limestone grassland occupy the plateau above the steep Cotswold escarpment (an AONB). Broken by patches of woodland and scrub, and containing a number of ancient earthworks and archaeological remains, the commons (designated an SSSI) are still grazed by the cattle and horses of local graziers exercising their historic rights as commoners. The area is also popular for walking, jogging, golf and kite-flying. The Bulwarks, an Iron Age hill fort above the village of Amberley, commands splendid views across the Cotswold landscape to the Welsh Hills.

Both commons are recognised for the importance of their wildlife, and among the many flowers and grasses are the common rock-rose, eyebright, cowslip, pyramidal and common spotted orchids, stemless thistle and bird's foot trefoil. Butterflies include chalkhill and small blues, dark-green fritillary and Duke of Burgundy, and juniper bushes on the steep slopes also attract a number of interesting insects. Dog's mercury and bluebell flourish in the ash, oak and beech woodland remnants.

Rodborough Common, with its small coombes and spurs, contains a number of specific habitats which support a wide range of plants and associated invertebrates. Although the commons form one of the richest grassland systems in the country, the flora at Rodborough is suffering from a decline in grazing, and species such as the rare pasque flower have declined considerably, while rank tor grass has increased phenomenally. The growing number of visitors is causing problems, particularly at Minchinhampton.

[⏫] Open access; network of footpaths and minor roads across commons.

[P] Parking areas on edge of commons and on Rodborough Common.

[★] Information boards; leaflets.

[⛺] 235 ha (580.5 acres) between Stroud and Nailsworth, E of A46 and SW of A419.   [162:SO850038 and 850010]

Park Hall Moor   Derbyshire

Merging with the Kinder Scout massif in the High Peak Estate west of Kinder Downfall, Park Hall Moor is a large tract of heather moorland which falls away to the outskirts of Hayfield. The view across to the Kinder escarpment is impressive, and the foreground is dominated by enclosed spurs dissected by cloughs or river valleys.

Park Hall Moor has been managed for red grouse, sheep and wildlife since the early nineteenth century, and the shooting cabin and adjacent shooting butts are in regular use today. Other popular activities include rambling. During the Kinder Scout mass trespass in 1932 the demonstrators walked along Snake Path (which opened in 1897) to reach Kinder and enforce their claim for access to open country. The Trust now safeguards this right of access for ever.

There are good expanses of wet and dry heathland here. Bilberry, crowberry and cowberry are three species associated with the drier heath, and hare's tail and common cotton grasses, *Sphagnum* moss and sedges with the wet heath. Special protection is given to the rare bog rosemary, and an excellent assemblage of upland birds breeds in the area. Rowan and birch trees are scattered up the steep river valleys. The Trust is working to control the spread of invasive rhododendron onto the moor.

The whole of Park Hall Moor was incorporated in the Royal Forest of the Peak around the time of the Norman Conquest.

🚶 Open access; network of footpaths; the Pennine Way.

🅿 Roadside parking; parking at Bowden Bridge and Hayfield.

★ Local facilities; camping at Bowden Bridge.

🏛 653 ha (1613 acres) W of Kinder Downfall, E of A6242.   [110:SK035885]

Sherborne Park Estate   Gloucestershire

This large agricultural estate on the Cotswold plateau (part of the Cotswold AONB and the Sherborne and Windrush conservation areas) contains large areas of former parkland and has good views across the Windrush Valley.

Within the estate is Lodge Park, a seventeenth-century deer-coursing lodge set within a park and currently being renovated by the Trust. The landscape is peppered with copses and coppiced woodland, some on ancient wooded sites. The remnants of a number of meadows along the river were once part of a more extensive system of flood meadows, an old practice which allowed the river water to flow over the grassland during the winter months, releasing its nutrients and warming the land.

A colony of the scarce Duke of Burgundy butterfly inhabits an area of unimproved rich limestone grassland, and mature trees in the parkland harbour some rare beetles and lichens associated with old-established woodland. The copses, woodlands and sheltered belts of trees provide invaluable habitats for birds. The rare lesser horseshoe bat roosts in the older buildings, and on the river are water vole and birds such as little grebe, sedge warbler, reed bunting and mute swan.

Lodge Park contains a fine neolithic chambered tomb, and other evidence of prehistoric life exists on the estate, though Bronze Age barrows have been ploughed down over the years and other settlement evidence lies in cultivated land. An unusual survival is Windrush Camp, a defended settlement of the later prehistoric period (not open to the public).

🚶 Confined to roads, bridleways and footpaths; waymarked routes.

🅿 Car park at Ewepen barn N of A40.

★ Leaflets; information boards in Ewepen barn; waymarked walks.

🏛 1677 ha (4144 acres) 3ml E of Northleach, each side of A40.

[163:SP162138]

Shugborough Staffordshire

Set within the former Forest of Cannock, this estate, administered by Staffordshire County Council, is dominated by parkland, farmland and plantation woodlands. A few relics of the old hunting forest still survive, such as Haywood and Great Haywood parks, and include old oak pollards of biological and historical importance which support a range of beetles found only on trees associated with primeval woods. A variety of birds such as pied flycatcher, woodcock, lesser spotted woodpecker and wood warbler can be seen in small areas of oak and birch woodland, as well as the barn owl (a nationally declining species); there are interesting displays of fungi in the autumn.

Shugborough Park Farm is now a working agricultural museum, recreating nineteenth-century farm life with displays, demonstrations and livestock. Its close proximity to the River Trent and its fragile wetland habitats of marsh, fen and alder carr enhance the value of the wildlife of the area.

There are over four miles of river frontage, and the wetland sites harbour reed bunting, sedge warbler, moorhen and coot. Insects such as dragonflies and damselflies inhabit the reeds and sedges.

[🚶] House, museum and farm open seasonally; park open daily; footpaths; station at Stafford and bus service from Stafford and Lichfield.

[P] Car park.

[★] NT shop and tea-room; WCs (including disabled); guided walks and trails; visitor centre with audio-visual display; play area; museum and farm accessible to wheelchairs.

[▦] 364 ha (899 acres) 5½ml SE of Stafford on A513, entrance at Milford.
[127:SJ992225]

Snake Pass and Hope Woodlands Derbyshire

Located between the two large moorland massifs of Kinder Scout and Bleaklow, Snake Pass and Hope 'Woodlands' (a misnomer since very little of the valley is wooded) form part of 13,500-hectare Trust property of the High Peak Estate, and include substantial blocks of moorland, hidden valleys and woods surrounding the rivers of Ashop, Alport and Westend which run down to Ladybower Reservoir.

Crossed by the bleak and high road between Manchester and Sheffield, it is often blocked by snow in winter. As in other areas of the High Peak, the deep blanket peat of the moorland is bare and exposed in many places due to pollution, fire and sheep damage over the past 300 years, which has affected the growth of the protective layer of *Sphagnum* moss, cotton grass and other bog species. Management by the Trust to reverse these effects is now underway, aimed particularly at reducing the amount of bare peat, especially along footpaths. However, excellent expanses of upland heath remain on the plateau.

The plateau is dissected by deeply incised valleys or cloughs where the soil is less peaty and acid, and here there are relict woodlands, grassland and bracken. The moorland supports a mosaic of grassland, bogs, wet flushes, eroded peat hags as well as the expanses of heather moor. Hare's tail and common cotton grasses, purple moor grass, bilberry, cowberry, crowberry, bell heather, cross-leaved heath, ling and the rare bog rose-mary provide habitat for a rich upland bird community which includes merlin, short-eared owl, red grouse, golden plover, dunlin, curlew, wheatear, skylark and meadow pipit. Woodlands and rivers provide additional habitat and shelter for many birds such as goldcrest, nuthatch, dipper and common sandpiper, and the inaccessible rock outcrops and pockets of natural oak woodland harbour a rich diversity of wildlife. The alternating bands of gritstone and shales are unstable in places, resulting in dramatic landslips such as the one at Alport Castles, reported to be the largest in the country.

The moors have been heavily grazed since the medieval period (Hope Woodlands have been utilized as rough grazing for sheep since this time), although grazing pressure has been controlled by the Trust over the last ten years. The moorland is crossed by a Roman road (north of the Snake Inn), and the large ditch known as 'Devil's Dike' is thought to have been cut by the monks of Basingwerk in Cheshire as a boundary for their land. Of interest in Snake Pass are several vernacular gritstone buildings, once part of the Chatsworth and Hardwick Hall Estates and which have been recently repaired by the Trust, and some old drove roads and sheep folds.

🏃 Open access; network of footpaths; property includes sections of the Pennine Way.

🅿 Roadside parking by A57.

★ Local facilities; camping.

🚌 6718 ha (16,600 acres) 10ml E of Glossop, both sides of A57.

[110:SK100939]

Styal Estate and Country Park   Cheshire

Styal Country Park, one of the first in the country to be established, is set in the wooded valley of the River Bollin. The woods of beech, oak and ash, some on ancient woodland sites, have a history of industrial use, with the coppicing of the underwood for stakes and the production of charcoal, and the periodic removal of mature timber for building, creating a specific community of wild flowers, birds and other wildlife.

Arthur's Wood on the northern slopes of the river contains some giant redwoods, and in spring bluebells cover the ground. The river cuts down into a steep gorge, exposing a geologically interesting succession of rocks. Great spotted woodpecker, woodcock and tawny owl may be seen, with grey wagtail and the occasional kingfisher along the riverside, which is rich with mosses, ferns and liverworts, attractive damselflies and dragonflies.

Much of the woodland was planted by the Greg family who founded Quarry Bank Mill in 1784, now a working museum of the cotton industry. Styal village, an old industrial settlement at the centre of the property, was also built by the Gregs. It is one of the few remaining unaltered factory colonies of the Industrial Revolution, and includes housing for workers and apprentices, a school, shop and two chapels.

ⓘ Country park open all year during daylight hours; circular walk from main car park; footpath across property (approximately 3ml); walks through woods and along river; station at Styal.

ⓟ Large car park (free to members) at Quarry Bank Mill; local authority car park at Twinnies Bridge.

★ Shop and restaurant (not NT) at mill; WCs (including disabled); information boards with maps at all entrances to property; country park guide with details of walks available from car park kiosk, mill and estate office in village; guided walks; picnic areas; wheelchair route from car park at Twinnies Bridge (central and western woodlands are steep with several flights of steps, stout footwear required). Dogs must be kept under close control at all times.

⬛ 121 ha (300 acres) 1½ml NW of Wilmslow, off B5166.   [109:SJ835836]

Wenlock Edge and Wilderhope   Shropshire

Approached from the west, the famous narrow limestone escarpment of Wenlock Edge in Shropshire runs for fifteen miles from Craven Arms to Ironbridge. The limestone, of international repute as an example of old coral reef deposits, supports an array of richly flowered grassland and ancient woodland, making the area an important SSSI.

Throughout the woods and along the scarp is an area of industrial and agricultural activity, with evidence of quarrying and limestone workings. Lime kilns and coppice woodland used to produce charcoal for firing the burners are clearly seen. On the Wilderhope Estate are the remains of old ridge and furrow in a number of fields. The Trust has acquired recent plantings of conifers, which changed the character of the Edge; now the balance is being redressed by replacing the conifers with the broadleaved trees natural to the area.

Several woods on the scarp slope are on ancient woodland sites, rich with unusual flora and shrubs. Small- and large-leaved limes, ash, hazel, wych elm and field maple are some of the trees to be seen, and the woodland flora includes the nettled-leaved bellflower, spurge laurel, yellow archangel, soft-shield fern, early purple orchid, common dog violet, dog's mercury and woodruff. Along the rides or in newly coppiced areas the flowers grow in greater profusion and attract many butterflies. Badger and dormouse inhabit the woods, and woodcock, nuthatch and spotted flycatcher are among the woodland birds. Buzzard can be seen overhead.

The herb-rich grassland along the upper edge of the wooded scarp supports pyramidal orchid, common gromwell and basil thyme. The estate of Wilderhope, situated in the remote and pastoral countryside on the southern slope of Wenlock Edge, surrounds a splendid, unspoilt Elizabethan manor built of limestone and now leased to the Youth Hostel Association. The landscape of wooded stream valleys, herb-rich grasslands, ancient woodlands, copses and old hedgerows forms the setting for Mary Webb's Shropshire country novels of the early years of this century.

Ash, oak, spindle, spurge laurel and yew grow in the ancient woods. Stanway Coppice is notable for its variety of woodland plants such as great woodrush, wood sorrel and foxglove (in the wetter areas). Dog's mercury, broad buckler fern and wood melick are common along the wooded streamsides, and the remaining unimproved limestone grasslands support a wide range of flowers, including eyebright and salad burnet. The hedges along the old trackways are thick with hazel, dogwood, rose, elder and blackthorn, and a small area of alder carr in a damp flush is a refuge for golden saxifrage, mosses and sedges.

[🚶] Footpaths and bridleways; Wilderhope Manor open seasonally; permitted routes in Wilderhope; Shropshire Way runs along Wenlock Edge; circular paths; station at Church Stretton.

P 2 car parks; lay-by parking; car park at Wilderhope Manor.

★ Local facilities; leaflet describing routes; viewpoints; easy access route.

⬛ 318 ha (786 acres) between Ironbridge Gorge and Craven Arms,
    NE of A49, via B4371 crossing the ridge; Wilderhope 6ml SW of
    Much Wenlock, 5½ml E of Church Stretton.
                    [127:SJ605002, 138:SO595988, 570965 and 545929]

The Winnats and Mam Tor   Derbyshire

Winnats Pass (the name is a corruption of 'wind-gates') is a deep and
impressive gorge which cuts into the limestone escarpment west of the
Norman village of Castleton. It contains many characteristic features of
a limestone landscape, with imposing crags, steep grassy shoulders and
cavern openings which disguise a network of caves and old workings of
lead, Blue John spar and calcite mines, and form this classic karst
scenery.

The pass leads out on to a plateau landscape of pastures enclosed by
typical grey limestone walls to the west, and the popular walkers' and
cavers' centre of Castleton to the east. Old pack-horse routes cross the
area. The grassland of the steep slopes and crags is rich in many lime-
loving plants, with Jacob's ladder, pansy, rock-rose, small scabious, harebell, thyme and many species characteristic of the Derbyshire limestone.
Shady rock crevices are colonised by woodland species such as wood sage
and dog's mercury. The crags harbour many unusual plants that survive
where grazing pressure is light.

Mam Tor, less than a mile to the north of the pass, dominates the head
of the Hope Valley and is known as the 'shivering mountain' because of
the frequent landslips of grit and shale on the south-eastern side. It is
popular for windswept walks with panoramic views for miles around,
towards Kinder Scout and to Lose Hill on the eastern edge of the ridge
(also owned by the Trust). The old A625 below the Tor was closed many
years ago after a substantial landslip severely disrupted the road, but this
is now an impressive attraction for sightseers.

Few visitors realise that the grassy slopes of the summit conceal the
remains of one of the best-preserved Bronze/Iron Age hill forts in the
county. The Tor is also the site of two Bronze Age barrows. The (until
recently) very heavily grazed acid grassland does not have the varied
flora of the nearby limestone grasslands of Winnats Pass, but the steep
gullies that have in the past escaped the pressure of grazing support ferns,

mosses and woodland herbs. Pockets of oak woodland at the base of the slopes add to the diversity of wildlife interest.

[†] Open access; footpaths from west and from the ridge.

[P] Car parks in Castleton, Mam Nick and below Mam Tor on old A625; no parking in Winnats Pass.

[★] Facilities in Castleton; National Park information centre; leaflet; caravans and camping at Losehill; farmhouse B&B at Dunscar Farm, Castleton.

[▣] 316 ha (780 acres) 2–3ml W of Castleton.   [110:SK135826 and 126836]

Woodchester Park   Gloucestershire

Originally landscaped during the eighteenth century to provide a setting for Woodchester Mansion, the park is located in a large and tranquil valley close to the Cotswold scarp. The Georgian house was replaced during the Victorian era, and the later mansion (not NT) can be seen together with the ruins of several earlier outbuildings around the former gardens.

The property is very diverse, ranging from disused quarries to grassland and extensive woodland, and includes a chain of picturesque lakes. There are several uncommon plants associated with ancient woodland, including bird's nest orchid, stinking hellebore, angular Solomon's seal and lily-of-the-valley. The woods are also home to many species of bird, with breeding buzzard, sparrowhawk and three species of woodpecker.

The lakes contain a well-established fish community, with carp, pike, roach and tench all present, and in summer white water-lilies adorn the surface of the water. Waterbirds include kingfisher and mandarin duck. An early nineteenth-century boathouse can be seen on the south side of Middle Pond.

The valley is renowned as a site for bats, with five species regularly recorded, and probably has one of the highest densities of badger setts in Britain.

[†] Park open daily; waymarked walks (1, 3 & 7ml), some sections strenuous so stout footwear required; station at Stroud.

[P] Car park (charge) accessible from Nympsfield road, 300m from the junction with B4066.

[★] Leaflet.

[▣] 202 ha (499 acres) 4ml SW of Stroud off B4066.   [162:SO797012]

Arnside Knott

Cumbria

This shapely limestone hill is set between Silverdale and the Kent estuary, and includes dry valleys and steep cascades of scree, scattered with boulders and slabs of concrete-like breccia. Over the limestone is a skim of fine soil, encouraging the development of heathland among the mosaic of scrub, woodland and tussocky grassland. Centuries of common grazing and treeplanting have modified the natural vegetation, but significant communities of plants and animals survive.

The areas of open pasture and woodland are home to large numbers of butterflies, most notably the nationally endangered high brown fritillary, and important plants and trees include herb Paris and small-leaved lime. Sessile oak, yew and hazel dominate the woodland, with a coppiced area being used to produce charcoal.

The property is especially notable as a place at which north and south meet. Arctic-alpine species, such as the Scotch argus butterfly, are found alongside inhabitants of more temperate zones, such as the southern wood ant, here at the most northerly edge of its range.

[🚶] Footpaths; station at Arnside; local bus services.

[P] Car park above Larch Grove; parking also in village.

[★] Local facilities; leaflet (includes self-guided walks).

[▦] 107 ha (264 acres) 1ml S of Arnside, reached via B5282.

[97:SD456775]

Borrowdale

Cumbria

It is hard to believe that this valley, now part of a National Park, was once a hive of industrial activity with iron-smelting, charcoal-burning and mining for copper and graphite. Scattered hamlets reflect the Nordic influence in their names, while stone walls and vernacular buildings chronicle centuries of farming. Today farmers struggle to make a living and visitors play an important role in sustaining the local community.

There is much of historical and literary interest in the area, including the late neolithic Castlerigg Stone Circle just east of Keswick, and the medieval pack-horse bridge at Ashness. It has long been a favourite haunt of writers and artists. Friar's Crag, at the Keswick end of the lake and one of the most famous viewpoints in the Lake District, is where John Ruskin awoke to aesthetic experience as a child, and St Herbert's Island, sanctuary of a hermit in the seventh century, was Beatrix Potter's 'Owl Island' in *The Tale of Squirrel Nutkin*.

Leading south from Derwentwater, Borrowdale is surrounded by rugged crags, inviting fells, old mine workings and wooded valleys with clear rivers. The fine sessile oak woodlands are of particular ecological interest, and the damp, western climate supports internationally important lichens, mosses and insects. An alder woodland and marsh along the shores of Derwentwater provides ideal nesting sites for wildfowl and waders. Brandelhow, on the west shore of Derwentwater, was the first large property to be bought by the Trust in 1902.

Borrowdale splits into three valleys, Watendlath, Stonethwaite and Seathwaite, each with its own distinctive character. The Trust's estate also includes the western half of Derwentwater and half the western shore with the fells behind, the eastern shore up to the watershed with Thirlmere, and the land around Seatoller up to the Honister Pass, with Seathwaite and Stonethwaite. There are a number of farms within the three valleys, managed by tenant farmers.

Many of the fields are edged with pollarded ash trees, some of which support rare lichens. Some of the fells support important expanses of upland heath, a habitat which has declined in England and Wales because of heavy grazing by sheep.

The gills or ravines in which streams cascade down from the fell tops are rich with woodland and mountain vegetation including alpine lady's mantle, mountain sorrel, columbine and starry saxifrage. Birch woodlands have colonised old quarry workings.

The upland heaths are important for moorland birds such as red grouse; peregrine and raven can be seen on the fells, with pied flycatcher, redstart and wood warbler in the oak woods.

By road (congestion in high season, particularly on road to Watendlath); access over Honister Pass; well-marked footpaths and bridleways; launch service on Derwentwater.

Numerous car parks and lay-bys; no parking on roadside.

Footpaths; WCs; leaflets on valley walks, general information and off-road cycling from Lakeside Information Centre; information centres at Lakeside, Keswick (S) and Seatoller (S); camping and caravan sites; youth hostels; boating and fishing facilities (for further information contact regional office); disabled access to Crow Park and Friar's Crag.

11,806 ha (29,173 acres) 3ml S of Keswick, access from B5289 extending from S shore of Derwentwater to Honister Pass.   [89:NY2514]

The Buttermere Valley   Cumbria

The Buttermere Valley lies in precipitous lakeland scenery with few settlements, and encompasses three lakes, Crummock Water, Buttermere and Loweswater, all owned by the Trust. Buttermere was once linked to Crummock Water to the north-west, but flash-floods after the last Ice Age caused a band of alluvial deposits which now divides the two. Loweswater, north-west of Crummock Water, has several woods on its shores, while Buttermere is surrounded by Red Pike, Haystacks and Fleetwith Pike, which fall steeply down to the lakes and display the classic glacial features of corries, tarns, ridges and hanging valleys. (The Trust protects all the fells east of Buttermere and Crummock Water.)

The area is of great ecological interest, and the Buttermere Fells support the largest area of upland heath on Trust land in the Lake District, with rare plants such as the montane shrub bearberry. Buzzard, peregrine, raven and ring ouzel inhabit the fells.

Notable woodlands include Scales Wood (not owned by the Trust), above the apron of alluvial deposits between Buttermere and Crummock Water, which is nationally important for the rare lichens and mosses growing on the oak and ash trees. Lanthwaite Wood includes some old oak coppice and scrub oak, and glades support many interesting insects. Other broadleaved woods include Holme, Ghyll, Long How and Nether How.

The lakes are of particular interest for wildlife. Buttermere is low in nutrients, and supports a variety of rare Crustacea and fish, including char (an Ice Age relict fish), a deepwater trout which requires low temperatures. Loweswater's rich plant life provides good cover for great crested grebe and other water birds, including merganser, coot, mallard and goldeneye.

Among the sites of historical interest are a number of prehistoric settlements and evidence of fifteenth-century enclosures.

🚶 By road; limited access to Loweswater; network of footpaths.

🅿 Car parks and lay-bys; no parking for coaches.

⭐ Local facilities; mountain rescue point at Gatesgarth Farm; boating facilities (for further information contact NT Regional Office).

🛏 2934 ha (7250 acres) and covenants over 4650 acres (1882 ha) 9ml S of Cockermouth, via B5289 from Cockermouth or Keswick. [89:NY175170]

The Coniston Valley   Cumbria

The best way to view Coniston Water and its surrounding panorama is from the steam yacht *Gondola*, restored by the Trust in the late 1970s, which since the mid-nineteenth century has regularly taken visitors down this glacial lake, past Peel Island at the southern end of the lake (the inspiration for Arthur Ransome's 'Wild Cat Island' in *Swallows and Amazons*). The 'Old Man of Coniston' can be seen rising up behind the village of Coniston and Coniston Old Hall. The eastern shore is characterised by a contrasting mosaic of steeply rising conifer and mixed deciduous woodland containing the rare small-leaved lime.

At the head of Coniston Water (famous as the site of Donald Campbell's fatal attempt to beat the water-speed record in 1967), north-east of the village lies Tarn Hows, bought and sold on to the Trust by Beatrix Potter, a favourite place for excursions and with magnificent views of the mountains. It was landscaped to look like a Swiss lake in the nineteenth century. The shallow tarn has some important habitats, including a boggy area rich in wetland plants, with marsh cinquefoil, bogbean, common spotted orchid, sweet gale and hare's tail cotton grass. The slopes of Coniston Old Man (not Trust land) are scarred by old copper mines and slate quarries, and the remains of enclosures and bloomeries are evidence of a thirteenth-century monastic community. The Tilberthwaite mine is now colonised by various species of tree, moss and lichen.

The fells are covered in the ubiquitous upland grassland of mat grass, fescues and bents, with juniper on the screes and some fellsides. Characteristic oak woodlands, are of great ecological importance and support a wide range of mosses, lichens and invertebrates. Many pitsteads remain in the woods where charcoal was produced from coppicing. A scattering of ash, oak, rowan, hawthorn and Scots pine now covers the intake land of the fellsides, and in-bye fields in the valley bottom include some meadows rich in wild flowers.

[🚶] Via minor roads; network of footpaths; open access to shore; steam yacht *Gondola* sails from Coniston Pier (timetable available locally); no wheelchairs on *Gondola* but guide dogs admitted; vehicle ferry across Windermere.

[P] Plentiful car parks.

[★] WCs at Coniston car park (north end of lake); leaflets on Coniston Valley and Tarn Hows; caravan and camp sites.

⊞ 2226 ha (5500 acres) 9ml SE of Ambleside on A593, minor road to E of
Coniston Water, 12ml W of Windermere across ferry on B5285 through
Hawkshead.   [96 and 97:SD304964]

Dunnerdale   Cumbria

Running south-west from the central lakes, the remote and beautiful
Duddon Valley is isolated from the heart of the Lake District by Wrynose
Pass, lying between Langdale and Coniston fells. All the land on either
side of the Pass road, west of the Three Shires Stone, is protected by the
Trust.

In its upper reaches the river pours down the valley through resistant
volcanic rocks with frequent rock pools, its course punctuated by forestry
plantations. The valley widens out after High Wallowbarrow with farmsteads and enclosed wall pastures on either side, low craggy fells to the
east and rich oak woodlands to the west.

The broadleaved Duddon Woods (coppiced in the past for charcoal) are
of particular ecological interest, lush with mosses, ferns, lichens and
invertebrates. Birds include wood warbler, blackcap, treecreeper,
nuthatch and great spotted woodpecker. Birds on the fells include raven,
carrion crow, meadow pipit and wheatear, and buzzard are often seen
above the valley hunting for small mammals.

Heavy grazing has reduced the heather cover and interest of the
upland grasslands, but a few important areas remain. Bogs and mires,
containing mosses and damp-loving plants fill the hollows among the
fells. Patches of juniper scrub are of particular interest for wildlife, and the
River Duddon (part-owned by the Trust) provides valuable stretches of
open water.

Of historical interest are cairns, cairn fields and standing stones from
the Bronze and Iron ages, remains of Roman trade and military routes,
and the remains of copper mining and quarrying (local names sometimes
reflect past industries, as in Wallowbarrow Coppice and Kiln Bank).

The Trust's ownership is more patchy here than in other valleys:
Baskell Pikeside, Hazel Head, Wallowbarrow, Tongue House and Troutal
Farms, Cockley Beck and Blackhall Farms at the dale head, and Fenwick
Farm on Thwaites Fell.

🚶 Via narrow gated road; network of paths.

🅿 Informal parking.

★ Local facilities.

🖼 940 ha (2323 acres) reached by minor road between Little Langdale to Duddon Bridge, NW of Broughton-in-Furness, off A595.

[89:NY246016 and 96:SD223968]

Eaves and Waterslack Woods   Lancashire

Overlooking Bank House Farm and Morecambe Bay, this wooded limestone escarpment is of great wildlife interest. Waterslack Wood, towards the east of the property, is known to be an ancient woodland site.

Although partly modified by later planting of conifers (which are not being replaced), the older wooded areas have a number of plants and insects indicating continuity of tree cover, such as herb Paris, small-leaved lime, wild service tree, lily-of-the-valley, dog's mercury, ramson and bluebell. Evidence of traditional woodland management is visible throughout the woods, with hazel coppice below the standard trees.

Elsewhere, dense thickets of self-sown yew and scrubby woodland disguise important areas of limestone pavement (a habitat that in other places has been much destroyed by removal for rockeries over recent years), and limestone grasslands, which were once grazing land. The Trust is now undertaking a sensitive programme of tree clearance, coppicing and scrub removal to restore larger glades and open areas.

The limestone grasslands have some good anthills which provide food for green woodpecker, and associated plants include rockrose, quaking grass, spring cinquefoil and autumn gentian. Bloody crane's bill and hart's tongue fern grow on the limestone pavement. Butterflies, including high-brown fritillary, are abundant, and wild animals can often be seen in the woods, notably roe deer.

Of historical interest are the 'Pepper Pot', a monument to Queen Victoria's Golden Jubilee, and an old gamekeeper's cottage.

🚶 By minor road; network of paths.

🅿 Small car park.

★ Facilities at Silverdale; leaflet; viewpoint; picnic site.

🖼 43 ha (106 acres) 4ml NW of Carnforth, 1ml N of Silverdale.

[97:SD465758]

Ennerdale   Cumbria

The difficult access to Ennerdale protects it from over-visiting, and it remains one of the more secluded and quiet valleys. Great Gable, Pillar,

Steeple, Haycock and Red Pike, some of the highest peaks in the Lake District, rise above Ennerdale Forest (Forestry Commission) which dominates the valley towards the east.

The Trust manages land around Ennerdale Water above the Forestry Commission land, as well as Kinniside Common, a bleak expanse of fell. As with Wastwater, the lake is of interest for its purity and low nutrient levels, and provides an important habitat for char, aquatic crustaceans and unusual plants. The poorly drained mire adjacent to the lake is rich in invertebrates and damp-loving plants.

The damp, western broadleaved woodlands, notably Side Wood, of sessile oak and upland birch abound in mosses, lichens and ferns, and on the crags, in the gills and on rock ledges are mountain plant communities which include saxifrages, alpine lady's mantle and heather. The region also contains an interesting expanse of heathland, illustrating the gradation in vegetation from lakeside margin through broadleaved woodland to heather moor. A huge re-walling project has recently been completed to separate this valuable heath from the overgrazed and grassy Kinniside Common.

Of historical interest are a neolithic settlement on Kinniside Common and medieval settlement patterns. There is a long history of bloomeries and iron-ore mining in the area.

🚶 No vehicle access beyond Bowness Knott car park; network of footpaths; circular walk round lake.

🅿 Limited parking; Forestry Commission car parks; North West Water car park.

🚾 WCs at Bowness Knott car park; youth hostels; no camping.

▦ 2428 ha (6000 acres), excluding Kinniside Common, approached from the W off minor roads from A5086 via Ennerdale Bridge. [89:NY093164]

Eskdale   Cumbria

A significant Roman military road follows this remote valley from Ravenglass to Ambleside, with the remains of the Hardknott Roman fort (managed by the Trust) dominating the head of the valley. The varied terrain reflects the difference in the underlying rock structure, with the crags, screes and corries of the upper Esk of volcanic rocks, and the whaleback fells in the lower stretch of coarse-grained granite.

Before the establishment of the National Park, Eskdale and the Duddon Valley were part of a great controversy, with plans to plant large areas of fell with conifers; as a result it was agreed that in order to retain the open character of the landscape the central fells should not be planted. Drystone walls enclosing intake and in-bye fields are typical of the area; grey stone (volcanic rock) is more common but red-stone (sandstone) walls occur further down the valley. The river follows a sinuous course in places, bordered by old wooded banks and single holly trees creating characteristic features. Dipper and grey wagtail are typical of the birds to be seen along the river, and buzzard, peregrine and kestrel are common. The ravines have interesting relict woodland vegetation and plants that have escaped grazing by sheep (saxifrages, alpine lady's mantle, wood sage, heather and unusual ferns).

There are a number of herb-rich meadows with plants such as greater burnet, betony, knapweed, ox-eye daisy and a variety of grasses. On the fells, a number of valley mires and bogs support interesting mosses, grasses and sedges. The white downy heads of common cotton grass are quite distinct, and bog asphodel, sundew, butterwort, cross-leaved heath and marsh cinquefoil are also found.

The monasteries of Fountains and Furness held granges with extensive sheep walks in this area of the Lake District, and a medieval wall can still be seen at the valley head, defining the boundary of the monastic sheep farm. Also of historic interest are the Boot corn mill and the Woolpack Inn (neither are owned by the Trust) where the Fell Dales Sheepbreeders' Association (formed in 1864) holds its annual show on the last Saturday in September.

Eskdale retains evidence of the iron-ore mining industry, and visitors may enjoy a trip on the Ravenglass & Eskdale Railway, known locally as the 'Ratty', which started as an iron ore line in 1875.

The Trust owns all the land east of Penny Hill Farm to the Three Shires Stone, east of both Hardknott and Wrynose passes, arguably the most dramatic road in the Lake District, and also the fell to the north, including Harter Fell at the valley head.

🚶 Via narrow road from west; road from east over Hardknott and Wrynose Passes always impassable to caravans in winter; network of footpaths, particularly around Boot; Ravenglass & Eskdale Railway.

🅿 Lay-by at Hardknott; informal parking.

★ Local facilities.

🏛 1714 ha (4235 acres) reached by minor road from A595, 2ml N of Broad Oak to Hardknott Pass on the road to Little Langdale.   [89:NY3201]

Formby   Sefton

Part of the fourth largest sand dune system in Britain, this Merseyside nature reserve includes inter-tidal sand flats and both high yellow dunes and fixed dunes. Home to the nationally rare natterjack toad and designated an SSSI, it lies within a Ramsar site and forms part of the Sefton Coast Candidate SAC.

The reserve is constantly changing as natural forces mould the mobile dunes and foreshore. Pine woodlands were planted from the turn of the century onwards in an attempt to stabilise the dunes and provide shelter. At one time areas within the dunes were levelled for growing asparagus, although only the field pattern survives. Sheep are now grazed on some of these fields in order to conserve the developing dune grassland.

The frontal dunes roll back as sand is blown inland, whilst vigorous marram grass pushes up new shoots, trapping sand and consolidating the dunes. The more stable open dunes support creeping willow, dewberry and sand sedge, with scrub developing in places where grazing by rabbits is not too intense. Hawthorn, wild rose and birch scrub are maintained, whilst balsam poplar, white poplar and sea buckthorn are removed. Nationally notable plants include both dune and green-flowered helleborine, Portland spurge and seaside centaury, with bee and pyramidal orchids adding colour.

Many waders, gulls and migrant birds feed along the shoreline, with skylark, wheatear and kestrel among the species that may be seen inland. The pine woodland supports an important red squirrel population.

The semi-fossilised hoofprints of red deer, roe deer and aurochs, which grazed the saltmarshes during the Neolithic period, are sometimes exposed in inter-tidal sediments. 160 human footprint trails have also been recorded since 1990.

🚶 Open access all year; footpaths through woods and to beach; walk around squirrel reserve; coastal footpath from Crosby to Southport; local stations at Formby and Freshfield.

🅿 Car park (free to members).

★ Information panel; leaflets; picnic sites; wheelchair walk on boardwalk across dunes; wheelchair access to red squirrel reserve.

❗ No barbecues, fires or camping (to avoid fire risk).

�'200 ha (494 acres) W of Formby, of A565(T).   [108:SD275080]

Grasmere
Cumbria

Approached from the north over Dunmail Raise, the picturesque landscape around Grasmere is an impressive sight, with heaps of glacial debris, drumlins and *roche moutonée* (a glaciated type of rock surface) littering the U-shaped valley of the River Rothay, which flows down to Lake Windermere.

To the west, the Trust protects Grasmere Common, descending to Loughrigg Fell and including Grasmere Lake, and to the east the estate extends up to Seat Sandal and Fairfield, then down to White Moss Common and the southern half of Rydal Water. Here, in a condensed version of other grander valleys, Wordsworth's village is surrounded by a varied landscape which includes a number of small lakes, areas of broadleaved and coniferous woodland, scree slopes and lichen-covered crags, drystone walls skirting the fells and bracken-covered commons crossed by many footpaths. There are historic pack-horse routes over the fells.

Grasmere and Rydal in particular are important for overwintering wildfowl, and goosander, red-breasted merganser, pochard, common sandpiper and grey wagtail can be seen. There are many different aquatic plants in Rydal Water, and the reedbeds provide a good habitat for small nesting birds. A variety of rare snails and insects live among the tussocks of sedges and rushes, which form excellent stands of fen along the lake edges where there is no grazing.

The higher fells are covered predominantly by grassland and bracken, but with some fine stands of juniper, and the narrow ravines support relicts of woodland with rowan, ash, birch and many mosses and ferns. The islands in Rydal Water (only Little Isle is protected by the Trust) have interesting examples of ungrazed ancient woodland, with small-leaved lime as well as later-introduced exotics.

[🚶] Network of footpaths; open access to fells.

[P] Car parks in Grasmere and White Moss Common.

[★] Family walks and valley information leaflets; WCs (including disabled) in Grasmere and White Moss Common car park; information board at White Moss Common; no camping; boating and fishing facilities (further information from NT Regional Office).

[⛉] 2702 ha (6677 acres), access off A591 and minor roads.   [90:NY337077]

Heald Brow   Cumbria

Acquired in 1999, this property comprises three parcels of land within the Arnside and Silverdale AONB and includes significant areas of exposed limestone pavement. A series of footpaths leads across the property and the top of the Brow affords dramatic views over Morecambe Bay.

A number of nationally rare plants occur here, with the dark and humid grikes of the limestone pavement allowing the presence of species more usually associated with woodland. The grassland supports an important population of butterflies, and the site is also notable for the number of anthills, some of which may be more than a century old. The local soil is particularly fine and can be easily moved by the ants. It is also ideal for wild thyme, which grows in profusion on top of the anthills, resulting in a dramatic purple display in summer.

[🚶] Network of footpaths; station at Silverdale; local bus service connects Heald Brow with Eaves Wood and passes close to Jack Scout.

[P] Parking in Silverdale.

[★] Local facilities.

[▣] 170 ha (420 acres) 1¾ml S of Silverdale on minor road.   [97:SO742467]

Heysham Head   Lancashire

A sandstone headland mainly comprised of coastal heathland with some woodland, Heysham Head offers dramatic vistas across Morecambe Bay to the Lakeland fells. The area on the head known as Barrow's Field is important not only for its wildlife interest but also archaeologically. An SAM, it contains the 8th-century St Patrick's Chapel and, adjacent, several unique rock-cut graves.

The heathland here is a typical mix of grassland and scrub, including extensive bracken and bramble cover with bluebells below. The tangled mix of gorse and bramble on the seaward slopes provides a natural protective cloak and habitat for many species of animal and insect. A few small patches of heather heath survive. The cliff faces support communities of two uncommon ferns, royal fern and sea spleenwort, and are the only location in Lancashire for the latter species. Although dominated by sycamore, the woodland areas also include oak, ash and wych elm.

[🚶] Open access.

[P] Car park in village; limited informal parking near chapel.

[▣] 8 ha (19 acres) at Heysham, off A683.   [97: SD419618]

The Langdales
Cumbria

Dominated by the magnificent Langdale Pikes, Pike O'Blisco and Crinkle Crags, the two valleys of Great and Little Langdale have quite distinct qualities. Great Langdale, a sweeping, glaciated valley with steep, rugged sides and an ice-scoured wide, flat bottom, provides direct access to the surrounding fells. Little Langdale, a smaller valley with less dramatic landscape, is ideal walking country, a combination of rough fells, undulating valley floor, isolated tarns, meadows and a patchwork of woodlands.

The Trust's estate includes part of Great Langdale east of Millbeck and all the valley to the west, extending over to Little Langdale, south of Blea Tarn, together with the land around and including Little Langdale Tarn.

There is a wide variety of historical interest within this ancient landscape, with the 'Thing Mount' (the remains of a Viking parliamentary site), slate farmhouses with bank barns dating from the seventeenth and eighteenth centuries, and a thirteenth-century stone wall surrounding the head of Great Langdale. The disused coppermine at the head of the Greenburn Valley has left a fascinating historical footprint of a vanished industry.

The plants of the high fells reflect the acid soils, heavy grazing pressure and underlying volcanic rocks. A thick mat of purple moor grass, wavy hair grass, mat grass and fescues covers most of the tops. Bogs and mires occupy damp hollows, with *Sphagnum* moss, common and hare's tail cotton grasses, butterwort, common sundew, and many sedges and rushes. Juniper scrub reaches high levels on the fellside. Only small areas of heather have survived.

The ravines support interesting woodland relict and montane communities, with saxifrages, alpine lady's mantle, wood sorrel, wood anemone and heathers. Elterwater Tarn (not owned by the Trust) and Little Langdale Tarn are valuable sites for wildfowl and goosander, and breeding sites for little and great crested grebes.

Throughout the summer swallow and swift swoop and feed over the water, and the surrounding reedbeds, carr and woodland attract many nesting birds including nuthatch, treecreeper and warblers. A number of hay fields still have a wide range of flowers and grasses (betony, ox-eye daisy, cuckoo flower, heath spotted orchid, great burnet, wood crane's bill and lady's mantle).

[🚶] By road (narrow roads unsuitable for caravans and congestion to be expected in Little Langdale); network of footpaths and bridleways; open access to fells.

[P] Car parks where signed; lay-bys; no parking on roadside or in gateways.

[★] WCs at Elterwater, Chapel Stile and Stickle Ghyll; Leaflets on Little Langdale walks, Greenburn mine and valleys; information boards in car parks; viewpoint from Blea Tarn towards Langdale Pikes; canoeing; camping.

[!] No boating or fishing permitted on Elterwater or Little Langdale Tarn. The south screes of the Langdale Pikes are dangerously unstable because of erosion.

[⛺] 429 ha (1060 acres) W of Ambleside, from A593 and B5343 to Elterwater and Little Langdale. [89:NY2906]

Sandscale Haws Cumbria

Sandscale Haws is one of the best sand-dune systems in Britain. Within its very extensive area there are dunes of varying ages, from newly forming ones nearest the sea, high 'yellow dunes' with marram grass, to old stable grass-covered dunes inland. It also has a superb series of slacks, or wet depressions between the dunes. A large freshwater marsh with willow scrub behind the dunes, and developing saltmarsh on the foreshore add further valuable habitats.

The calcareous sand of the dunes and the slacks supports an exceptionally rich flora, with over 600 plant species recorded, including several orchids such as the rare coral-root orchid. The freshwater marsh has different species, such as yellow flag, meadowsweet, and numerous sedges and rushes. It is important, with the grassland behind, for nesting waders.

Sandscale has a thriving population of the rare natterjack toad. A special pool has been constructed near the car park so that visitors can see the toads and hear the remarkable call of the males on evenings in April and May.

The Duddon Estuary is of international importance for its birdlife, with shelduck, mallard, merganser, eider duck, goldeneye, cormorant, dunlin, redshank, grey plover and ringed plover. Along the shoreline, plants able to establish themselves in the constantly changing conditions created by the tidal system include sandwort, sea rocket, saltwort, sea holly and Ray's knotgrass.

Grazing is essential for maintaining the rich flora of the dunes, slacks and grasslands. Some small fenced enclosures in the slacks, erected in 1970, illustrate what the effects of cessation of grazing would be.

Sandscale Haws holds a key to the importance of this coastal stretch throughout history. Stone axes from the Langdale axe factory sites have been retrieved from the area, and the word Sandscale comes from the Scandinavian *sandra* (beach) and *skali* (hut); *haws* is a Norse word for hills. Evidence of iron workings can be found over much of the area but in particular at Nigel Pit, next to the car park.

[↟] Bridleway along coast; Cumbria Coastal Way; Hawthwaite Lane leading to beach.

[P] Car park, signed Roan Head.

[★] Beach shop (seasonal) and WCs at car park; information board; guided walks; leaflet; disabled access from car park to beach and natterjack pool.

[!] There are dangerous gullies in the estuaries; check tides before venturing too far.

[▆] 282 ha (651 acres) 3ml N of Barrow-in-Furness, off A595 Dalton to Askam road.
                                                              [96:SD1875]

Silverdale   Lancashire

Bank House Farm is a working, organic farm set in an attractive situation overlooking Morecambe Bay and the salt marshes of the Kent Estuary. The surrounding farmland is crossed with light-grey limestone walls and a number of the fields are bordered by layered hedges. The whitewashed house has an unusual window facing the coast, through which it is thought a guiding light would shine for travellers crossing the dangerous sands.

Morecambe Bay is of international importance for its birdlife, with the biggest population of overwintering waders in Britain. Here it is fringed by clifftop grasslands and grazing marshes, lying within the shelter of a wooded limestone escarpment. The grassland supports flowers such as common rock rose, sea fern grass, hawkweed, crested hair and quaking grasses, small-leaved cotoneaster, green-winged orchid and autumn lady's tresses, as well as some unusual whitebeams. Several small plantations provide shelter and additional tree cover; the wood between George's Lot and the grazing marsh includes oak, ash, wych elm and a few specimens of the rare Lancaster whitebeam.

Jack Scout is a wooded limestone cliffline on the southern point of the

Silverdale peninsula, overlooking the Wharton Sands of Morecambe Bay, and was the first coastal property north of the River Ribble to be owned by the Trust. There are impressive views across the bay from the 'Giant's Seat' at the highest point.

The richness of these limestone habitats, with notable pockets of limestone pavement, woodland and grassland, make this an ecologically important site, and of historical interest is an old lime kiln, recently renovated by the Trust and now occasionally fired.

A varied scrub woodland of ash, birch, holly, hazel, juniper, yew, oak, old man's beard and guelder rose creates dense thickets in places, and soft-shield fern, lords and ladies, wood anemone and wood sorrel are among the many flowers to be found on the woodland floor. A number of self-coppiced small-leaved lime are of note. The grassland, which has been invaded by gorse and bracken in parts (now being cut and controlled) supports limestone-loving flowers and grasses, including crested hair grass, blue moor grass, salad burnet, carline thistle, small scabious, lady's bedstraw and early purple orchid.

[🚶] From Silverdale; footpaths along cliffline and crossing Bank House Farm.

[P] Informal parking off road (avoid blocking gateways or lanes).

[★] Information panel at Jack Scout.

[♿] 33 ha (82 acres) 7ml NW of Carnforth, W of Silverdale; 7ml NW of Carnforth, 1ml S of Silverdale.   [97:SD460752 and 459737]

Sizergh Castle   Cumbria

Although more widely known for its castle and garden, the Sizergh estate is an attraction in itself and is rich in wildlife. Traversed by a network of footpaths, the area has flower-rich limestone grassland, ancient woodland and reclaimed mossland containing relicts of raised bog. Parts of the estate give commanding views over the Kent Estuary and Morecambe Bay, the Howgill and Lake District fells, and the Pennines.

Helsington Barrows is an SSSI supporting limestone-loving plants, including orchids, and scattered woodland including juniper and yew. Brigsteer Wood is most famous for its spring display of wild daffodils, yet it also contains various plants indicative of ancient woodland. It is actively managed to maintain and improve its conservation value, through such work as coppice cycles and glade creation, thereby encouraging butterflies, insects and spring flowers.

- 🚶 Open access.
- 🅿 Car park at castle; informal car parks at Brigsteer Woods and St John's Church, Helsington.
- ★ Refreshment kiosk (seasonal) in castle car park; walks leaflet available from NT shop at castle.
- 🚐 633 ha (1563 acres) 3ml S of Kendal, off A590.   [97: SD498878]

Speke   Liverpool

Gardens, mixed woodland, farmland, small lakes and relics of a former heathland surround this magnificent timber-framed manor house on the outskirts of Liverpool. Estate walks provide good views of the house and at the southern end of the property a steep climb up a grassy bank reveals the River Mersey (an SSSI and Ramsar site of international importance for wildfowl), the Wirral Peninsula and the mountains of North Wales.

Parts of the woodland were previously pasture woods associated with the historic manorial estate, but most have been replanted. Stocktons Wood and the Clough are known to be ancient woodland sites and so have a varied flora, including beautiful displays of bluebells in spring. Stocktons Wood also has nationally rare species of deadwood beetles.

- 🚶 Open seasonally; walks through woods; no path to estuary; local stations at Garston and Hunt's Cross.
- 🅿 Car park; special parking for disabled.
- ★ NT shop and tea-room; WCs (including disabled); woodland path suitable for wheelchairs; leaflets; picnic area in orchard.
- 🚐 40 ha (98 acres) on N side of River Mersey, 8ml SE of Liverpool, 1ml S of A561.   [108:SJ419825]

The Stubbins Estate and Holcombe Moor Lancashire

Perched above the Irwell Valley, this walled, improved pastureland links the industrial Pennine communities of Rossendale with Holcombe Moor, a bleak open moorland typical of the Lancashire Pennines. The country-side is made up of deeply incised and wooded valleys, pastureland, low moorland and rushy hollows, characteristic of the acid soil overlying the Millstone Grit.

In the cloughs beech, oak and birch woodlands provide valuable cover for a number of birds. There are several small areas of unimproved herb-rich grassland, and curlew, meadow pipit and skylark can be heard calling over the rough tussocky upland grassland during the spring and summer months.

A network of footpaths crosses the farmsteads overlooking the valley and leading up to the moorland. The buildings and drystone walls are built from local gritstone and some farm buildings date back to the seventeenth century.

[†] Footpaths; Rossendale Way (route established by Groundwork).

[P] Informal parking.

[★] Local facilities.

[⚓] 547 ha (1313 acres) W of Stubbins, 5ml N of Bury, 1ml N of Ramsbottom, each side of B6214.   [109:SD785177]

Ullswater   Cumbria

One of the most beautiful lakes in the Lake District, Ullswater follows a sinuous course along a glaciated valley with classic features such as upland tarns, ridges, U-shaped valleys and screes. The Trust estate is concentrated around the head of the valley at Brotherswater and to the north and west of the lake around Glencoyne Wood, Park and Farm, Gowbarrow Park and Aira Force (impressive waterfalls surrounded by a pinetum and landscaped parkland).

Beyond the steep valley sides lie the imposing fells of Helvellyn, Fairfield and Great Dodd. This historic landscape was divided into manors in medieval times, and has been strongly influenced by the large estates. Farming has continued to be the main land use, as can be seen from the traditional farmhouses, hogg houses and walls dating from the sixteenth century. Glencoyne Farmhouse dates back to at least 1629. There is probable evidence of medieval deer parks at Gowbarrow and Glencoyne.

Ullswater has a literary link with the poet Wordsworth: after a walk along the shore of the lake he wrote, 'I wandered lonely as a cloud'.

It was the success of the Trust in acquiring a stretch of shoreline at Gowbarrow that started a more concerted effort in preserving the beauty of the valley. The increased numbers of nesting birds, including goosander and cormorant on the lake are a result of limiting the use of power boats. Brotherswater is also of great value to overwintering wildfowl, and the marginal reed vegetation attracts many breeding birds. Buzzard, raven and red grouse are also seen in the area.

The area contains a variety of other wildlife habitats of great interest. On the fell tops and mountain sides a good range of upland plants can be seen, including saxifrages, northern bedstraw and sedges. Dry and wet heaths occur in pockets, with heather, bilberry, *Sphagnum* moss and common and hare's tail cotton grasses. Excellent ancient woodlands and wood pastures occur above Brotherswater and at Glencoyne, Glencoyne Park and Gowbarrow. The last site includes some very fine old ash, elm, oak, yew and small-leaved lime. The oak woods are rich in mosses, ferns and lichens. This is a good area for red squirrels.

🚶 By road; network of footpaths and bridleways; steamers run on Ullswater (seasonal); station at Penrith.

🅿 Car parks and lay-bys.

★ Tea-rooms (not NT) at Aira Force and Side Farm; facilities at Glenridding and Patterdale; WCs at Glenridding, Aira Force and Patterdale; leaflet on Aira Force; information boards at Cow Bridge car park (N of Brotherswater) and Aira Force; NT information vehicle at Aira Force (seasonal); caravan and camping sites; boating and fishing facilities (for further information contact NT Regional Office).

🗺 5059 ha (12,500 acres) SW of Penrith, N of Windermere on A592 running along N shore of lake.   [90:NY386170]

Wasdale   Cumbria

Wasdale is one of the few seemingly wild areas left in the Lake District, quiet, remote, yet dramatic. Wastwater, England's deepest lake (Arctic char still survive in the pure and nutrient-poor waters), is bounded on the south-east by impressive scree slopes (the main area of dramatic scree is from Whin Rigg to Illgill Head), and some of the highest peaks in the Lake District (Scafell Pike, Great Gable, Great End and Red Pike) form a striking horseshoe around the head of the valley, their grey shapes and steep fans of unstable scree reflected in the calm surface of the lake. The Trust owns all the valley land, including the 400-hectare Nether Wasdale Estate, the bed of the lake and all the surrounding fells. Wasdale Hall, at the foot of Wastwater, is let to the Youth Hostels Association.

The flood plain of Lingmell and Mosedale becks at Wasdale Head has an especially notable pattern of thick drystone walls, while the screes are of particular importance for plants including dwarf juniper, alpine lady's mantle, purple saxifrage and a number of rare mountain plants.

The area contains a large expanse of upland grassland and grassy heath with mountain flowers and mosses. Bogs and mires are found in the hollows, with damp-loving plants such as sundew, cotton grasses, sedges and yellow mountain saxifrage.

Like much of the Lake District, the area contains a great deal of historic interest, with Bronze Age cairns, Iron Age and Roman settlements, and prehistoric field patterns.

[🏃] By one road only (no through road); well-marked footpaths and bridleways; open access to fells.

[P] 3 NT car parks.

[★] Facilities in local villages; WCs at Wasdale Head; NT camp site; youth hostel; boating facilities (for further information contact NT Regional Office).

[⛴] 7000 ha (17,298 acres), access from A595(T) via minor roads NE of Santon Bridge.   [89:NY162066]

Windermere   Cumbria

In the centre of the Lake District, this is probably the busiest and most heavily populated valley. More mountainous in the north, it opens out to a wide lake, ten miles long, with sheltered bays, wooded islands and knolls, many in Trust ownership. The wildlife interests of the lake are threatened by pollution and disturbance from boating and water-borne leisure activities and are the subject of constant reviews by the Trust, together with the National Park Authority and various conservation organisations.

The Trust owns some of the most secluded, wooded shoreline and valley side along the west shore, from Wray Castle through Arthur's Wood, Heald Wood, Belt Ash Coppice to the ferry-crossing point to Windermere. From the early Middle Ages the coppice woodlands of oak, ash and alder clothing the lake's shore were cultivated for the production of charcoal, especially by the monks of Furness Abbey (the old monastic courthouse still stands near Hawkshead).

On the islands of Rampholme and Lady Holme are ungrazed broadleaved woodlands with an inland cormorant roost, and other important wildlife sites include Skelghyll Wood, an ancient woodland on base-rich rocks which contains snails and insects characteristic of its antiquity; Wansfell Pike, east of Ambleside which commands good views across the lake; Borran's Field (the site of the remains of a Roman fort) which has some important reed-beds with a wide range of plants, including rushes, marsh bedstraw, purple loosestrife, sneezewort, greater burnet, marsh marigold and bur reed. The woodlands along the east shore include ash, yew, oak and hazel, and good numbers of small-leaved lime trees.

The local farmland has some excellent traditional hay meadows, rich flushes and pastures, all with a very rich flora, and the lake itself is an important site for a variety of overwintering wildfowl which congregate in undisturbed sanctuaries, including pochard and tufted duck and the strikingly-marked goldeneye. Coot, moorhen, common sandpiper, goosander and mute swan can be seen along the shoreline.

Cockshot Point near Bowness-on-Windermere and Queen Adelaide Hill are popular and easily accessible sites on the shore of the lake, and nearby Troutbeck, with its village and farms centred on the stream of the same name, is well worth a visit. The farmhouse of Hill Top at Near Sawrey, between the lake and Esthwaite Water, was the home of Beatrix Potter and the setting for many of her stories. The house was bequeathed by her to the Trust in 1944.

🚶 Network of footpaths; access to lake by boat (several boat-hire companies); station at Windermere, and Lakeside and Haverthwaite Railway connected to Windermere station by boat trip across lake.

🅿 Car parks at Ambleside for Borran's Field and Skelghyll; Wray Castle and Belle Grange for west shore; Bowness and Windermere for Cockshot Point and Queen Adelaide Hill.

★ Facilities at Ambleside, Bowness, Waterhead and Windermere; café, WCs, rowing-boat hire; NT camping at Low Wray; NT Country Park at Fell Foot, near Newby Bridge; boating and fishing facilities (for further information contact NT Regional Office).

🛏 953 ha (2356 acres) on W side of B5286 Ambleside to Hawkshead road, on E side of A591.

[89:SD397911, 90:NY414010, 90:SD410998, 96 and 97:SD404958 and 396964, 96:SD386951, 97:SD422996 and 424995]

Allen Banks and Staward Gorge   Northumberland

Surrounded by the characteristically exposed Northumbrian landscape, the River Allen, a tributary of the Tyne, carves its way through a deep ravine clothed in trees.

A network of paths leads through the mixed woodland and a suspension bridge crosses the river, offering the chance to catch sight of a dipper or grey wagtail flitting down the gorge. A longer walk leads south to Staward Gorge sssi.

Staward Wood, to the south in the Allen Valley, contains the dramatic ruins of Staward Pele, a medieval fortified tower-house and gateway.

The ground flora, including moschatel, wood fescue, ferns, ramson and bluebell, suggests that parts of the woodland are of ancient origin. Red squirrel, once holding its own in the north of the country, is becoming increasingly rare, but the valley is Britain's most northerly location for the dormouse.

[ⓚ] Open all year (charge); main entrance at northern end of property.

[P] Car park in old kitchen garden.

[★] WCs; information board and interpretation panel; self-guided walks; picnic facilities; no caravans or camping; coaches must book (tel. 01434 344218).

[▣] 202 ha (500 acres) 3ml W of Haydon Bridge, ½ml S of A69, near junction of Tyne and Allen rivers.   [86 and 87:NY798640]

Bellister   Northumberland

The ruins of Bellister Pele Tower and Castle, once the hub of a large agricultural estate, are prominent features of this historic countryside in the valley of the South Tyne.

The property has an interesting flora, and wildlife habitats range from open rough pasture and moorland to improved pasture and mixed woodland, some parts of which are ancient. Barnfoot River Shingles sssi is an important area for wildlife. A number of interesting earthwork remains have escaped modern agricultural improvement.

[ⓚ] Footpaths.

[P] Informal parking.

[★] Leaflet for Hadrian's Wall walks; Burnside camp site.

[▣] 453 ha (1120 acres) S of A69, both sides of Haltwhistle to Alston road.   [86:NY699631]

Bridestones Moor, Blakey Topping and Crosscliff

N. Yorkshire

Steeped in local folklore and legend, the Bridestones are curiously shaped ancient sandstone stacks rising above the moor (an SSSI managed by the Trust as a nature reserve). They overlook a landscape of heather moorland dissected by steep-sided ravines or 'griffs'. The heather was once more extensive, but agriculture and forestry over the past few decades have considerably changed the landscape.

Blakey Topping, the geological curiosity of a heather-covered conical hill rising above a sea of forest, stands to the east adjoining Crosscliff Moor. Both Bridestones and Crosscliff contain important heath communities, under pressure from changing land use.

Heather, crowberry, bilberry, sedges, grasses, mosses and lichens grow in the mixture of wet and dry heath on the open moor, and of particular interest are the pockets of mature heather which ensure the regeneration of this essential habitat for its associated insects, birds and lichens. Emperor moth feed on the heather, and can be seen occasionally, with lizards and slow worms found in the open patches. Maidenhair and black spleenworts, and wall rue grow in the rock crevices. Birch and rowan scrub are scattered across the moor. Both scrub and invasive bracken are controlled in order to protect the important moorland habitat.

The ancient oak woodland of Dovedale Wood has a lush growth of mosses, ferns, primrose, dog's mercury and honeysuckle, and birds such as great spotted woodpecker, great tit and redstart can be seen. The dale grasslands have a rich flora and fauna, with grazing and mowing now established for their protection.

The Forest Drive follows the course of the Staindale Beck to the south of the property, which is bounded by forest to the east. Of historical interest are some prehistoric barrows hidden among the heather of Grime Moor.

[🚶] Via Forestry Commission toll road; open access to moors; permitted paths to Blakey Topping and Crosscliff Moor; North Yorkshire Moors Railway runs from Grosmont to Pickering (seasonal).

[P] Forestry Commission car park off Dalby Forest Drive at Staindale Lake; car park at the Hole of Horcum.

[★] WCs and picnic site (Forestry Commission); NT information panel; leaflet (from Low Dalby Forest Centre); guided walks; viewpoint.

[▦] 501 ha (1237 acres) 12ml S of Whitby, 1ml E of A169, via toll road through Dalby Forest Drive.   [94:SE877906]

Brimham Rocks   N. Yorkshire

High on a windswept escarpment above Nidderdale, Brimham Rocks and Moor are a combination of spectacular rock formations (of national geological importance) and rugged heather moorland designated an sssi, providing rich habitat for an array of plant and animal life.

Brimham House, built as a shooting lodge in 1792 and now housing an exhibition room and National Trust shop, is by virtue of its prominent position on the hillside the perfect spot to view the property and surrounding countryside.

The moor is dominated by ling and bell heathers, and bilberry is also present in large quantities. The less common cross-leaved heath is found in the wetter areas, as are bog asphodel, cranberry and the insectiverous sundew.

Grouse, snipe and curlew are frequently seen on the moorland, whilst jackdaw predominates in the main rock area and red deer can occasionally be seen. Pheasant, willow warbler, green woodpecker and chiffchaff can be heard in the wooded areas.

Evidence suggests that the area was once heavily wooded, and natural regeneration still occurs, with silver birch, rowan, oak and crab apple present. Holly trees on the edge of the escarpment attract the holly blue butterfly, a rare visitor to Yorkshire.

[⅄] Open access to moors; footpath to rocks; Nidderdale Way long-distance footpath passes through; station at Harrogate.

[P] Car parks at property entrance (no parking on roadside).

[⊠] NT shop and exhibition room in shooting lodge; light refreshments; WCs (including disabled); limited wheelchair access to rocks; leaflet; guided walks.

[⊞] 156.5 ha (387 acres) 8ml SW of Ripon off B6265, 10ml NW of Harrogate off B6165.   [99:SE206650]

Cayton Bay and Knipe Point   N. Yorkshire

The popular beach of Cayton Bay is sheltered by the sandstone headland of Knipe Point to the north, and surrounded by impressive cliffs and areas of landslip which create a wide range of interesting habitats in this sssi, with herb-rich grassland, scrub, woodland, pools and wet flushes. Extensive woodland and grassland management schemes are being undertaken to improve the nature conservation interest.

The woodland on the drier upper slopes contains ferns, orchids, wood avens and red campion, and on the grassland grow harebell, small scabious, yellow rattle, grass of Parnassus, woolly thistle and orchids. Meadowsweet, angelica and sedges are found in the wet flushes.

- 🚶 Access to beach through woods; steps to the south; Cleveland long-distance footpath; station at Scarborough.
- 🅿 Car park ½ml S, off A165.
- ★ Local facilities.
- ⬛ 35.5 ha (88 acres) 3ml S of Scarborough, E of Osgodby. [101:TA063850]

Cragside Estate   Northumberland

Situated in the secluded valley of the Debdon Burn, a tributary of the River Coquet, and surrounded by wild Northumbrian moorland, is an unusual pleasure ground created by Sir William Armstrong, the extraordinary Victorian inventor, engineer and industrialist from Tyneside.

Established originally as a weekend retreat, and subsequently a country mansion, the romantic and picturesque house stands on a heathery hillside which was transformed into a park by planting expanses of conifers (including some unusual varieties in the pinetum below the house) and rhododendrons, and the laying out of an elaborate network of carriageways, footpaths and bridges. Streams cut their way through deep ravines, with steep banks softened by luxuriant ferns, which give glimpses of naturally wooded concealed valleys.

Armstrong used his knowledge of engineering to create five large lakes which supplied water, hydraulic power and hydro-electricity for the house (Cragside was the first house in the world to be electrically powered in this way); he built roads, dammed streams and cleared the heather and scrub wilderness to plant a very large rock garden and more than seven million trees, mostly conifers. These woodlands harbour many birds, including woodcock, spotted and pied flycatchers, wood warbler, siskin, tree pipit and both great spotted and green woodpeckers.

Sparrowhawk hunt in the woods, and red squirrel, roe deer and adder can also be seen. There are still some remnants among the trees of the former heathland cover, with plants such as heather (including the cross-leaved species), bilberry and purple moor grass. Flocks of goldcrest, tit and finch inhabit the conifers, young pioneer birch woodland and rhododendron scrub. Five species of bat, including the rare Leisler's, are found in the old buildings and trees. On the moors above Cragside Woods seventy Bronze Age barrows can be seen.

The long-established wetland vegetation (fragrant agrimony is among the more unusual plants) beside the lakes attracts various birds and insects, including dragonflies. Dipper are common along the streams, where it is possible to find plants associated with the old woodland.

[⚲] House, garden and estate open seasonally; entrance on Rothbury to Alnwick road; permitted paths; 30 miles of footpaths; bus service from Morpeth and Newcastle, alight Reivers Well Gate.

[P] Car and coach parks.

[★] NT shop and restaurant; WCs (including disabled); visitor centre; leaflets and guidebook; information centre and boards; power circuit with tour of restored hydraulic and hydroelectric machinery; adventure playground; pinetum; rock garden and formal Victorian garden; guided walks; labyrinth maze; viewpoints suitable for wheelchairs.

[⊞] 405 ha (1000 acres) 1ml NE of Rothbury on N bank of River Coquet, off B6344 Morpeth to Rothbury road. [81:NU073022]

Craster, Embleton Links and Low Newton-by-the-Sea
Northumberland

This estate includes some of the finest scenery along the Northumberland coast, from the busy fishing village and kippering centre of Craster, with a sweep of grassland leading up to the spectacular ruins of the fourteenth-century Dunstanburgh Castle (under the guardianship of English Heritage) on an outcrop of the great Whin Sill, the precipitous cliffs behind, and much of the coastal strip as far as Newton Point on the other side of Embleton Bay.

There are some important historical remains, including interesting earthworks around the castle, with a medieval or post-medieval farm-stead and impressive relics of former open-field cultivation preserved under permanent pasture, and some evidence of Romano-British settle-ments. Near Craster are the buildings of a Second World War radar station, part of the country's first early-warning system. There is also a Rocket Life-Saving Apparatus Post, used in the past to train the local volunteer life-saving brigade and once a common feature of all rocky coasts.

Embleton Bay, another potential landing beach, was heavily defended in the Second World War, and there is an interesting collection of wartime pillboxes which have survived by chance because the demolition squads were refused access across the golf course.

At Newton Pool and Point are remains of some probable post-medieval farmsteads or cottages, and at Low Newton, a picturesque eighteenth-century planned farming and fishing village with a natural harbour protected by an offshore reef, there is a nineteenth-century coastal lookout (now a holiday cottage owned by the Trust).

The property includes a variety of habitats supporting a wide range of wildlife. The freshwater Newton Pool is a nature reserve of special ornithological interest which attracts many species including over-wintering wildfowl, passage migrants, waders and breeding birds such as sedge warbler and reed bunting in the fringes. It also harbours some interesting invertebrates and amphibians. Waders and water rail are attracted by the open pond margins. The cliffs of the Whin Sill are home to seabirds such as fulmar, shag and at least 700 pairs of kittiwake. Eider duck inhabit the inshore waters.

The castle is surrounded by herb-rich limestone grassland, with purple milk-vetch, field madder, spring squill, wild thyme, bloody crane's bill and clover. The sand dunes also support a variety of plants, with the newer ones stabilised by lyme and sea couch grasses. In the grassland between the established dunes grow bloody crane's bill, restharrow, burnet rose, harebell and primrose, with common butterwort and tufted centaury in the damp patches.

Low Newton and Newton Links have an important series of coastal habitats which support a variety of plants and animals. A colony of little tern, protected during the breeding season, just manages to survive here. The tidal zone, with its important sandy and rocky shore, and the marine environment beyond are of great ecological interest and are leased by the Trust for conservation purposes.

[i] Footpaths.

[P] Car parks at Low Newton (vehicle access to Low Newton Square restricted to residents only), Craster and Embleton.

[★] WCs (including disabled at Craster) at all 3 sites; leaflets; information panels; guided walks (details from regional office); birdwatchers' hide at Newton Pool with access for wheelchairs; dogs under control at all times.

[⛴] 306 ha (756 acres) on coast between Craster and Beadnell, off A1 via B1339.   [75:NU258220, 236417 and 243235 to 243240]

The Durham Coast: Noses Point to Lime Kiln Gill   Durham

The Trust acquired these properties with a view to reclaiming the landscape from the scarring caused by mining over the years. With its raised beaches, wooded denes or valleys, floristically rich magnesian limestone grassland and extensive broadleaved woodland, the area is of great ecological interest.

It includes Beacon Hill, the highest point on the Durham coast and used as a navigation aid for shipping from the Middle Ages, with impressive views across to the Cleveland Hills and along the coast. Some mesolithic worked flint has been found, and there is evidence of old field systems around the hilltop, with the remains of two farmsteads.

Hawthorn Dene is one of the most extensive and varied areas of broadleaved woodland on magnesian limestone in the county. There is an eighteenth-century lime kiln on the beach and the ruin of a nineteenth-century coastguard station above the valley. The area of Hawthorn Towers house and garden is now a hay meadow. Blue House Farm is also of interest, and some old field boundaries can be seen. The acquisition of Warren House Gill near Easington marks a major landmark for Enterprise Neptune. Given for a nominal fee of £1 by British Coal in 1987, it was the 500th mile of coastline to come to the Trust. Now, more than one in every six miles of coastline in England, Wales and Northern Ireland is owned by the Trust.

There are some possible First World War clifftop trenches, and a Second World War pillbox at the head of the beach. A dramatic nineteenth-century railway viaduct crosses the dene and is still in use.

Despite the impact of industrial activities, the area has a wide range of wildlife. The woods are made up of ash, oak and sycamore, with alder, yew, wych elm and hornbeam also present. Foxes and roe deer can be seen, with birds such as kestrel and tawny owl. Bluebell, wood anemone, cuckoo pint, ramson and sanicle flourish. The grassland includes the unusual dyer's greenweed, a small shrubby plant with narrow leaves and yellow flowers, so called because of its use as a source of dye.

On the exposed clifftops the limestone vegetation is influenced by its closeness to the sea, and wild thyme, bloody crane's bill, rock-rose and pyramidal orchid can be found. There is a wide variety of seabirds, including fulmar and kittiwake. A number of damp fen areas, a scarce habitat in the county, add to the wildlife interest of the properties.

[i] Via Easington on rough dirt tracks; network of footpaths from Easington Colliery, Hawthorn and Seaham, and along clifftop; Durham coastal path.

[P] Small car parks near Fox Holes Dene and Noses Point, Seaham.

[★] Local facilities; line fishing from coast.

[≋] 162 ha (400 acres) 5ml S of Sunderland, 15ml SE of Newcastle-upon-Tyne.   [88:NZ437480 to 455408]

The Farne Islands   Northumberland

The Inner and Outer Farnes are two groups in a scatter of about thirty virtually uninhabited basalt islands (an AONB, NNR and Heritage Coast) separated from the mainland by Inner Sound. They are renowned for their early Christian and medieval monastic settlement (the enclosure is an SAM), their history of shipwrecks, and their immense wildlife interest. The Farne Islands are accessible by boat only, and visits are dependent on weather and sea conditions.

Inner Farne, the largest island, is the site of St Cuthbert's hermitage in the seventh century, and the fourteenth-century chapel (restored in 1848) built in his memory can still be seen. The fifteenth-century pele tower, once used as a lighthouse burning coal on the roof, now houses the Farne Islands seasonal wardens (the islands have been protected as a nature reserve, and now a sea-bird sanctuary, since 1925). The island supports a wide variety of flowering plants.

There is also a nineteenth-century lighthouse (not open to the public), and on Brownsman Island the ruin of another coal-burning lighthouse and its replacement stump which was succeeded by the Longstone Lighthouse, made famous by Grace Darling who rescued survivors from the wreck of the *Forfarshire* in 1838. There are also some old ridge and furrow cultivation terraces, now obvious only from the air.

A good range of birds can be seen, with the cliffs of the resistant Whin Sill (encased in lichen and in places eighty feet high) used by thousands of breeding birds. More than twenty species have been recorded, with 6000 pairs of kittiwake, 22,000 pairs of guillemot and a smaller number of razorbill. Four species of tern (common, Arctic, roseate and Sandwich) arrive for the summer breeding season. The Arctic terns are famous for their dive-bombing of sightseers between mid-May and early July, as they protect their nests and young. Some 34,000 pairs of puffin nest in burrows and eider breed in any suitable habitat.

Atlantic grey seal, which can be seen all year round lounging on the rocks, use the islands as a breeding site in the autumn, with the pups born between September and December.

[⟨⟩] Seasonal, depending on weather, by boat daily only to Inner Farne and Staple Island from Seahouses (landing fee not included in boatmen's charges); footpaths.

[P] Car park in Seahouses.

[★] NT shop and information centre in Seahouses; WCs (including disabled) on Inner Farne; nature walks on Inner Farne; disabled access possible on Inner Farne, not recommended on Staple Island; local station at Chathill and bus service connecting Seahouses with trains.

[!] Hats advised mid May to early July when terns can be aggressive.

[⛺] 33 ha (81.5 acres) 2–5ml off coast opposite Bamburgh.   [75:NU230370]

Gibside   Gateshead

The core of the Gibside Estate was laid out by Sir George Bowes from 1720–1760, and is one of the finest surviving eighteenth-century landscapes in the North East. Trust ownership covers most of the historic estate and includes the chapel, a fine 1760s Palladian building by James Paine, the Avenue or Great Walk and the surrounding parkland, designed by 'Capability' Brown. Visitors can enjoy long circular walks giving access to the eighteenth-century vistas which lead to 'eye-catchers' such as the Statue to British Liberty, banqueting house and stable-block.

The parkland and the extensive woodlands, with recent plantings now reaching maturity, are of interest for their variety of wildlife, and an eighteenth-century plantation of beech, oak, ash and sycamore is an additional refuge for birds and mammals including red squirrel.

[⟨⟩] Open April to Oct, daily except Mon and in winter on Sun; circular walks and permitted footpaths; woodland walk; local station at Blaydon.

[P] Small car park.

[★] Shop; tea-room; WCs (including disabled); guided walks; picnic area in car park.

[⛺] 5.5 ha (14 acres) 7ml SW of Newcastle, 20ml NW of Durham, off B6314.
[88:NZ172583]

Hadrian's Wall Estate and Housesteads Fort
Northumberland

Marching along the precipitous outline of the Whin Sill, Hadrian's Wall is a spectacular reminder of the Roman occupation of Britain. The wall was constructed between AD122 and 125 as the northern most frontier of the Roman Empire, to defend against the unruly tribes from the north. Flanked with a ditch and vallum (earth rampart), at intervals along the wall are milecastles and forts, one of the best-preserved of which is Housesteads, owned by the Trust and under the guardianship of English Heritage. The wall is a World Heritage Site, an SSSI and SAM, and lies within the Northumberland National Park.

The Trust owns some four miles of the central sector of the wall, and has carried out much work over recent years in excavating, recording and consolidating the structure of the wall and its milecastles, which have suffered from erosion caused by the many visitors.

While the history of the world-famous wall, which is seventy-five miles in length and links Wallsend with the Solway Firth, is well documented, the countryside around is often overlooked. Isolated farmsteads, in-bye fields enclosed by whinstone walls, expanses of grassy moorland, willow carr, shelter belts of windswept trees, damp hollows (mires) and glacial lakes include a range of habitats with associated wildlife.

The lakes offer a refuge for overwintering wildfowl; teal and tufted duck are common. The luxuriant, well-developed heathland and fen communities are the remains of shallow glacial lakes where the high rainfall and impeded drainage has resulted in a patchwork of *Sphagnum* moss concealing rare and beautiful plants and invertebrates. The open water, marsh, fen, raised bogs, willow carr and damp grassland supports an interesting range of plants, such as unusual sedges, grass of Parnassus, early marsh orchids and stag's horn club moss. The crags of the Whin Sill contain a rich flora which includes mountain male and parsley ferns, fir club moss, woodrush and a variety of lichens.

There are spectacular views across the open landscape to the Pennines in the south, and to the Kielder and Wark forests in the north.

⚐ Wall and Housesteads Museum and Fort open all year; shop and information centre open seasonally; path beside wall; stations at Bardon Mill, Hexham and Haltwhistle, and seasonal bus service from Hexham and Haltwhistle stations.

P Car parks at Housesteads, Steel Rigg and Cawfields (operated by

Northumberland National Park on pay-and-display basis).

★ Shop and refreshments at Housesteads; WCs (including disabled) at Housesteads car park; information centre at Housesteads (seasonal opening); Roman Wall display in information centre; leaflets; National Park centre at Once Brewed; guided walks by NT and National Park Authority.

▣ 909 ha (2247 acres) 4ml NE of Haltwhistle, 2½ml N of Bardon Mill on B6318 (the Military Road).   [87:NY790688]

Hardcastle Crags   W. Yorkshire

In the heart of the Pennines the two wooded valleys of Hebden Dale and Crimsworth Dean lead down from Heptonstall and Wadworth moors. Hardcastle Crags, weathered stacks of gritstone, overlook a woodland of oak, birch, beech and rowan surrounding Hebden Water. On the south-facing slope is 'Slurring rock', where children used to slide down on wooden clogs carved out of alder or 'clog' wood. The local names, old mill ponds, stone packhorse routes ('causeys') and Gibson Mill (a former water-powered spinning and cotton-weaving mill) are evidence of the industries that once dominated the valleys. There are also some charcoal-burning platforms and remains of an old railway used in the construction of the reservoirs on the moors above.

A network of waymarked walks leads through the woods, along traditional paths and beside Hebden Water. Many of the woods have individual names, such as Foul Scout, Shackleton and High Greenwood, and old records suggest that part of the area is ancient woodland, although most was planted in the nineteenth century. Carpets of bluebells cover the ground in spring, and birds such as great spotted woodpecker, spotted and pied flycatchers and tawny owl have been recorded.

Piles of pine needles camouflage the chambers and tunnels of wood-ant nests. Gnawed cones are signs that squirrels are present. Dragonflies, grey wagtail and dipper are seen along the river.

Bilberry, ling and purple moor grass grow on the rough moorland on the valley sides and at Blakedean at the head of Hebden Dale.

⊼ Network of waymarked footpaths.

P 2 car parks.

★ Facilities at Hebden Bridge; leaflet showing 4 waymarked walks and routes of varying lengths; list of monthly guided walks; main track accessible for wheelchairs but rough and undulating, so help needed – otherwise steep ground.

▣ 174 ha (430 acres) 1½ml NW of Hebden Bridge, off A6033, 5ml NW of Todmorden.   [103:SD988291]

The Leas and Marsden Rock   South Tyneside

The 'flagship' of this property is the lighthouse complex at Lizard Point, an example of what was in its heyday a technologically very advanced aid to navigation just south of the busy entrance to the River Tyne. It also provides a focus for what is otherwise open clifftop space, although in the past there was a colliery village close by. The area has become famous through the novels of Catherine Cookson.

At the north end of the property there has been extensive limestone quarrying at Trow Point, and there are some remains of nineteenth-century coastal defences with the mounting for an experimental 'disappearing gun', a replica of which is on display, and the site of a gun battery overlooking Frenchman's Bay. There is also an impressive array of lime kilns from the nineteenth and twentieth centuries opposite Souter Lighthouse, the first lighthouse to be powered by alternating electric current.

The area has a long history based on fishing and smuggling, and points of interest include the eighteenth-century Marsden Grotto Pub (not NT).

The stretch of unspoilt coastline with its broad band of grassland was given to the Trust in 1987 by South Tyneside Metropolitan Borough Council. It is famed for its classic features of coastal erosion, such as natural rock arches, stacks, caves and wave-cut platforms, with cliffs and bays carved from the magnesian limestone. Divers and guillemot can be seen offshore.

Marsden Bay is recognised as one of the most important mainland sites for seabird breeding colonies between the Tweed and the Tees, and Marsden Rock is particularly popular, with nesting cormorant which have been increasing in numbers since they were first seen to use the stack in 1955. The cliffs support breeding kittiwake, fulmar, petrel, herring gull and razorbill.

The rocky and sandy foreshore is rich in marine life, and purple sandpiper and turnstone can be seen darting across the rocks in winter. The cliffs and grassland support a wide variety of plants such as cowslip, burnet saxifrage, thrift, sea plantain, bee orchid, wild thyme, small scabious and autumn gentian.

⚐ Open access; footpaths (those on the Leas are suitable for wheelchairs).

P 4 car parks.

★ Local facilities; WCs at Marsden car park; restaurant, information, shop and video display at Souter Lighthouse (seasonal opening); steps and lift to shore; viewpoint; guided walks.

▣ 120 ha (296 acres) E of A183 South Shields to Sunderland road, 10ml E of Gateshead.   [88:NZ388665]

Malham Tarn Estate   N. Yorkshire

Malham Tarn, England's highest freshwater lake, lies at the centre of the estate, within the classic limestone landscape of the Yorkshire Dales. It is an internationally important wetland site and also an NNR, managed jointly with English Nature and the Field Studies Council.

Trapped in a bowl of impermeable slate, the tarn is bordered by willow carr, fen and raised peat bog, which support a wide range of damp-loving plants, including cranberry, cloudberry, bog rosemary, cross-leaved heath, *Sphagnum* moss, round-leaved sundew, bog asphodel and meadowsweet. Great crested grebe, common sandpiper and coot nest along the shores.

The extensive estate includes expanses of typical karst scenery – limestone pavements of clints and grykes, dry valleys and crags with open moorland on the overlying blanket of peat. Ferns and lime-loving plants thrive in the fissures, and wild thyme, bird's foot trefoil, mountain pansy, eyebright, sedges and bird's eye primrose form a tight grassland sward. Kestrel and peregrine may be seen hunting, and the woodlands provide valuable shelter for birds. Upland breeding birds include curlew, lapwing, redshank, wheatear and golden plover. A web of drystone walls and field barns crosses the open landscape, with ancient field patterns and early industrial remains illustrating Man's long association with the area.

🚶 Footpaths and bridleways cross tenanted land; Pennine Way long-distance footpath; Yorkshire Dales cycle path; some areas of open access.

P Car park at Malham; informal parking.

★ WCs at Malham; leaflet about the NNR; guided walks; birdwatchers' hide at north-east corner of tarn; wheelchair access along estate road from Streetgate to Waterhouses; exhibition at Townhead Barn, Malham.

▣ 2900 ha (7200 acres) 6ml NE of Settle in Upper Craven.   [98:SD898633]

Marsden Moor Estate
W. Yorkshire

Extending from Buckstones Moss in the north to Wessenden Moor in the south, the estate covers a large area of unenclosed and registered urban common moorland, dissected by steep-sided valleys known locally as cloughs. Although this is wild, open country taking in the northern tip of the Peak District National Park, it has a surprising diversity of interest including valleys, reservoirs, peaks and crags, as well as archaeological remains dating from pre-Roman times to the great engineering structures of the canal and railway age.

Although seemingly bleak and inhospitable, the windswept landscape supports classic moorland birds such as golden plover, red grouse, curlew and twite. These birds breed here in such numbers that the estate is designated an SSI and is part of an international SPA.

[i] Registered commonland; open access on foot.

[P] Car parks at Buckstones Edge and Wessenden Head; roadside parking.

[★] Leaflets, including details on six self-guided walks; guided walks and events (details from Estate Office, The Old Goods Yard, Marsden, Huddersfield HD7 6DH, please enclose s.a.e.).

[⚑] 2300 ha (5685 acres) W, S and E of Marsden, 8ml SW of Huddersfield, both sides of A62.   [109:SE016136 and 077076]

Roseberry Common
Redcar & Cleveland

This popular site is dominated by the bent pinnacle of Roseberry Topping, which owes its peculiar shape to a major rockfall caused by undermining of the local sandstone for building material. As well as the Topping, the Trust owns Roseberry Common, Cliff Rigg Quarry and Newton and Cliff Ridge Woods. Newton Wood is designated as ancient woodland and Cliff Rigg Quarry is an important geological and archaeological site. The property also contains two SSSIs and lies within the North York Moors National Park.

Roseberry Common is grazed by sheep, and in parts is dominated by bracken. While farming is the main industry in this area, there is a local history of ironstone and whinstone mining, the latter being a very hard igneous stone used for road-building. The semi-precious stone jet was also once mined in the vicinity, but all previously known sites are now worked out.

The whole area is important for wildlife. Newton and Cliff Ridge Woods are of particular interest for birds, with nesting great spotted woodpecker, sparrowhawk, pied flycatcher and tawny owl. Wood sorrel, red campion and greater woodrush are among the plants to be found in the woodland, which is notable in late spring for a spectacular display of bluebells, which create a sea of blue across the site.

[↟] Network of footpaths; Cleveland Way long-distance footpath. North Yorkshire Middlesbrough-Whitby line, nearest station at Great Ayton (good views of Topping from train).

[P] Car park.

[★] WCs; information panel; Captain Cook Monument (not NT) E of Great Ayton.

[▣] 124 ha (306 acres) 8ml SE of Middlesbrough.   [93:NZ575124]

St Aidan's and Shoreston Dunes   Northumberland

This stretch of the sweeping Northumberland coast (an AONB and Heritage Coast) has magnificent views across to the Farne Islands, north to the dramatic profile of Bamburgh Castle two miles up the coast, and west to the Cheviot Hills.

A narrow ridge of dunes and rough dune grassland backs the foreshore which is of a considerable extent at low tide. The dunes are dominated towards the sea by the coarse spikes of marram grass, with a more varied range of plants inland. Wild clary and purple milk-vetch are among the more unusual, together with the typical dune grassland plants of resthar-row, burnet rose, sand sedge, harebell, bird's foot trefoil, lady's bedstraw and bloody cranesbill.

Monk's House, which marks the northern boundary of the property, was once the mainland store house and ferry landing stage for the monks of the Farne Islands. Also of interest is an old lime kiln at Seahouses harbour, linked to the town by a disused railway line.

[↟] Open access; footpaths; local station at Chathill.

[P] Car park at Seahouses; informal parking on verges.

[★] NT shop, information centre and WCs at Seahouses; grazing animals present, please do not feed, close gates and keep dogs under close control.

[▣] 24 ha (60 acres) 2ml SE of Bamburgh, just N of Seahouses.
          [75:NU204335]

Staintondale and Robin Hood's Bay   N. Yorkshire

Lying within the North Yorkshire Moors National Park, these crumbling cliffs of sandstone, shale, limestone and ironstone (a Heritage Coast and SSSI) are of considerable botanical interest, with habitats ranging from dry heath and bracken, scrub, woodland and wet flushes. Herb-rich grassland covers the open crags.

The variety of flowering plants provides food for many bees, hoverflies and other insects, and birds such as stonechat, whinchat and linnet nest in the dense scrub. Part of the commonland is well-wooded, with a rich flora of sweet woodruff, mosses and ferns including soft-shield fern (at Hayburn Wyke). Spotted flycatcher and treecreeper are among the many woodland birds.

Much of the spectacular clifftop farmland is protected by the Trust. The fields of Bay Ness Farm run down to the cliffs overlooking Robin Hood's Bay to the north, and Rigg Hall Farm, between Hayburn Wyke and Ravenscar, also includes more than 1000 metres of cliffline. Hayburn Wyke is an attractive small bay with delightful walks through woodland and a stream tumbling down to a boulder beach above the impressive undercliff of Beast Cliff (not owned by the Trust).

At Bay Ness, the steep hillsides and incised valleys include some grassland with many herbs and wild flowers, and the cliffs are used by nesting seabirds such as fulmar, herring gull, kittiwake and cormorant. Boggle Hole is a steeply incised inlet in the middle of Robin's Hood Bay, and from Bay Town there are impressive views of the headland of Ravenscar with its cliffs of eroded sandstone, gently sloping undercliffs and rough cover of scrub, heath, grassland and bracken.

The vegetation partly conceals old brickworks and quarries where shale was extracted during the sixteenth century for the alum used in fixing dyes and curing hides. The remains of alum works are now being consolidated by the Trust and represent the best surviving example in the country of this early chemical industry – an important monument to a way of life which once dominated this strip of the North Yorkshire coast.

[🚶] Via Cleveland Way long-distance footpath; access by car to Ravenscar and Robin Hood's Bay; network of footpaths; bridleway and cycle path along disused railway line (owned by Scarborough District Council).

[P] Car parks at Robin Hood's Bay and Ravenscar; roadside parking.

[★] Shop and NT coastal centre at Ravenscar; WCs at Ravenscar and Robin

Hood's Bay (town); 2 information panels beside Cleveland Way explaining alum industry; restored Old Coastguard Station (opens July 2000) in Robin Hood's Bay with displays, exhibits, education centre and holiday cottage.

▣ 348 ha (860 acres) 15ml N of Scarborough on A171.   [94:NZ980013]

Upper Wharfedale

N. Yorkshire

This large property lies in the valley of the River Wharfe, within the Yorkshire Dales National Park, and is part of the Pennine Dales ESA. The attractive landscape of pale grey limestone crags, drystone walls and vernacular buildings is offset by green pastures, herb-rich meadows, wooded slopes and moorland. There are some prehistoric field patterns and remains of old lead mines.

The grasslands support a variety of lime-loving plants, such as ox-eye daisy, yellow rattle, betony, knapweed, sedges, self-heal, orchids and many grasses. The ungrazed ledges on the crags are rich in mosses, ferns and tall herbs.

The gill woodlands are particularly important for their rich bryophyte flora. Historical evidence, and studies of the lichen and invertebrate communities, have shown that parts of the valley have been managed as pasture-woodland for centuries.

In the woods ancient oaks, ash, wych elm, hazel, bird cherry, rowan, holly and birch can be seen. Above the valley sides the plateaux are covered in peat, with the resulting grassland and peat bogs of particular interest for their plant and bird communities.

[🚶] Footpaths and bridlepaths cross tenanted land; some areas of open access; Dales Way long distance footpath.

[P] Car parks at Kettlewell and Buckden; informal parking.

[★] WCs at Kettlewell and Buckden; walks leaflet; guided walks; exhibition at Townhead Barn, Buckden.

▣ 2470 ha (6100 acres) N of Kettlewell, both sides of B6460.

[98:SE968722]

The Wallington Estate

Northumberland

This superb estate spans several parishes, with evidence of a complex sequence of past agricultural and industrial land-use reflected in the varied landforms and the increase in elevation away from the Wansbeck

Valley. It includes the extensive grounds, partly the work of 'Capability' Brown (who was born nearby and went to school on the estate), of a handsome eighteenth-century sandstone country house, the former seat of the Trevelyan family. There is a fine conservatory in the walled garden, landscaped grounds with artificial lakes, enclosed farmland with small woodlands, sheltered river banks and exposed moorland beyond.

Two walks lead across the estate; one beside the river and the other along disused railway lines. There are views into Redesdale, to the slopes of Simonside and the Cheviot Hills to the north.

The woodlands around the house have good breeding populations of treecreeper, pied flycatcher, summer migrants and nuthatch (this is their most northerly breeding area). The woods next to the river are of interest for riverside birds such as grey wagtail, dipper and kingfisher.

The reduction in grouse-shooting has led to the deterioration and decline of the heather moors, but a number of unimproved meadows have a rich flora which includes the melancholy thistle, globeflower and northern marsh orchid.

The landscape holds much of archaeological interest, with many hundreds of sites dating from the Bronze Age to the recent past, including some SAMs. Of interest is the eighteenth-century Paine's Bridge (not owned by the Trust) over the Wansbeck, two prehistoric camps, old lime kilns and milestones, and the village of Cambo (now a conservation area), which was built as a model village in 1740 and is still almost unchanged. The oldest building, a medieval fortified vicarage, is now the post office, and there are some attractive houses and farmhouses. Winter's Gibbet, near Harwood, is a stark reminder of past events.

[⚹] House open seasonally; grounds open all year; walks round estate open June to October (Wannie Line and Greenleighton Moor Walks); extensive network of rights of way; station at Morpeth and bus service from Newcastle.

[P] Car parks at house and at NT Regional Office at Scot's Gap, from where Wannie Line Walk starts.

[✹] NT shop and restaurant; WCs (including disabled); leaflets; information centre; grounds and terrace of walled garden suitable for wheelchairs.

[≅] 5463.5 ha (13,500 acres) 12ml N of Morpeth, 6ml N of Belsay, E of A696 Jedburgh road, 1ml S of Cambo off B6342.   [81:NZ030843]

Aberdeunant   Carmarthenshire

Aberdeunant is a testament to four centuries of Welsh rural life and has
survived as a working farm. The traditional thatched cruck-framed farmhouse is possibly a rebuilt medieval hall house. The outbuildings include
a barn, cowshed, stable and implement shed; they are largely of stone and
slate construction and date partly from the 18th and 19th centuries.

Located in unspoilt rolling countryside, the farm has been managed in
a low intensity way for several generations and is valuable for its unimproved habitats, including flower-rich hay meadows. A permitted circular path leads around the property.

[⌖] Footpaths.

[P] Parking at farm.

[★] Local facilities.

[▦] 60 ha (147 acres) at Taliaris, nr Llandeilo.   [146:SN672308]

Aberglaslyn   Gwynedd

This famous Snowdonia beauty spot includes the spectacular Aberglaslyn Pass, the racing waters of the Afon Glaslyn (popular for salmon
fishing) the steep wooded slopes above the Pass and an expanse of mountainous land. There are good views from Pont Aberglaslyn, the stone
bridge at the narrowest point of the gorge.

Heath, grasslands and mires create a range of wildlife habitats. The
heath is unusual as it contains several species usually found at lower alti-
tudes, such as western gorse, grayling butterfly, bloody-nose beetle and
stonechat. It also has some excellent expanses of bell heather. The mires
include local plants such as the insectivorous oblong-leaved sundew and
white-beaked sedge, while the gorge itself is important for its mosses on
riverside rocks.

The woods at Aberglaslyn include some areas of ancient oakwood and
some more recent plantations, but rhododendron is invading both the
wood and the sides of the gorge. When established, it completely shades
out the native flora and so much time and expense is being devoted to its
control.

The property also includes some rushy fields on the previous estuary of
the Afon Glaslyn, once a navigable waterway which was reclaimed at the
beginning of the nineteenth century. The remains of the old harbour by
the deep pool which gives the river its name are now several miles from

the sea. Dotted throughout the landscape is evidence of previous settlements, ranging from Bronze Age shelters to the cableways, pits and stops
which are the remains of a copper-mining industry.

In the village of Beddgelert is an ancient cottage named Llywelyn
Cottage, once a public house known as Tŷ Isaf and now a National Trust
shop. From here it is possible to set off on a network of paths which lead to
the grave of Gelert, the brave dog of Prince Llywelyn. Continuing past the
grave, the path joins the route of the old Welsh Highland Railway.

- ⓚ Network of walks through the pass and to Gelert's grave; Ffestiniog
  Railway runs between Porthmadog and Ffestiniog (seasonal).
- Ⓟ Car parks at Beddgelert and Nantmor.
- 🌠 WCs at Beddgelert and Nantmor; leaflet for Aberglaslyn.
- 🕿 390.5 ha (965 acres) 12ml SE of Caernarfon, on A4085, extending S for
  1½ml from Beddgelert.   [115:SH595463]

Abergwesyn Common   Powys

This extensive and remote moorland in central Wales has escaped the
blanket afforestation of much of the surrounding countryside. Drygan
Fawr and Gorllwyn are the highest peaks along the central ridge with the
western and northern slopes of the plateau cut by deep river valleys.

This large upland area exhibits some of the problems of managing
upland commons, with heavy sheep-grazing, burning and spread of
bracken. Nevertheless, there are some very valuable habitats here. The
summit plateaux support upland heath and blanket bog with an important community of breeding birds which include dunlin, golden plover
and red grouse. The slopes, where not too bracken-infested, have dry
heath of heather and gorse, rich flushed grasslands and small areas of
alder and other semi-natural woodland. The area is feeding territory for
the rare mid-Wales speciality, red kite.

At least fifty prehistoric cairns are scattered across the moors, re-built
in the nineteenth century into beehive structures as markers for
commoners, and evidence of the ancient use of these wild open spaces.
Other features of historic interest are the standing stones, stone align-
ments and old drove roads which cross the property.

- ⓚ Main access points north of A483; easy access from Abergwesyn and
  Llanwrtyd Wells; network of footpaths across plateau.
- Ⓟ Informal parking.
- 🌠 Local facilities.

⚓ 6678 ha (16,500 acres) in the Cambrian Mountains, W of Llandrindod Wells, extending from Irfon Gorge to the Wye Valley.

[147:SN841551 to 967620]

Begwns   Powys

A beautiful upland common along a hill ridge with panoramic views of the Black Mountains, Brecon Beacons and the Carmarthen Fans. Surrounded by valleys on all sides, the common provides an attractive backdrop to the fertile lowlands and small towns and valleys of the upper Wye Valley. Birds include curlew, lapwing, skylark and buzzard, and the nationally rare pill wort occurs in ponds scattered across the hill. There are a number of archaeolgical sites, including an abandoned village, probably medieval.

🚶 Open access for walkers over common. Limited access for mountain bikes following legal routes.

🅿 The common is crossed by 3 tarmac roads with parking allowed in lay-bys and on grass verges.

★ Local facilities; information on the area is available in the TIC in Hay-on Wye.

⚓ 523.5 ha (1293½ acres) 4ml NW of Hay on Wye.   [148:SO163442]

Berthlwyd Farm   Powys

A traditional sheep farm including an sssi and ranging from high craggy grazing with rocky outcrops to areas of indigenous oak woodland over ancient pastures and wetland. The spectacular red kite may be seen here, and plants of note include yellow rattle, ragged robin and lesser butterfly orchid. The abundant insect life includes the rare marsh fritillary.

🚶 Via public highway then by public footpath.

🅿 Limited roadside parking.

⚓ 66 ha (163 acres), 2ml from Ystradfellte, Brecon.   [160:SO913133]

Bishopston Valley   Swansea

This deeply incised and sheltered valley has one of the best and most extensive areas of ancient woodland on Gower, with a great variety of trees such as ash, oak, small-leaved lime, holly, field maple and wild service tree; hazel, spindle and dogwood occur as shrubs. There is a rich ground flora, including soft shield fern, columbine, tutsan, wood anemone and wood spurge.

The underlying geology is carboniferous limestone, and here it displays karst features such as swallow holes, pot holes, dry valleys, collapsed caverns and limestone screes.

Apart from ancient woodland, this valley has an excellent diversity of habitat, with wet meadows, herb-rich limestone grassland, bracken, scrub and stream (above ground in part of the valley) where nesting dipper can occasionally be seen. An Iron Age promontory fort, hidden by trees, is perched on the east side of the valley and derelict quarries and lime kilns also offer clues to the past.

[🚶] Footpath through valley.

[P] Small parking area (not NT) by church at Kittle.

[★] Leaflet.

[🚌] 62 ha (153 acres) on Gower Peninsula, 6ml SW of Swansea via A4067 and B4436.   [159:SS575894]

Braich y Pwll   Gwynedd

This wild and beautiful extremity of the Llŷn Peninsula is the point from where the first pilgrims set off during the Middle Ages to Ynys Enlli. The ruins of St Mary's church, once used by these medieval pilgrims, and remains of medieval field patterns with ridge and furrow can still be seen. In the spring and summer numerous birds such as fulmar, cormorant, great and lesser black-backed gulls, herring gull, kittiwake, razorbill, guillemot, kestrel, raven and, notably, the rare chough nest on the most inaccessible ledges of the high cliffs, which are made up of ancient precambrian rocks. Grey seal breed in the caves and coves.

A variety of plants, such as golden samphire and sea spleenwort, grow among the cliffs, and there are some important maritime lichens on the rocks. On the clifftops stonechat, wheatear, whitethroat, linnet and meadow pipit can be seen. Ecologically, the highlight of this part of the Llŷn Peninsula is the superb expanse of coastal heath, one of the best examples in Europe. Bell heather, heather and western gorse are the dominant species, clipped short and waved in places by the prevailing winds, and the bell heather and gorse create spectacular colour in July and August. This short heath provides the all-important summer feeding habitat for the rare chough. Heavy grazing and heather burning on commonland has led to loss of heath, and its replacement by gorse or acid grassland and bracken, but there are still excellent strands on Trust land.

The farmland behind the cliff zone, where the chough feed in winter, has areas of ancient field patterns bounded by earth walls or stone hedges known as cloddiau.

[⋏] Network of footpaths.

[P] Car park.

[★] Small information centre in old coastguard hut at Mynydd Mawr; local facilities at Aberdaron; leaflet.

[⛵] 49 ha (122 acres) at tip of Llŷn Peninsula near Aberdaron, 18ml W of Pwllheli via B4413. [123:SH140254]

The Brecon Beacons Powys

This impressive landscape of glacial valleys cutting into an escarpment of old red sandstone rocks is dominated by the flat-topped summits of Penyfan and Corn Ddu, the highest points in southern Britain. To the east Cribyn, although lower, makes an equally dramatic skyline. On a clear day, a walk to the summits will afford spectacular views as far as the Devon coast, Herefordshire and Plynlimon.

The upper slopes are heavily grazed by sheep and horses, resulting in a uniform grassland which includes matt and purple moor grasses, but the flora becomes more interesting on the steep north-facing slopes where sheep cannot venture. Here, plants such as purple saxifrage are a reminder of the last Ice Age. The wide-open tracts also provide a habitat for many upland birds including raven, buzzard, ring ouzel and red grouse. In places, remnants of heathland blanket bog add to the diversity of habitats.

Run-off from the upper slopes channels down rocky gullies, through bracken-covered lower slopes, to form tumbling streams which flow through the oak and hazel woods of the valley floor. Piles of moss and lichen-covered rocks beside deep depressions in the Beacons mark the sites of old quarries, the source of stone for sheep pens and miles of dry-stone walls. Older tracks, still in use today, mark the Roman and Norman routes across the escarpment, and high on the summits of Penyfan and Corn Ddu lie burial mounds dating from the Bronze Age.

[⋏] Unrestricted rights of way over commonland.

[P] NT car park at Cwm Gwdi; local authority car parks at Pont Ar Daf and Storey Arms.

★ Facilities at Brecon.

▣ 3,290 ha (8,150 acres) 5ml S of Brecon, E of A470.   [160:SO012216]

The Carneddau Estate   Conwy/Gwynedd

This large estate includes some of the finest scenery in the Snowdonia
National Park. There are numerous lakes, including Llyn Idwal, at 373
metres above sea level, which is part of the Cwm Idwal National Nature
Reserve. The estate lies both sides of the A5, which runs through the Nant
Ffrancon and Nant y Benglog valleys, surrounded by the rugged peaks of
the Carneddau and Glyderau massifs. Among the peaks, which rise to
over 900 metres above sea level, are Carnedd Llewelyn, Tryfan, Glyder
Fach and Glyder Fawr and Carnedd Dafydd.

Typical upland features abound, such as drystone walls, ancient
sheepfolds and isolated farmhouses, many of which have been farmed by
the same families for generations. Clues to even earlier habitation is
evident in the numerous archaeological remains, such as mountain-top
cairns, stone circles, standing stones and ancient hilltop forts.

Indications of past glacial activity such as hanging cwms, stone-strips
and glacial striations can be seen. Geology, climate and management
dictate the diversity of vegetation in this complex area. The main Carneddau ridge is the largest area of montane grassland in Britain south of
the Cairngorms. Bogs and mires are rich in mosses, insectivorous plants
such as sundew and butterwort, rare sedges and other damp-loving
plants. The heavily grazed mineral soils support acres of acid grassland,
but some upland heath survives where grazing pressure is not too great.
The steep, base-rich cliffs, inaccessible to sheep, support an almost unique
Arctic-Alpine flora, including rare saxifrages and the well-known but
rarely seen Snowdon lily, found in Britain only at a few sites in Snowdonia.

There are many footpaths, some of which are showing signs of numerous visitors with large erosion scars, on which sensitive remedial work
has to be undertaken.

⊼ Network of footpaths.

P Car parks along A5 between Capel Curig and Bethesda.

★ Refreshments at Ogwen Cottage; WCs.

▣ 7,036 ha (17,385 acres) 8ml SE of Bangor, both sides of A5, near Capel
Curig.   [115:SH649604]

Carreg and Porthorion
Gwynedd

A continuation of the magnificent Llŷn Peninsula coastline with its bevelled profile of headlands, islands and bays, this property commands spectacular views along the coast and on a clear day across to Ireland. The two tiny tidal islands and the adjoining cliffs of Dinas Fawr and Dinas Bach are overlooked by Mynydd Carreg. The absence of woodland is notable on this very exposed wind-clipped landscape, although streams, flushes and ungrazed ledges provide valuable protection from grazing, leading to rich areas for plants and insects.

Grey seals are common along the coastline, as well as a variety of seabirds. The uncommon chough can be seen feeding in the area.

The cliffs and rocky outcrops are covered with maritime lichens, some of importance for their rarity, and the coastal grassland, heavily grazed, is floristically rich in places. Spring squill, kidney vetch, thyme, rock spurrey, thrift, primrose, burnet saxifrage and restharrow are some of the many flowers to be seen.

[🚶] Footpath; access to islands at low water only.

[P] Car parks at Porthor and Carreg.

[★] Local facilities.

[⛴] 75 ha (184 acres) 3ml NW of Aberdaron.   [123:SH156290]

Cemaes
Ynys Môn

The land at Cemaes includes a stretch of the northern Anglesey coast with two rocky headlands, bays, cliffland and a harbour wall and promenade to the north of Cemaes. Characteristic landscape features include small fields bounded by walls and old lime kilns used to make slaked lime for top dressing fields, and a small area of saltmarsh to the north of Cemaes, an unusual habitat along this particular stretch of coast. To the north an old church dedicated to St Patrick has links with local legends and folklore. The Wylfa Nuclear Power Station looms above the shingle bay.

Popular with geologists because of the range of rocks and structures revealed in the cliffs, Cemaes has a classic cliff section through the ancient precambrian 'Mona Complex' rocks, contorted lavas, limestones and grits, baked and compressed at least 1000 million years ago.

There is also much of wildlife interest. At Llanbadrig Point exposures of ancient rocks are covered with rare and unusual lichens. Rock samphire, kidney vetch, thrift, sea spleenwort and sea campion fill the crevices of the rocks. A small disused cliff quarry, now colonised by heath and grassland, attracts a number of butterflies including wall brown, grayling and gate-keeper, while the regular mounds of yellow meadow ant nests indicate the antiquity of many of the clifftop grasslands. Thickets of scrub create valuable habitats for typical clifftop birds such as stonechat, whitethroat and dunnock and although the cliffs are too low for nesting seabirds, common tern, herring gull, cormorant, redshank and oystercatcher can be seen.

⬚ Open access to cliff; coastal footpath.

P Small car park; car park at St Patrick's church.

★ Facilities at Cemaes.

⬚ 21 ha (51 acres) on E side of Cemaes Bay, 8ml W of Amlwch on A5025, Anglesey.   [114:SH375937]

Coed Cae Fali   Gwynedd

Overlooking the Dwyryd Estuary in the Vale of Ffestiniog, this property on a steep valley side within the Snowdonia National Park consists of a mix of ancient oak woodland with more recently planted beech and conifers such as larch and Norway spruce. It was bought by the Trust with the express purpose of restoring the semi-natural oak woodland, of which there are many important examples in the Ffestiniog area.

The extensive replanting has shaded the woodland floor, much reducing the wildlife interest and entirely changing the character of the wood; beech and conifers are now being selectively removed. The invasive rhododendron, a problem throughout Snowdonia if not controlled, prevents new tree growth and shades the woodland flora, which includes wood sage, hard fern, cow-wheat and common polypody. A rich community of mosses can also be seen on the woodland floor, while bilberry, ling, cross-leaved heath and bell heather grow in the more open areas of the wood. Birds nesting in the woodlands include pied flycatcher, redstart, wood warbler and tree pipit – the four classic upland oakwood birds.

There is evidence throughout the woods of traditional methods of woodland management, such as hazel and oak coppice stools, and old walls and barns are a reminder of a time when woodland clearings were farmed.

⬚ Footpaths; Ffestiniog Railway runs between Porthmadog and Blaenau Ffestiniog (seasonal).

P Parking in lay-by off A487.

★ Nature trails.

♨ 191 ha (472 acres) off A487(T), 7ml E of Porthmadog, E of Penrhyn-
    deudraeth.   [115:SH635403 and 124:SH635403]

Coed y Bwnydd   Monmouthshire

A large, wooded iron age hill fort (an SAM) and associated woodland on a
hilltop with views of the Usk valley. The site is noted for its spring flowers,
which include a spectacular display of bluebells. In autumn and winter,
when the vegetation has died down, the interesting archaeological
features can be appreciated more fully.

⋔ Open access; circular path around site; footpath to site linked to car
    park at Clytha.

P Layby at entrance to site on country lane (parking for 3/4 cars); site
    linked to car park at Clytha.

★ Seasonal interpretation panels erected when goats are grazing the site.

♨ 10 ha (25 acres) 4ml north of Usk.   [161:SO365068]

The Colby Estate   Pembrokeshire

The Colby Estate, in the Pembrokeshire Coast National Park and SSSI,
adjoins Carmarthen Bay either side of Amroth, a little holiday village on
the Pembrokeshire border. Reaching $1\frac{1}{2}$ miles inland to a ridge of
carboniferous limestone, it surrounds and protects a beautiful wooded
valley which runs north from the sea and forks at Colby Lodge. Farmland,
cliffs and coastal pastures, steep wooded valleys with fast-running
streams, abandoned fields regenerating to oak and ash woods, overgrown
quarries and mine workings provide important habitats for a rich variety
of animals and birds.

Overlying the Pembrokeshire coalfield, the estate was extensively
mined for its anthracite until the middle of the nineteenth century. It
takes its name from John Colby, an industrial entrepreneur of the early
nineteenth century, who built Colby Lodge. Along the footpaths and in
the woods, the evocative remains of the industry lie scattered beneath the
peace and tranquillity of the present landscape.

⋔ Excellent network of footpaths; Colby Woodland Garden open
    seasonally; local station at Kilgetty and bus service from Tenby.

P Car park.

⊠ NT shop and refreshments at Woodland Garden; WCs; part of Woodland Garden accessible to wheelchairs.

▣ 394 ha (973 acres) immediately NW of Amroth.   [158:SN155080]

Craflwyn   Gwynedd

This estate has a rich and varied past. Once owned by Llwelyn Fawr, a former Prince of Wales, it became a fashionable retreat in the latter half of the nineteenth century, during which time many ornamental trees and shrubs were planted in the woodland. The complex of fishponds, rock-lined streams and mossy waterfalls further demonstrates the owner's efforts to keep abreast of contemporary trends in landscape design. This attractive habitat now supports a wealth of insects and birds, with an area of heathland (known as Cocyn Craflwyn) adding diversity.

⊡ Network of footpaths

℗ Small car park (£1 donation appreciated)

⊠ Education centre with guided walks and other activities by arrangement; leaflet; information panel; local facilities at Beddgelert

▣ 93 ha (230 acres) 1ml NE of Beddgelert on A498   [115:SH600490]

Cregennan   Gwynedd

The Cadair Idris massif, in the south-western quarter of the Snowdonia National Park, is an impressive mountainous landscape with a wide range of nationally important upland habitats (lakes, crags, heath, mires, scree and open grassland) and classic features of a glaciated mountain terrain. Cregennan lies to the north-west of the summit with views of the massif and across the Mawddach Estuary to Barmouth Bay. Dinas Oleu, an area of cliffland above Barmouth, was the first property to be acquired by the Trust.

The clear waters of the two lakes, known jointly as Llynnau Cregennan, are fed by streams running off the mountains, creating a network of wetland habitats. A combination of mosses (including club mosses), sedges, heather, cross-leaved heath, bilberry, crow-berry and lichens make up these valuable habitats; Cregennan Bog, in particular, is covered with *Sphagnum* moss and bog myrtle.

The ungrazed islands on the lakes contain examples of the vegetation that could grow without grazing pressure, such as vigorous tall heathland plants. There are also some significant areas of bushy dry heath around the lake, with bilberry, cross-leaved heath, mosses, grasses and lichens, and peregrine, raven and buzzard are a common sight overhead. A small area of woodland, dominated by ash, forms a landmark and there is also an interesting area of upland hazel scrub. The crags and rock crevices support important wildlife communities, inaccessible to sheep grazing, with mossy and starry saxifrages, Wilson's filmy fern, rose-root and beech fern.

Recent archaeological surveys have uncovered a succession of significant remains scattered over the landscape, dating back to a prehistoric age, including standing stones, rectangular huts and ring cairns, evidence of a continuous pattern of settlement in what appears to be a wild and inhospitable terrain. A network of dry-stone walls and vernacular farm buildings dotted throughout the valleys reveal more recent efforts to make a living from farming in these mountains.

[↟] Minor gated metalled road; footpaths around northern edge of lake; car access through property.

[P] Car park at Llynnau Cregennan.

[★] WCs at Llynnau Cregennan; youth hostel at Abergwynant.

[⬚] 332 ha (820 acres) 1ml E of Arthog, A493 up steep winding road or Cadair Idris road from Dolgellau.   [124:SH660140]

Dinas Island   Pembrokeshire

With dramatic views across Cardigan Bay, this prominent headland provides an important nesting site for seabirds, including guillemot, razorbill, fulmar and gulls, especially on Needle Rock. The rare chough and raven may also be seen here, and grey seals swim off the headland, which is linked to the 'mainland' by a valley – a glacial meltwater channel, now filled with thick peat deposits.

Interesting maritime grassland, open rock communities and extensive heathland occur on the cliffs, although there are large areas of less notable coarse grassland and bracken. Thrift clearwing moth and small blue butterfly are among the interesting invertebrates.

[↟] Circular walk around headland; permitted path across farmland.

[P] Car parks to W and E.

[★] Facilities at Pwll Gwaelod; WCs; leaflet from Dyfed Wildlife Trust.

[⬚] 4 ha (9½ acres) 7ml NE of Fishguard, off A487(T).   [157:SN010404]

Dinas Oleu   Gwynedd

A gorse-covered hillside with small areas of young sycamore and oak,
Dinas Oleu was the very first property to be passed to the National Trust.
Given in 1895, it was the foundation stone for a conservation charity
which now owns over 240,000 hectares of countryside.

On the more open areas of the hillside warm breezes provide idea habitat for plants such as stork's-bill and knotted clover. Some rare liverworts
and mosses have been recorded on the thin, well drained soils. Cae Fadog,
adjoining Dinas Oleu, is dominated by heath, and the scarcity of lowland
heath gives it special importance. Plants found here include birds foot
trefoil, and wild thyme. The frequency of flowering herbs is an important
feature, providing good nectar for insects such as solitary bees and
hoverflies.

Walkers can sit and contemplate the magnificent view from a
commemorative stone seat, in the shape of centenary "C", built on the top
of Dinas Oleu in 1995 to mark the 100th anniversary of the gift of the
headland to the Trust.

👤 Footpath from centre of town; network of paths on site.

P In Barmouth town centre.

★ Leaflet available from local TIC.

♿ 2 ha (4½ acres) on hillside above Barmouth.   [124:SM615160]

Dinefwr Estate   Carmarthenshire

Dinefwr Park has had a significant involvement with the early medieval
history of Wales; the old Dinefwr Castle which overlooks the Tywi Valley
was the capital of Deheubarth, one of the three ancient kingdoms of
Wales. Newton House has been the ancestral home of the modern
Dynevor family since around 1500. The old castle is now a ruin, owned
by the Wildlife Trust West Wales and managed by Cadw.

The surrounding parkland is also a medieval feature and includes
parks enclosed for deer and white park cattle. The park still contains
descendants of the wildwood, and is a very important site for species of
lichen and insect which are confined to sites with an unbroken continuity
of ancient trees. The park and adjacent farmland were landscaped in the
eighteenth century, when much tree-planting was carried out.

As well as the park, valuable features at Dinefwr include the banks of
the River Tywi, its flood pastures and old ox-bows, which have a rich

aquatic flora including scarce pondweeds, floating marshwort, nodding bur-marigold and greater bladderwort. The flood plain and ox-bows are part of a site of international importance for wintering birds, including ten per cent of the British population of white-fronted geese (down-stream) and teal, wigeon, shoveler, curlew, lapwing and other waders.

[†] Via minor roads; station at Llandeilo.

[P] Car park in park near Newton House.

[★] Parkland walks, including boardwalk; bird hide.

[⊞] 196 ha (450 acres) off A40(T), entrance at Llandeilo.   [159:SN615225]

The Dolaucothi Estate   Carmarthenshire

In the remote Cothi Valley, gold has been mined from these wooded slopes since Roman times. The gold mines are the main focus for a visit, but the estate is large and encompasses eleven tenanted farms and part of Pumpsaint village.

Oak and alder woods are rich in woodland plants. Llandre Carr, an alder woodland, is of note for its abundance of mosses and lichens, and pockets of old sessile oak woodland provide important cover for numerous breeding birds. The majestic red kite may also be seen over the woods.

[†] Walks around mines and woodlands; local station at Llanwrda.

[P] Car park near mines.

[★] Mines open seasonally; leaflets; booklets; trails; volunteer base camp; visitor information centre in village.

[⊞] 1,021 ha (2,522 acres) between Llanwrda and Lampeter at Pumpsaint, off A482.   [146:SN6640]

The Dolmelynllyn Estate   Gwynedd

This extensive and varied estate on the slopes of Y Garn in the Rhinog Mountains, within the Snowdonia National Park, includes parkland, two farms and two sheep walks. Wooded fringes, hay meadows and pastures lie along the River Mawddach, where royal fern and globe flower can be found in places.

Oak woodlands on the steep lower slopes include Coed Berthlwyd and Ganllwyd, the latter a National Nature Reserve of great interest for its mosses and liverworts. Woodland plants include hay-scented buckler fern, lemon-scented fern, Wilson's filmy fern and the mountain male fern, while birds in the woods include breeding nuthatch and buzzard. Rare lichens occur on well-lit trees at woodland edges, along the tracks and in the park, indicating a long continuity of woodland cover in this area and an unpolluted, humid atmosphere.

Cefn Coch and Berthlwyd gold mines, dating from the nineteenth century, are among the many relics of the mining history of the area. Small dry-stone enclosures, field barns and abandoned farmsteads make up the landscape of the lower hill slopes, while upland shelters or 'hafotai' can be seen on higher ground. Many of the fields have unimproved grass-lands, rich flushes and mires, and an abundance of the diminutive ivy-leaved bellflower is a feature.

The Rhiniogau heather moors of Derlwyn and Y Llethr to the west are of interest, with excellent expanses of cross-leaved heath, bell heather, bilberry, cowberry, crowberry and a very varied under-storey of mosses and lichens beneath the dwarf shrubs, as well as ungrazed crags with tall herb ledges and small mountain lakes and pools.

[🏃] Well-used footpaths through woods.

[P] Car park at nature reserve; Forestry Commission car park on opposite side of river.

[★] WCs; leaflets; information panel; old mine site open to the public; fishing with permits.

[▆] 546 ha (1,350 acres) 5ml NW of Dolgellau, W of A470.   [124:SH728243]

Gamallt   Gwynedd

This remote moorland is overlain by a thick layer of peat, and much valued for its well-developed dry heathland, upland lakes and an exten-sive 'blanket' bog which includes dwarf shrubs of heather, crowberry, cowberry, cotton grass and luxuriant carpets of *Sphagnum* moss. Heather flowers are an important food source for specialist upland invertebrates which include moths and bees, while the lakes, low in nutrients (olig-otrophic), provide an important habitat for a number of rare water beetles. Common sandpiper, ring ouzel, wheatear and meadow pipit are present, and Gamallt also supports an important upland breeding bird community.

Many notable archaeological remains are scattered across the moor, including a large Iron Age settlement with huts and enclosures. A Roman road known as Sarn Helen crosses the property.

[🏃] On foot only, by track one mile from Ffestiniog on Bala road; Ffestiniog Railway runs between Porthmadog and Blaenau Ffestiniog (seasonal).

P Informal parking.

★ Local facilities.

⬛ 122 ha (300 acres) 3ml NE of Ffestiniog.   [124:SH722423]

Glan Faenol   Gwynedd

Bordering the Menai Strait between the mainland and Anglesey, this property includes an area of woodland and improved farmland associated with Vaynol Hall, the remains of one of the largest estates in North Wales. Views to the mountains of Snowdonia and across this beautiful, rocky, wooded, tidal strait (now an important marine nature reserve) have been depicted in a famous mural by Rex Whistler at Plas Newydd.

The parkland around the Hall has small pockets of natural deciduous woodland which are important for wildlife, and the Trust is gradually converting the conifer plantations to broadleaved woodlands and the arable land to pasture. A number of follies and estate buildings survive, with a round tower built to rival the column on Anglesey and a family mausoleum. Old lime workings are now colonised by a covert of ash, elm, birch, holly, hazel and dog's mercury, and the estate wall around the park is also of historic interest.

⬛ Footpaths; station at Bangor.

P Small car park.

★ Local facilities.

⬛ 127 ha (314 acres) 3ml SW of Bangor, 7ml N of Caernarfon off A487.
                [114 and 115:SH530695 and 534698 for car park]

Good Hope   Pembrokeshire

Lying on the rugged coastline east of Strumble Head, this traditional farmed landscape includes narrow fields, historical field boundaries ('Pembrokeshire banks') and vernacular farm buildings.

The farmland consists of a patchwork of dry and wet pasture, scrub, rushes, gorse and bracken. Adder's tongue fern, a plant typical of old damp unimproved pastures, exists within a number of fields with many orchids, yellow bartsia, ragged robin, wild angelica, marsh bedstraw and lesser spearwort. The hedgebanks, an important feature of the landscape, add to the ecological interest of the property. Overgrown willow, black-thorn and bramble attract birds such as willow warbler, chiffchaff, grasshopper warbler, whitethroat and wren. An old green lane divides the farm into two.

The unfarmed clifftop includes areas of coastal maritime grassland and heath rich in plants such as heather, thrift, kidney vetch, ox-eye daisy and sea campion, which attract many insects. The rare chough, a speciality of coastal grasslands and heaths in Pembrokeshire and the Llŷn Peninsula, can also be seen regularly.

[🚶] Pembrokeshire coastal path; footpath through farmland.

[P] Car park at Strumble Head (1½ml to W); no parking on property.

[★] Facilities at Fishguard.

[🏠] 39 ha (97 acres) E of Strumble Head, 3ml NW of Fishguard on the Pembrokeshire coast.   [157:SM912407]

Graig Fawr   Denbighshire

This limestone hill supports an outstanding variety of flowers and butterflies. The northern brown argus butterfly, a rare species in north Wales, is found here, its larvae feeding on the common rockrose. A ½ mile walk to the summit offers panoramic views over the Vale of Clwyd and along the coastline to Snowdonia.

[🚶] Network of footpaths

[P] Small car park

[★] Local facilities; leaflet

[🏠] 1ml S of Prestatyn off A457 by the village of Meliden.   [116:SJ062800]

Hafod y Llan and Gelli Iago   Gwynedd

The Hafod y Llan and Gelli Iago estates lie in the heart of Snowdonia and are of national and international importance. Both were acquired in 1998 following a public appeal. The Hafod y Llan estate covers a rugged landscape rising from the shores of Llyn Gwynant and the Afon Glaslyn to the summit of Yr Wyddfa (Snowdon). The Gelli Iago estate faces north west towards Snowdon and rises to the summit of Cnicht.

Yr Wyddfa (Snowdon) is the second largest National Nature Reserve in England and Wales and 55% of it lies within the Hafod y Llan estate. Hafod y Llan and the Snowdon massif in general has outstanding examples of landforms formed during the last Ice Age, including corries, aretes, moraines and blockfields, which combined form some of the best documented and spectacular landscapes in Wales. The vegetation is principally that of mountain and moorland, with acid grassland the dominant vegetation in terms of area. There are five types of semi-natural woodland dominated by ash, oak and alder, and the property has the largest population in Wales of the mountain juniper, a rare sub-species of the common juniper.

Gelli Iago has a gentler and more undulating landscape than Hafod y Llan – a consequence of the underlying rocks. Two thirds of Gelli Iago is composed of sedimentary rocks, more easily eroded than the harder igneous rocks which dominate Hafod y Llan.

The estate includes six lakes and drainage is sufficiently poor in places to support a variety of mire communities. 10% of the Gelli Iago estate is designated an SSSI.

[⌖] One of the principal access routes up Snowdon, the Watkin Path (opened in 1892) runs in its entirety through the Hafod y Llan estate.

[P] Car park in lay-by on A498.

[★] Local facilities in Beddgelert.

[🚌] Hafod y Llan 1,025 ha (2534 acres) 4ml NE of Beddgelert; Gelli Iago 627 ha (1549 acres) 3ml E of Beddgelert.

[115:SH629513 and 633484]

Henrhyd Falls and Graigllech Woods   Powys

Situated on the southern edge of the Brecon Beacons National Park, this area contains a complicated series of river capture and rejuvenation at the head of the Neath and Tawe rivers which has produced narrow, steep-sided gorges and waterfalls. One such gorge and waterfall can be seen here on the Nant Llech, a tributary of the Tawe. This impressive beauty spot is crossed by the course of the nineteenth-century Brecon Forest Tramroad, an early railway used to transport minerals.

The 'dingles', or woods on either side of the gorge, are rich in wildlife. Evidence of past woodland management is visible in the form of old coppice stools, and the woods to the north, dominated by oak, ash and hazel, also contain remains of coppicing. To the south there is little coppicing, and the trees include wych elm and small-leaved lime. The remains of a Roman fort (not owned by the Trust) among the woods nearby add further historic interest.

Rocks around the waterfalls are covered in mosses, ferns and liver-worts, and on ledges tall herbs such as tutsan, meadowsweet, common valerian and lady's mantle occur. Many other more local plants are present in the Nant Llech valley as a whole.

- 🚶 Footpath to gorge.
- 🅿 Car park N of gorge through Coelbren, off minor road.
- ★ Local facilities.
- ❗ Care must be taken to avoid landslips.
- ⛁ 76 ha (188 acres) N of Coelbren junction, midway between A4067 and A4109.   [160:SN855122]

The Kymin   Monmouthshire

A wooded garden on a hill above Monmouth, with extensive views across the Wye Valley. A banqueting house called 'The Round House' was built here in 1794 by a dining club. The Naval Temple, erected by the same club in 1801 in honour of the Royal Navy, is open all year. The whole site lies within the Wye Valley AONB.

- 🚶 Public footpaths to site linking with walks in Forest of Dean; Offa's Dyke crosses the site.
- 🅿 Car parking interspersed in wooded area at entrance to site.
- ★ WCs & shops in Monmouth; interpretation panel on site; leaflet available at TIC and NT shop in Monmouth.
- ⛁ 4 ha (10 acres) 1ml E of Monmouth between A466 & A4136.
                                                       [162:SO528125]

Lan-Lay Meadows   Vale of Glamorgan

A series of unimproved wetland meadows alongside the River Ely, which is an SSSI. The meadows comprise several small fields enclosed by mature neglected hedgerows with superb mature oaks and chestnut trees. This habitat was once common within the Vale of Glamorgan, but much has been lost due to agricultural improvement.

- 🚶 Open access; public footpath alongside River Ely and one crossing site.
- 🅿 Limited parking; preferable to park in village and walk to site.
- ★ Local facilities. Please keep dogs under control as livestock graze this site.
- ⛁ 8.5 ha (21 acres) on the outskirts of Peterstone Super Ely, 8ml W of Cardiff.   [170:ST079759]

Lawrenny

Pembrokeshire

This ancient oakwood stands on the east bank of the Daugleddau Estuary between its two branches, Garron Pil and the Cresswell River. The estuary is of importance for its wildfowl and waders, and is of marine biological interest because of the change in plants and animals upstream as the saltwater merges with fresh.

The coppiced sessile oak woodland supports a rich association of beetles, mosses, lichens, woodland plants and the wild service tree, all indicators of the antiquity of the site. Breeding birds include redstart.

Permitted footpaths on NT property.

Car park at Lawrenny Quay.

Facilities at nearby Lawrenny Quay.

29 ha (71 acres) 16ml SE of Haverfordwest, W of A4075 to Lawrenny.
[157 and 158:SN017068]

Little Milford

Pembrokeshire

Situated on the west bank of the tidal mouth of the Cleddau River, a branch of the Daugleddau Estuary, this wooded property fringes an important estuarine bird sanctuary with impressive wintering populations of wildfowl and waders, including redshank, dunlin and ringed plover. Good numbers of greenshank can be seen on migration.

The wooded slopes of conifer and broadleaved trees include pockets of oak coppice with a rich woodland flora and fauna. Woodland plants include great woodrush, moschatel, common cow-wheat and the local hay-scented buckler fern, here near the northern edge of its distributional range in Britain.

The estuarine and alluvial flats are fringed by a small area of ungrazed saltmarsh, and a reedbed.

Network of footpaths and 2 bridleways cross property.

2 small car parks, near entrance to property off main Haverfordwest to Freystrop road and just before Hook village.

Local facilities in Haverfordwest.

29 ha (72 acres) 3ml S of Haverfordwest, Pembrokeshire.
[158 and 157:SM967118]

Llanrhidian Marsh and Whitford Burrows

Swansea

These properties are outstanding both for their landscape beauty and for their wildlife. Llanrhidian Marsh is one of the best examples of a salt-marsh in Britain, and Whitford Burrows one of the best dune systems.

Llanrhidian Marsh is a high saltmarsh, only inundated by very high tides, which has been built up into the Burry Inlet far out in front of the old fossil limestone cliffline, a very distinct feature backing the marshes. It is commonland, heavily grazed by sheep and ponies, and provides an interesting contrast with the ungrazed marshes nearby, which have a very different saltmarsh flora. The site is of international importance for its huge populations of over wintering wildfowl (over 14,500) and waders (over 38,000) including oystercatcher, knot, turnstone, pintail, curlew, golden plover, grey plover, teal, shelduck, shoveler, dunlin, sanderling and redshank.

Whitford Burrows is a very extensive dune system. Although partly planted with pines to stabilise the dunes (a practice now known to reduce significantly the interest of sand dunes, mobile and fresh sand being essential for their natural functioning) the Burrows have an excellent series of dune habitats. These include embryo (new) dunes, yellow dunes with marram grass, stable dune grassland, superb damp hollows or slacks, and very interesting dune-to-saltmarsh transitions. The flora is exceptional, and includes many rare and local species, including early marsh orchid, fen orchid, early sand-grass, golden dock and dune gentian. Whitford Burrows was the first Trust property to be acquired under the Enterprise Neptune appeal.

[🚶] Via minor roads.

[P] Informal parking in farmers field.

[★] Information from Countryside Council for Wales at RVB House, Llys Felin Newydd, Phoenix Way, Enterprise Park, Swansea SA7 9FG.

[⛶] 514 ha (1,271 acres) on N and NW coast of Gower peninsula, from village of Crofty, 6ml W of Swansea off minor roads to Cheriton from B4295.   [159:SS439937]

Longhouse

Pembrokeshire

This property includes an impressive rocky headland with small offshore islands, sea stacks, sheer cliffs, unimproved clifftops and farmland.

Traditional hedgebanks rich in wildflowers surround some of the small fields, and herb-rich coastal grasslands, cliffledges and scrub encircle the farmland.

The headlands include some important grasslands and rock crevices which support spring squill, kidney vetch, tormentil, pink thrift, rock spurrey, sea campion, sheep's bit and many other species. Of historic interest is a promontory hill fort which can be seen at Castell Coch and Ynys Castell.

[🚶] Coast path; circular walk.

[P] Limited parking at Abercastle and Trevine (care must be taken to avoid blocking gates and lanes).

[★] Facilities at Trevine; WCs at Abercastle; leaflet.

[▦] 82 ha (203 acres) 14ml NE of St David's, just NE of Trefin off A487.

[157:SM853337]

Lydstep Headland   Pembrokeshire

This impressive coastal promontory overlooks the island of Caldey and protects Lydstep Haven. It is made up of carboniferous limestone which forms high cliffs, deep inlets and caves.

The cliffs are important for seabirds such as fulmar, razorbill and guillemot, which nest on the rock ledges, and the uncommon chough can be seen quite frequently.

Clifftop grasslands are a mass of colour with cowslip, spring squill, wild thyme, ox-eye daisy, autumn gentian and the occasional green-winged orchid. A disused limestone quarry, possibly used to export limestone in ships across the Bristol Channel, is now being colonised by lime-loving plants.

[🚶] On foot via public footpath from Lydstep village; Pembrokeshire Coast Path crosses property; stations at Manorbier, Penally and Tenby.

[P] Car park on headland.

[★] Nature trail leaflet.

[▦] 22 ha (54 acres) 4ml SW of Tenby on A4139, 3ml E of Manorbier.

[158:SS090976]

Marloes Sands and Deer Park   Pembrokeshire

The most westerly section of the Dale-Marloes Peninsula is surrounded by a dramatic coastline with complex geological structures and a sweep of sands to the south. The rocks include unusual volcanic lavas, and a good example of the junction between the Silurian and Devonian geological periods. The name Deer Park refers to an enclosing wall built during the eighteenth and nineteenth centuries, although there is no evidence that deer were ever introduced.

On the south coast between Gateholm and the Deer Park, herb-rich unimproved grasslands, heath, scrub and lichens of national importance cover the rocks. The heath includes prostrate broom, a rare coastal plant.

Marloes Mere, leased to the Wildlife Trust West Wales, is an extensive bog dominated by rushes with many other plants such as common cotton grass and ragged robin, and a rich habitat for birds.

Wintering wildfowl and waders include wigeon, shoveler, pintail, curlew and lapwing, with whimbrel on migration. Gateholm Island and promontory, the site of an ancient fort, lies to the west of Marloes Sands. Gateholm, together with Midland Island and the Deer Park, were bought with Enterprise Neptune funds in 1981.

On the north coast scrub and coarse grassland provide good feeding and nesting sites for stonechat, whitethroat, dunnock, linnet, yellowhammer and wren. The patches of heath, which are pruned and 'waved' by the strong salt-laden winds, attract insect feeding on heather, such as the oak eggar moth and heather beetle. The Trust has reintroduced grazing to the Deer Park to maintain short grassland and heath habitats, very important for chough which breed on the cliff ledges and feed on the cliff tops.

Public access to Marloes Sands and Martin's Haven beach; long-distance path along coastline.

P Large car parks at Martin's Haven and above Marloes Sands.

★ WCs at Marloes village; leaflet for Marloes Peninsula; interpretive centre at Martins Haven, Lockley Lodge, run by the Wildlife Trust West Wales; youth hostel at Runwayskiln, Marloes.

212 ha (524 acres) SW of Haverfordwest, off B4327. [157:SM770085]

Mwche and Pentowyn Carmarthenshire

The marshes at Mwche and Pentowyn lie on the east bank of the Taf estuary, opposite Laugharne and surrounded by delightful rolling countryside. The ruined bell house at Black Scar used to contain the bell by which travellers would summon the Laugharne ferry. To the south and south-east are the Taf-Towy estuary complex and the dunes at Pendine. The

whole area is an important habitat for birds, and the marshes are especially notable for their wintering wildfowl, including good numbers of
wigeon and occasional wild geese. An area of woodland adds ecological
diversity and supports a range of typical birds and plants.

[⫟] Network of footpaths, including along the old seawall.

[P] Nearest parking is on driveway to Lords Park Farm, 1ml SE (please park
considerately).

[⛵] 62 ha (153 acres) 3ml W of Llansteffan, via B4312.   [159:SN315107]

Mwnt   Ceredigion

This charming and safe family beach in a sheltered bay, bounded on the
north by the dramatic headland of Foel y Mwnt, is a geological SSSI and
part of the Ceredigion Heritage Coast. The maritime flora is more varied
than is typical here, and includes spring squill, hard rush and fifty species
of lichen (in contrast to the average of fifteen for this part of the coastline).
In spring the headland has a glorious carpet of pink thrift.

Birds of prey hunt over the surrounding agricultural pastureland, and
gulls and fulmar occupy the precipitous cliffs. Grey seal, bottle-nosed
dolphin and terns frequent the waters of the bay.

The bay is the site of a battle in 1155, when an invasion of Flemings
was repelled by the Welsh. The church of the Holy Cross was built in the
thirteenth or fourteenth century on the site of an old Celtic saint's cell, on
the pilgrimage route to Bardsey.

Imported lime, used to sweeten the acid soil of this west-coast
seaboard, was burnt in the old kiln.

[⫟] Steps down to beach.

[P] Large car park, free to members.

[★] WCs and refreshments (seasonal). Dogs are not allowed on the beach
during the summer.

[!] Care should be taken near the treacherous cliff edges.

[⛵] 40 ha (98 acres) 4ml NE of Cardigan, off A487.

[145:SN190520]

Mynachdy, Clegir Mawr and Cemlyn   Ynys Môn

This varied stretch of coast from Cemaes to Clegir on the north side of
Anglesey is designated a Heritage Coast because of the unspoilt beauty of

its small shingle beaches, rocky inlets, grassy headlands, islands, inshore water, farmed landscape and the numerous remains of an industrial and maritime past.

The landscape consists of drumlins, or small rounded rocky hillocks formed in the last Ice Age, often surrounded by narrow bands of arable land, pasture or, in some of the hollows, by bog and fen. The grassy and heathy headlands have a rich flora, with spring squill, kidney vetch, harebell, thyme, knapweed, devil's bit scabious, restharrow, bloody crane's bill and bird's foot trefoil.

Cemlyn, a lagoon created by the impounding of brackish water, attracts winter populations of wildfowl and a colony of Arctic and common terns during April to July; it is managed as a nature reserve by the North Wales Wildlife Trust.

Mynachdy includes a fine stretch of the north-west corner of Anglesey with many coves, and views to Holyhead Bay. Old settlement sites and the remains of derelict copper mines can also be seen here.

Clegir Mawr and Cemlyn consist of gently undulating farmland with typical drystone walls surrounding small fields, rocky sea cliffs, headlands and shingle beaches. the beaches are colonised by pioneer plants such as sea kale, sea radish and sea holly, while the cliffs, encrusted with unusual lichens, thrift, rocky spurrey and sea campion, include some spectacular folds and ancient volcanic intrusions. They also provide important nesting sites for chough, raven, jackdaw and peregrine. The rocks here are amongst the oldest in Britain, some 1000 million years old, and are of great geological interest. Earthworks and a twelfth-century church are of historic interest at Cemlyn.

🚶 Waymarked path along the coast; network of paths linking with coast.

🅿 Small car parks at Fydlyn and Hen Felin.

★ Leaflets; information boards.

📷 358 ha (884 acres) 2ml W of Cemaes Bay, off side roads from A5025 on N coast of Anglesey.
    [114:SH304915/316927 (Mynachdy); SH329936/SH337932 (Cemlyn)]

Mynydd Anelog   Gwynedd

This area of ancient commonland, with the remains of prehistoric hut circles, stands on one of the higher hills of the Llŷn Peninsula, with precipitous cliffs commanding spectacular views across to Ireland, the Snowdonia mountain range, Anglesey and south to St David's Head.

Like that at Braich-y-Pwll, the coastal heath is one of the best examples of its kind in Europe, and the three dwarf shrubs – heather, bell heather and western gorse – grow well where grazing is not too heavy and burning not too frequent. It provides crucial summer feeding-ground for the rare chough, a red-billed member of the crow family which is now found in Britain only on the Llŷn, Anglesey, in Pembrokeshire and in part of the western coast of Scotland. Like those on Anglesey, the Llŷn rocks are ancient pre-Cambrian metamorphosed lavas and sediments of great geological interest.

The clifftop moorland is scattered with rock boulders and outcrops, providing an ideal point to view the varied landscape of Llŷn – small-scale traditional farms, unimproved coarse grassland and heather enclosed by walls, fences and stone banks, ancient commons and scrubby pockets of woodland.

[↟] Footpath from Whistling Sands beach.

[P] Car parks at Carreg and Porthor.

[★] Local facilities.

[⬛] 47 ha (116 acres) 2ml NW of Aberdaron.   [123:SH150275]

Penarfynydd and Porth Ysgo   Gwynedd

On the south side of the peninsula, Porth Ysgo, a sandy beach surrounded by cliffs, looks towards Ynys Enlli and Ynysoedd Gwylanod. In marked contrast to the steep, exposed cliffs of much of the Llŷn, this site has soft, unstable cliffs which are low-lying, sheltered and scrubby. Penarfynydd is higher and has steep bracken-covered cliffs; there is also a mudflow here which supports some interesting grassland and heath. Breeding birds include fulmar, cormorant, shag, kittiwake, razorbill and guillemot.

The dark, volcanic intrusions exposed on the beach are covered with maritime lichens, and the surrounding clifftops are fringed with a herb-rich grassland, typically found around the relatively ungrazed parts of the peninsula. The underlying rocks strongly influence the plants; the more base-rich soils support finer grasses, with madder, rock sea lavender, thyme, sea campion and many species unusual to the Llŷn coast.

The heather, gorse and bracken along the clifftop attract small birds such as stonechat, linnet and yellowhammer, while chough feeds on the shorter grassland and gorse.

🔲 Footpaths.

🅿 2 small car parks.

⭐ Local facilities.

♿ 99 ha (245 acres) 2ml E of Aberdaron, access by minor roads.
[123:SH217265 and 208266]

Penbryn   Ceredigion

This gently sloping sandy beach, an sssi and part of the Ceredigion Heritage Coast, is approached via the picturesque Hoffnant Valley from the Trust's car park at Llanborth Farm.

There are steep cliffs to the south-west, and more unusual rock formations at the north-east end. Notable local plants include Portland and wood spurges and rocky stonecrop. The predominantly sycamore and ash woodland of the valley supports important fern communities and is rich in insect life.

The coastal scrub holds a good population of small birds including grasshopper warbler and whitethroat. Bottle-nosed dolphin are sometimes spotted from the beach.

The valley is referred to locally as Cwm Lladron or Robbers' Valley, and is said to have been much used by smugglers, while the Corbalani Stone, reputedly marking the grave of an early Celtic chieftain, has been loosely associated with the Arthurian legend.

🔲 Footpath down the Hoffnant Valley.

🅿 Car park, free to members.

⭐ Shop, café and WCs open seasonally at Llanborth Farm. Dogs not allowed on the beach during summer.

♿ 50 ha (124 acres) N of A487, midway between Cardigan and New Quay.
[145:SN295519]

Pennard Cliffs and Three Cliffs Bay   Swansea

This impressive carboniferous limestone coastline is of great importance for its fossil-rich rocks and variety of archaeological remains. Minchin Hole, a geological sssi, is an unusual cave cut into the calcareous rocks, and archaeologists and palaeontologists have found evidence of mammal bones and early man on this site.

High Pennard, one of the higher points along the cliffline, is capped with a prehistoric defensive hill fort, and Penmaen Burrows over Three Cliffs Bay contains a megalithic burial chamber, a pillow mound, a medieval tower and church, and some old lime kilns. A derelict limestone quarry at Pwll Du, from which stone was exported to Devon, is also of historic interest.

Steep cliffs, broad sands and a meandering stream make up Three Cliffs Bay. A small sand-dune system and area of saltmarsh, used by many field study groups, add to the wildlife interest of the area, with a number of characteristic plants such as sea spurge, sea holly, eel grass, glasswort and sea plantain. The intertidal zone is of marine interest, and the wide sandbanks on the stream provide an ideal feeding ground for waders and wildfowl. A rich diversity of plants along the clifftop reflects the underlying calcareous soils. Where the grassland has escaped agricultural improvement, a greater variety of flowers exists, with wild thyme, kidney vetch, violets, bird's foot trefoil, rock-rose and small scabious, and these attract a number of associated butterflies such as the dark-green fritillary, small blue, brown argus and grayling.

Heather occurs where the soil has been leached and is more acidic, and blackthorn scrub also occurs on the clifftop, attracting many small birds such as stonechat, linnet and whinchat. Fulmar, kittiwake, cormorant and guillemot nest on the cliffs.

⊞ Via minor roads; access to Three Cliffs Bay from Pennard Burrows or via Penmaen Burrows.

P Car park at Southgate; car park at Penmaen (limited space).

★ Village shop and WCs at Southgate; leaflets available from car park attendant at Southgate; no disabled access.

⊠ 100 ha (258 acres) 7ml SW of Swansea, extending E of Pwll-du Head to Southgate on Gower Peninsula.

[159:SS554873]

Plas-yn-Rhiw Estate   Gwynedd

The former home of the three Keating sisters, the manor of Plas-yn-Rhiw is surrounded by a comparatively well-wooded estate overlooking the long sweeping curved beach of Porth Neigwl. The sisters bought the property in 1939 and subsequently donated it to the Trust 'to save a unique area of natural beauty in memory of their parents'.

In one of the few woodlands on the peninsula, oak, elm and sycamore create a damp, shaded environment for a wealth of ferns, and a mixture of scrub and grassland attracts birds such as stonechat, whinchat and linnet.

Mynydd-y-Graig, the site of an ancient hill fort and some megalithic remains, is of historic interest and the subject of further archaeological studies.

🏃 Via minor roads; Plas-yn-Rhiw house open seasonally; station at Pwllheli and local bus service from Pwllheli and Aberdaron, alight at Botwnnog.

P Car park.

★ NT shop; WCs (including disabled); information point; picnic area; path through woods suitable for wheelchairs.

⬛ 168 ha (416 acres) near Pwllheli, access via minor roads off B4413.
[123:SH236285 and 228275]

Porthdinllaen   Gwynedd

Porthdinllaen, on the Llŷn Peninsula near Nefyn, is one of the most beautiful stretches of coastline in Wales. Its perfect crescent of sand is fringed by cliffs and rugged headland. The harbour – the only truly sheltered one on Llŷn's rocky north coast – was a busy little port in its own right. Records indicate that in 1861 around 800 vessels entered Porthdinllaen. It was also a safe haven for shipping during storms, protected by its headland from prevailing south-westerly and westerly gales.

In 1864, a station was established at Porthdinllaen by the RNLI. It continues in use to this day, keeping a watchful eye over Caernarfon Bay and the Irish Sea.

Porthdinllaen is noted for its marine and geological importance which is reflected in its designation as an SSSI. The rocky seashore on both sides of Trwyn Porthdinllaen is rich in marine wildlife. a particularly wide variety of habitats is present here between high and low tides, ranging from west-facing wave-exposed rocks to very sheltered stretches in the east – the latter are very rare on the Llŷn. A walk along the shore at low water can reveal an amazing variety of marine creatures, including barnacles, crabs, dog whelks, kelp, limpets, sea anemones, winkles and wrack. Seaweeds, which provide a home and source of food for many other species, are an important and colourful part of Porthdinllaen's marine life. Brown seaweeds form quite distinctive bands along the shore, while the delicate-looking red seaweeds are more abundant in low water or rockpools. The large rockpools around Trwyn Porthdinllaen are home to many prawns, fish, crabs and sea anemones. A large community of more obscure sea creatures – such as moss animals, sponges and sea squirts – lives on the undersides of boulders and amongst the seaweeds.

Eelgrass, the only flowering plant that lives in the sea around British coasts, can be seen in front of Porthdinllaen village, taking advantage of the shelter provided by the peninsula. This plant lives in sandy areas where it can form thick beds, much like meadows on land. Many marine species live in the eelgrass beds, which serve as important nursery areas for fish.

⟦⟧ On foot from car park to the village.

P Car park at Morfa Nefyn.

★ Refreshments and WC in village.

◪ 9 ha (22½ acres) 4ml W of Nefyn off B4417   [123:SH145265]

Porthor (Whistling Sands)   Gwynedd

From the sandy bay of Porthor a three-mile footpath leads to the heath-covered Anelog with its high cliffs and spectacular views. On a clear day Snowdonia, Anglesey, St David's Head in Pembrokeshire and Ireland can be seen from the summit. Remains of prehistoric hut circles are also found on this ancient common. The walk ends on the roadside near the Chapel at Uwchmynydd.

⟦⟧ Footpaths.

P Parking at Porthor and by the Chapel at Uwchmynydd.

★ Refreshments; WC at Porthor (seasonal); leaflet.

◪ 49.5 ha (73 acres) 2½ml NW of Aberdaron off B4327.   [123:SH166298]

Rhossili Down and Beach   Swansea

The impressive sweep of Rhossili Bay is backed by a solifluction terrace forming a rectangular terrace known locally as the Warren.

Rising above the platform, Rhossili Down (a large whaleback ridge of grass, heath and boggy hollows) commands good views across the Bristol Channel, the Gower Peninsula and towards Pembrokeshire. The expanses of shrubby heath support a number of insects including some uncommon butterflies, with small pockets of scrub attracting many migrant birds. To the north, a boulder field is of particular interest for its lichens, and some important mires and wet heaths on the lower eastern slopes are also of great conservation interest.

A range of archaeological features has survived in this important prehistoric landscape, with cairns and burial chambers, stone circles and early field boundaries.

🚶 From Rhossili village and from the N; well marked footpath.

🅿 Car park at Rhossili (not NT).

★ WCs; information centre at Rhossili.

🗺 215 ha (531 acres) 15ml W of Swansea, at end of Gower Peninsula.

[159:SS418883]

St David's Head   Pembrokeshire

One of the most famous headlands in Wales, this rugged coastline reveals renowned and excellent expanses of Ordovician volcanic intrusions, of great geological interest. Biologically, the headland is just as notable, with one of the largest expanses of coastal heath in Britain, continuing inland onto the rocky promontory of Carn Llidi. On the most exposed seaward slopes the heath consists of heather, bell heather and the rare hairy greenweed, and is wind-clipped and short. Maritime species such as kidney vetch, spring squill, thrift, sea plantain, sheep's bit and musk stork's bill occur in the heath and grasslands here, and in the rock crevices are orpine, sea spleenwort and wild chives.

Moving inland, western gorse becomes abundant with the other dwarf shrubs, and the heath is taller. Associated plants here include lousewort, heath bedstraw, heath-spotted orchid, heath milkwort and various sedges. There are wet areas with purple moor grass, bracken, bramble, common gorse scrub, pools and mires, the whole providing a superb expanse of semi-natural habitat.

The invertebrate fauna is very interesting, and includes both north-western and south-western specialities such as a rare pill woodlouse and the green hairy snail, with local heathland beetles, heather-feeding moths and other species. Nesting seabirds are scattered thinly all along the Trust's cliffs, but only the commoner species are represented. Jack-daw, raven, chough, peregrine, house martin and swift are more notable among the cliff-nesters, all present here or on Trust-owned cliffs in the St Bride's Bay area.

St David's Head and Carn Llidi are commonland, but until recently grazing had effectively ceased. The Trust is endeavouring to restore graz-ing so that the valuable heath and wetland does not become rank and scrub-invaded as it would, away from the windy coastal fringe.

The property is exceptionally rich in archaeological remains with prehistoric enclosures, forts and burial chambers at Coetan Arthur and on Carn Llidi, and an old field system behind the sheltered beach of Porthmelgan. Warrior's Dyke is a defensive Iron Age bank built to isolate the headland and create a coastal fortress.

[⚲] Coast path and footpaths from youth hostel at Whitesands Bay and Upper Porthmawr.

[P] Car park.

[★] NT shop, WCs and visitor centre at St David's; WC and café (not NT) at Whitesands Bay.

[▣] 210 ha (520 acres) 4ml NW of St David's, on B4583.   [157:SM730285]

Skirrid Fawr   Monmouthshire

This isolated hill of old red sandstone in the Black Mountains is largely covered with a coarse, tussocky grassland and there are also areas of heather and bilberry on the northern slopes.

The western slopes have two distinct semi-circular landslips, with a variety of plants such as parsley fern and green spleenwort growing in the crevices of the crags, contrasting with the unbroken slopes to the east.

Areas of woodland and scattered trees cover the western and southern slopes. In places the woods have a well-developed flora which includes hart's tongue fern, shining crane's bill, dog's mercury and a rich variety of mosses. Shrubs of hazel, holly and field maple occur within the woods. Woodland birds include woodcock, redstart, wood warbler and buzzard. Pont Skirrid and Caer Wood were formerly managed by the Forestry Commission. The Trust is now converting them from conifers to broadleafed species.

Footpaths lead through the oak woods and scattered scrub on the grassy summit, which commands impressive views of the Sugar Loaf, the Usk Valley and the Black Mountains.

[⚲] Footpaths from road to south of property; other footpaths provide access from small by-roads to the north; station at Abergavenny.

[P] Lay-by parking.

[★] Local facilities.

[▣] 83 ha (205 acres) 3ml NE of Abergavenny, 1½ml E of A465.

[161:SO330180]

The Stackpole Estate   Pembrokeshire

This extensive estate south of Pembroke is a coastal property of great contrast which includes eight miles of cliff, headlands, beaches and sand dunes, elongated lakes bordered by trees, sheltered bays and mature woodlands. The name Stackpole originates from the Norse *stac* for isolated rock and *pollr* for a small inlet.

The Bosherton Lakes and Stackpole Warren, together with the surrounding woodlands, are part of Stackpole National Nature Reserve, managed by the National Trust in partnership with the Countryside Council for Wales. The lakes were created between 1780 and 1840 by damming three narrow limestone valleys, two of which were formerly tidal. The central and western arms are calcareous marl lakes with extensive beds of stonewort and white water lily fed by underground springs. The eastern arm is stream-fed and is crossed by the handsome Eight-Arch Bridge. Lake wildlife includes otters, herons, wintering wildfowl and over twenty species of dragonfly. Eight species of bat live in the outbuildings of the former mansion of Stackpole Court and feed over the lakes and in the surrounding woodlands. Stackpole Warren supports internationally important lichen communities, as well as rich assemblages of duneland and calcareous grassland plants. There has been a rabbit warren on the dunes from medieval times; in recent years the grazing of the disease-struck rabbit population has been supplemented by sheep, cattle, ponies and goats.

The long stretch of limestone cliffs supports rich maritime grasslands, and is important for breeding seabirds including guillemot, razorbill, fulmar and shag, as well as resident chough.

Stackpole Quay is the collision zone between the limestone and the old red sandstone, which stretches a further two miles to the eastern extremity of the property. The quay area is an important geological site, and Greenala Point has a fine promontory fort. Another may be found on the promontory between the central and western arms of the lake.

The mansion was demolished in 1963, but a number of outbuildings survive and some have been converted to other uses. A small display in the former Game Larder illustrates the history of the house and lake.

[⚹] Property is traversed by the Pembrokeshire Coast Path; estate is served by an extensive network of footpaths (see estate map leaflet), with tracks for horses and mountain bikes in Castle Dock and Cheriton Bottom woods; wheelchair-accessible path runs along west bank of the eastern arm of the lakes, with accessible hide in the former boathouse.

P Car parks at Stackpole Quay, Broadhaven and Bosherton (for Lily Ponds); informal parking areas for estate woodlands.

★ Residential school basecamp ("Stackpole for Schools"); tearoom at Stackpole Quay; holiday cottages; fishing on lakes from designated fishing points (permit from NT and recognised outlets); WCs at Stackpole Quay and Broadhaven.

⬛ 806 ha (1992½ acres) 4ml S of Pembroke. [158:SR977963]

Sugar Loaf
Monmouthshire

This cone-shaped mountain has impressive views across the Bristol Channel, and to the Brecon Beacons, the Black Mountains and Herefordshire. The name refers to its shape, which resembles the sugar loaves which were once sold locally.

A number of important archaeological features can be seen including a boundary bank which encircles a former deer park linked to the Priory of Abergavenny, charcoal-burning sites and associated tracks, and coppiced trees which are evidence of the area's history of wood pasture.

The open moorland is covered with extensive areas of bracken, but also supports important upland heath. Parts are dominated by heather; other areas by bilberry, with cross-leaved heath, cowberry, common cow-wheat, hard fern and various grasses and mosses. There is a rich invertebrate fauna of heathland associates, and Sugar Loaf has a small breeding population of red grouse.

The woodland, dominated by oak, includes one of the most extensive tracts of ancient woodland in east Wales and forms a distinctive landscape feature for miles around. The now neglected coppice and mature trees include both sessile and pedunculate oak and beech. The latter is present as old pollards, indicating its probable native status here, which is interesting, since beech in most of Wales is planted rather than wild. Notable breeding woodland birds include pied flycatcher, redstart and wood warbler.

⏃ Access to car parks difficult (road steep and narrow); network of permitted paths and rights of way; station at Abergavenny.

P 4 car parks (limited).

★ Information panel in main car park.

⬛ 931 ha (2300 acres) 5ml NW of Abergavenny. [161:SO268167]

Tregwynt and Aber Mawr Beach
Pembrokeshire

The major feature of this property is the Aber Mawr Valley, which contains extensive development of semi-natural habitats, ranging from the shingle ridge at the mouth of the valley through tall, marshland vegetation and sallow carr into broadleaved woodland. The combination of the great diversity and extent of these semi-natural habitats makes the valley of great general wildlife value. Common and widespread species are present in abundance, but only a few more interesting species have been recorded. The scarcity of rarer species probably reflects the recent origin of the present mosaic of habitats, and of many of the individual habitats themselves.

The valley is rich in birdlife, with typical woodland breeding species such as chiffchaff, jay and buzzard; scrub birds such as linnet, whitethroat and garden warbler; and wetland birds such as sedge warbler and reed bunting. Badger are present and otter have been recorded.

In addition to the biological interest, the valley is also notable for its geomorphological and palaeo-geographical studies. Behind Aber Mawr beach there is a succession of deposits which provide much information about conditions here during the Ice Age. Sand martin nest in the low cliffs of Pen Deudraeth, and there is a submerged forest which is exposed at low tide.

Remains of a proposed nineteenth-century Irish sea port (a scheme put forward by the engineer Brunel) and a vernacular farmhouse are interesting historic features.

🚶 Long-distance coastal footpath; network of paths cross property.

🅿 Limited informal parking (avoiding blocking access).

★ Leaflet

🏛 101 ha (250 acres) 17ml NE of St David's, off A487.   [157:SM883346]

Upper and Lower Treginnis
Pembrokeshire

Coastal farms cover the south-west tip of St David's Peninsula, which commands spectacular views of Ramsey Sound and Island, St Bride's Bay, and (on a clear day) Snowdon and Ireland.

Traditional farm enclosures of small fields and hedgebanks cover the plateau. The unimproved coastal fringe consists of a variety of wildlife habitats, with grassland, heath and scrub masking many archaeological remains. The clifftop grasslands have patches of heather mixed with a profusion of wild flowers such as spring squill, thrift, sea campion, wild carrot, tormentil and hairy greenweed. The heath includes ling, bell heather, cross-leaved heath and gorse, which attract a number of moths, butterflies and other insects.

This property contains much of historic interest: a neolithic promontory fort, a chambered tomb, the Iron Age fort of Castell Heinif, old copper mine workings at Porthaflod, and quarries and lime kilns at Porthclais.

The high, vertical cliffs around Lower Treginnis, made up of igneous rocks, overlook sheltered inlets. Seals are commonly seen.

[⋏] Coastal footpath; waymarked permitted paths.

[P] Car parks at Porthclais and St Justinians.

[★] WCs at Porthclais; leaflets; refreshments (summer only) at Porthclais.

[�◨] 146 ha (360 acres) 3ml SW of St David's.   [157:SM725240]

Wharley Point   Carmarthenshire

Described in the work of Dylan Thomas, this gentle coastal promontory commands delightful views across the Taf and Tywi estuaries to Carmarthen Bay.

The cliffs of Wharley Point are scrubby, and this coast is sheltered enough to permit development of woodland as well. There are, however, open habitats of interest. Unimproved grassland occurs along the top of the cliff in the Lord's Park Farm area; interesting calcareous grassland occurs around some disused limestone quarries, and small areas of salt-marsh occur at the seaward mouths of valleys. The scrub includes many shrubs, such as blackthorn, hazel, hawthorn, gorse, privet, dogwood, holly and large ivy 'bushes', and the limestone grassland has the robust scrambling pea plant (everlasting pea), and calcicoles such as carline thistle, burnet saxifrage and ploughman's spikenard. Butterflies include common blue, brown argus and marbled white. There are important oystercatcher nesting areas in protected corners of the shoreline, a cormorant roost, and buzzard, raven and peregrine can be seen.

Several notable features of historic interest are the line of bulwarks of an Iron Age hill fort, the twelfth-century Llanstephan Castle (not owned by the Trust) and St Anthony's Well which supposedly has healing powers.

[⋏] Footpath from car park near St Anthony's Well; circular path.

[P] Car park at Llanstephan.

⊠ Beach and shops at Llanstephan.

⊞ 156 ha (386 acres) S of Llanstephan, off B4312 from Carmarthen.

[159:SN340093]

Ynys Barri   Pembrokeshire

This dramatic and rugged coastline between Abereiddi and Porthgain has much of industrial and archaeological interest. Porthgain (not owned by the Trust) has a well-documented history and was for many years a small port servicing a busy industrial region which exported slate, decorative stone and bricks. The remains of brick-works still exist at Porthgain, and tramways, workings, cottages and drowned quarry workings at Abereiddi, now overgrown by encroaching plants, provide a glimpse of this formerly prosperous area.

The bevelled, much indented coastline with its varying aspects and degrees of exposure supports a range of different vegetation types. Most notably, the clifftop has good areas of maritime grassland and coastal heath, the latter with the local petty whin, and both with dark green fritillary. Areas of exposed slate are particularly important for invertebrates. Cliffs and derelict slate quarries are used by nesting birds such as wheatear, peregrine, chough, fulmar and shag, and grey seal can be seen offshore. Some of the remaining hedgebanks have a rich flora, with cowslip, stonecrop and campion. A man-made basin drowned by salt water, the Blue Lagoon, is of particular marine biological interest with a fauna of active (rather than sedentary) suspension feeders which can cope with the amount of silt produced in the absence of any current, and are not dependent on a current for food supply.

[⋔] Coast path; path through Barry Island farm to cliffs.

[P] Car park at Abereiddi and Porthgain.

⊠ WCs at Abereiddi; telephone at Prothgain; bathing and beach at Traethllyfn; emergency telephone at Abereiddi.

[!] Care should be taken when bathing, because of dangerous undercurrents at south-west corner of beach.

⊞ 81 ha (200 acres) 9ml NE of St David's.   [157:SM805320]

The Argory
Co. Armagh

Overlooking the River Blackwater, this house dating from 1824 is an example of the lifestyle of the Irish gentry during the nineteenth and early twentieth centuries. The original gas lighting plant can still be seen.

Beyond the lawn and yew arbours, woodlands of oak (including evergreens) and birch cover much of the estate. Some of these contain interesting plants such as wood sanicle, common dog violet, lords and ladies, and yellow pimpernel, although rhododendron and laurel are causing problems in some areas by overshadowing the woodland floor. Willow warbler, woodcock, jay and chaffinch are some of the many woodland birds.

Argory Moss, a raised bog partially cut over for peat, is a valuable wetland rich in mosses, including *Sphagnum* moss, heather, notably the cross-leaved variety, lichens, cranberry and sedges, managed jointly by the Trust and the Ulster Wildlife Trust. The encroaching birch and Scots pine are controlled. The drainage ditches which lead to the river support many flowers and are the haunt of dragonflies (nine species have been recorded). The peatland areas attract many moths such as emperor, pebble hook-tip, drinker, double dart and brindled beauty; birds such as lapwing, snipe and curlew can also be seen feeding here and on the meadows.

[𝋡] Several walks around the house; track along banks of the Blackwater; house open seasonally; station at Portadown and bus service from Portadown, alight Charlemont.

[P] Car park.

[★] NT shop and tea-room; WCs (including disabled); driveways and special parking for disabled; adventure playground.

[⚏] 127.5 ha (315 acres) 4ml from Moy on Derrycaw road, 3ml from Junction 14 of M1.   [H872580]

Ballyconagan, Rathlin Island
Co. Antrim

Ballyconagan lies on the northern coast of Rathlin Island, overlooking the turbulent waters of the North Channel and giving wonderful views of the Scottish and Irish coasts and hills. It is farmed land on which the print of centuries of subsistence agriculture is firmly stamped, with ancient cultivation ridges and field marks clearly visible. The ruins of the thatched cottages that comprised the last settlement here lie in the lee of the low basalt cliffs, and on the exposed basalt tops the stone cairns formerly used for drying heather turf can be seen.

The area is rich in wildlife and boasts a diverse mosaic of wet and dry heathlands, small lakes, marsh and flower-rich grasslands. The western heath is the most northerly occurrence of its type in the British Isles and in late summer is ablaze with western gorse and bell heather. The flora of the lakes includes grass of Parnassus, marsh cinquefoil, bog bean and many species of sedge, which in turn provide habitat for rare craneflies, dragonflies, water bugs and beetles. The grasslands support communities of eyebright, heath spotted and early purple orchids, yellow rattle and devil's bit scabious. Breeding birds include skylark, linnet and wheatear, with buzzard, peregrine and raven regularly visiting. The Irish hare also breeds here.

🚶 Open all year; access on foot only via the East Light Road from Church Bay; waymarked track leads to coastguard lookout.

🅿 Available at the ferry terminal in Ballycastle.

★ Local facilities, including the Manor House Guest House, owned and managed by the Trust, with tea-room and overnight accommodation.

⛴ 65.5ha (155 acres) ½ml from Church Bay on Rathlin Island, 7ml from Ballycastle, access by daily ferry.   [D146520]

Ballykeel, Island Magee   Co. Antrim

This very attractive property, with its strong feeling of remoteness, overlooks Scotland to the east and the Copeland Islands at the mouth of Belfast Lough. It consists of coarse semi-improved agricultural grassland, bracken-dominated grassland, landslip faces supporting some interesting flowers, and undercliff scrub. The rocky shore varies from eroding boulder cliff faces to outcrops of Cretaceous limestone, with small areas of boulder and shingle beaches.

The property is accessible from a trackway leading down the cliff past a stone cottage restored for holiday use. The face of the cliffs is covered by thickets of fuchsia, blackthorn and hazel. Among the breeding birds whitethroat are particularly numerous.

Much of the grassland is coarse and invaded by bracken with primroses beneath. However, on the landslipped cliffs it becomes botanically rich with kidney vetch, harebell, greater burnet saxifrage, wild carrot, fairy flax, sea campion, field scabious and lady's bedstraw. Six-spot burnet moths are abundant.

[🚶] Pedestrian access only.

[P] Informal parking.

[★] Local facilities.

[⛴] 14.5 ha (36 acres) on outer east-facing shore of Island Magee, just south of Gobbins Cliffs, off B150.　　　　　　　　　　　　[J485965]

Ballymacormick and Orlock Point　　　　Co. Down

This low rocky shore along the mouth of Belfast Lough, a nature reserve and ASSI, has escaped encroachment by nearby Bangor. A network of paths leads through rocky outcrops covered in maritime heath and gorse.

Common pearlwort, sea aster, wild thyme, spring squill, rock spurrey, buck's horn plantain, bird's foot trefoil, thrift and many other more common plants are scattered among the rough grassland and heath of the clifftop and in the rock crevices. Butterflies include the small heath, common blue and wall brown. Stonechat, rock pipit, reed bunting and linnet breed among the scrub and gorse, and offshore there are large flocks of eider.

The property also includes areas of salt and freshwater marsh, as well as a tidal lagoon which attracts a number of migrant birds. The saltmarsh supports sea purslane (its northernmost occurrence in Ireland), lax-flowered sea lavender and saltmarsh flat sedge. In winter, cormorant and shag can be seen off the point, and oystercatcher and greenshank are among the many waders feeding on the mudflats. Turnstone and purple sandpiper may be seen on the rocks around the point.

The low cliffs of cleft rock are interspersed with shingle and sandy beaches. Cockle Island in Groomsport Harbour, an attractive place full of boats and framed by whitewashed cottages, has the sixth largest breeding population of Arctic tern in Ireland. Throughout the summer months they can be seen screeching overhead and diving for sand eels.

[🚶] Open access to saltmarshes; footpath along shore (poor in places), part of North Down coastal path; station at Bangor.

[P] Car parks at Groomsport and Ballyholme.

[★] Local facilities.

[⛴] 23 ha (58 acres) 1–3ml NE of Bangor, off A2 on S side of entrance to Belfast Lough.　　　　　　　　　　　　[J525837]

Bar Mouth   Co. Londonderry

The muddy sand and salt marshes of the Bann Estuary, sheltered from harsh weather by Portstewart Strand, on the south side of the estuary, are rich feeding grounds for waders and wildfowl.

In spring and autumn Bar Mouth is an important refuge for migrating birds, and the river provides a passage in May each year for elvers making their way to Lough Neagh for the summer, to return by the same route fully grown in the autumn. In summer, salmon have for many centuries travelled upstream to spawn (remains of fish-bones have been excavated from a nearby mesolithic camp).

The estuary mouth is of great historic interest, with the oldest occupied sand dune site in Europe. Many ancient dug-out canoes have also been found in the river mud.

The saltmarsh is covered in the grey and green of sea aster, sea milkwort, common saltmarsh grasses and sea rush. From November to January lapwing, golden plover, dunlin, redshank, curlew and oystercatcher rest and feed here, and offshore great crested grebe, merganser, shelduck, divers and auks can be seen.

[🯄] Open all year; access via path from car park to hide; station at Castlerock.

[P] Car park next to level crossing.

[★] Birdwatchers' hide with wheelchair access (key available from Warden).

[⬕] 11 ha (26 acres) on S side of River Bann, 1½ml E of Castlerock and 5ml NW of Coleraine.   [C792355]

Carrick-a-Rede, Larrybane and Sheep Island   Co. Antrim

Gaelic for 'Rock in the Road' (the road is the path of salmon on their westerly migration to the Bann and Bush rivers), Carrick-a-Rede has been the site of a salmon fishery for many centuries. During the season fishermen sling a precarious rope bridge across the 18-metre wide and 24-metre deep chasm between the mainland and the Island.

Those bold enough to cross the void are rewarded with views of the seabird colony on the sides of the island. The craggy rocks, covered with guano, form ideal nesting sites for fulmar, kittiwake, razorbill and guillemot. Designated an ASSI, this is also the site of complex and fascinating geology, with some volcanic rock and chalk deposits.

Larrybane Bay, wide and backed by chalk cliffs, links the headlands of Carrick-a-Rede and Larrybane Head. There are magnificent views from all the coastline around here, to the island of Rathlin and to the Hebrides beyond. A colony of house martin and swift nest in the old chalk quarry.

Off Larrybane Head, Sheep Island (designated an ASSI and SPA) supports large numbers of seabirds, including cormorant, black guillemot and eider.

A number of enclosed fields and the clifftop grassland, particularly on the mainland, support some interesting coastal plants, with spring squill, harebell, kidney vetch and several species of orchid. Snow bunting and twite winter on the stubble fields alongside skylark and linnet. A new footpath leads from Larrybane to Ballintoy.

⬚ From Larrybane only; rope bridge open seasonally in good weather.

P Car park (seasonal charge) at Larrybane.

✷ WCs; small tea-room; picnics; disabled access; dogs on leads only.

▣ 40 ha (99 acres) 5ml W of Ballycastle, 55ml from Belfast.   (D062450)

Castle Coole   Co. Fermanagh

Built between 1789 and 1795, this massive white palace lies within a fine wooded parkland surrounded by a landscape of rounded hillocks with scattered small lakes. The park is influenced by the eighteenth-century English style of naturalistic landscaping.

The woodlands attract a number of unusual birds, with blackcap, long-eared owl and jay. The glades in Flaxfield Wood are particularly important for invertebrates, including a number of uncommon hoverflies. Flaxfield and Lough Yoan woods also contain some interesting plants such as twayblade and broadleaved helleborine. These damp deciduous woodlands are also rich in bryophytes and lichens.

Breandrum Lough and Lough Coole are important wetland habitats, with cowbane, an unusual umbellifer, growing along the lake margins. The surrounding damp grassland is dominated by yellow flag, and provides valuable insect food for the many dragonflies hovering about the alder carr, reedbeds and fens. Lough Coole, the largest lake, has a varied shoreline with tussocks of sedge, bird cherry and spindle in the alder carr. Breeding ducks, red-breasted merganser and greylag geese inhabit the lough. A keen eye may spot the elusive water rail as it picks its way through the reeds, and curlew, snipe and lapwing may be seen on a small pocket of marshy grassland.

⟨⟩ House open seasonally; grounds open to pedestrians all year during daylight hours; local bus service from Enniskillen.

P Car park (seasonal charge).

★ WCs (including disabled) at visitor centre; picnics.

▣ 171 ha (423 acres) 1½ml SE of Enniskillen on A4 main Belfast to Enniskillen road.   [H260430]

Castle Ward   Co. Down

One of the great Irish country houses owned by the National Trust, Castle Ward is located on the shores of Strangford Lough. The original fortified tower house can be seen in Old Castle Ward farmyard. During the late nineteenth century it was the home of Mary Ward, a remarkable woman who pioneered the use of the microscope as well as being a naturalist, astronomer and artist.

The Gothick façade of the house overlooks an eighteenth-century landscaped park in the English style, with beeches and oaks leading down to the water's edge. The old quay was used to export lead and import the coal used to fuel the gas lighting. There is also an old ice-house in the grounds.

The farmyard contains evidence of the once-flourishing agricultural estate, with a sawmill, a cornmill (fully restored and driven by the water which fed Temple Water), barn, drying kiln and slaughterhouse. It was once a centre for the development of the linen industry and for innovative agricultural practices under Judge Michael Ward.

A number of walks, many in existence since the nineteenth century, lead through the farmyard to the woods of Old Castle Ward, and along the loughside past the square tower of the fifteenth-century Audley's Castle, built by an Anglo-Norman family.

The estate's close proximity to the lough and the variety of its landscape features have resulted in an interesting range of wildlife. The blocks of woodland, which in spring are carpeted in bluebells, are important for birds, with butterflies and hoverflies in the clearings. Wood sanicle and enchanter's nightshade flourish on the woodland floor. Temple Water, a man-made lake north of the house, attracts a number of birds from the lough.

Plants such as white water lily, spiked water milfoil, mare's tail and broadleaved pondweed grow in the nine freshwater ponds, as well as in Temple Water. At Mallard Pond seven species of dragonfly have been recorded. A grassland at the end of Temple Water supports nipplewort, ox-eye daisy and common spotted orchid. There is also a colony of pipistrelle bats in the estate buildings.

[🏃] House open seasonally; ground open all year during daylight hours; footpaths; bus service from Downpatrick to Strangford.

[P] Car park.

[★] NT shop and restaurant; WCs (including disabled); interpretation of house and estate in stable yard; educational study pack; guided walks organised by Wardens at estate office; Strangford Lough Wildlife Centre with audio-visual displays (seasonal opening); playground; Victorian pastimes centre; caravan site; base camp.

[⛴] 321 ha (794 acres) 7ml NE of Downpatrick, $1\frac{1}{2}$ml W of Strangford village on A25, on S shore of Strangford Lough, entrance by Ballyculter Lodge.

[J752494]

Collin Glen   Co. Antrim

On the west side of Belfast, the Glen River cuts a dramatic course through a great variety of rock types, descending in a series of impressive water-falls between the Collin and Black mountains on the edge of the Antrim plateau. The glen is situated at the north-western upper end of the river, and the lower slopes have been developed by the local community as a linear country park.

The upper glen, owned by the Trust, can be reached on foot from the country park. Of particular interest to geologists, this richly wooded gorge contains one of the Trust's most important broadleaved woodlands in Northern Ireland, and is especially of benefit because of its close prox-imity to the heavily populated city of Belfast. Despite recent modification with the planting of non-native trees, evidence of the wood's ancient origin remains in the abundant and varied wildlife.

Beneath the beech, wych elm and oak canopy, the woodland floor is lush with ferns, sweet woodruff, wood sanicle, wood sedge, early dog violet and broadleaved helleborine, with shrubs of blackthorn, hazel, holly and ash. There is a variety of rare molluscs and beetles, only associ-ated with such ancient woodlands.

Dipper, grey wagtail and kingfisher inhabit the course of the river, and the exposed rock faces of the gorge harbour many ferns, sedges, mosses and liverworts in the cracks and crevices. The silver-washed fritillary, rare in the east of the country, has been recorded.

[𝑅] Easily accessible from Belfast; network of well-made paths; access to river steep and difficult (impossible in places).

[P] Car park next to Glen Bridge.

[★] Viewpoints; limited access for disabled.

[⛴] 16 ha (39 acres) running from Glen road, 1ml SW of Falls Road boundary of Belfast, to foot of Collin Mountain.   [J270720]

The Crom Estate, Upper Lough Erne   Co. Fermanagh

This romantic landscape of islands, wooded peninsulas and ruins (including Crom Castle and Crichton Tower) lies on and around the tranquil waters of Upper Lough Erne. It has ASSI, SAC, SPA and Ramsar designations. Areas of deciduous woodland on Inisherk and Inishfendra, and in Reilly and Gole Woods are of great nature conservation value for their extent, the range of structure and age of the trees, and the numbers of breeding populations of birds. The woods are rare in Ireland as ancient sites, and over the millennia have developed special wildlife interest.

Oak and ash dominate the woodlands, with hazel, holly and spindle forming a dense shrub layer below the canopy. Rare mosses and lichens cloak the trees and the woodland floor. Woodland herbs and flowers are abundant, with wild garlic, wood sanicle, wood goldilocks, violets, twayblade and early purple orchid.

The oak woodland is the primary locality in Northern Ireland for the scarce purple hairstreak butterfly. Spotted flycatcher, garden warbler, blackcap and treecreeper all nest in the woods, and there is a heronry among the trees on Inishfendra. Many mammals also make their homes in the woodland: badger, fallow deer, red squirrel and pine marten may be seen.

Alder, willow and downy birch are common in the marshy fringes of the lough, with club rush, watermint, gipsywort, flowering rush, water horsetail, marsh marigold, yellow flag, yellow pimpernel and summer snowflake. Buckthorn, an uncommon shrub in Ireland, can be found along the lakeshore.

Great crested grebe are common; flocks of whooper swan feed on the improved pasture and cormorant roost in the winter months. The damp grasslands are important for breeding waders such as snipe, curlew and lapwing.

A study of the lichen and invertebrate communities has added to the national importance of the estate's historic parkland, wood pasture and lough shore, with the mixture of land and water leading to the many and varied habitats to be found. The area is threatened by land drainage, agricultural pollution and recreational damage.

⟨☆⟩ Crom Estate open seasonally; footpaths; bus service from Enniskillen-Clones (with connections from Belfast), alight Newtownbutler (3ml).

⟨P⟩ Car park. Public jetty for cruisers on Lough Erne.

⟨★⟩ Visitor centre; nature trails; WCs (including disabled); estate partly accessible to wheelchairs; picnics; holiday cottages; boat hire; dogs on leads only.

⟨▣⟩ 660 ha (1630 acres) 3ml W of Newtownbutler on the Newtownbutler to Crom road. [H36328, 361245 and 381232]

Cushendun   Co. Antrim

The picturesque village of Cushendun is a small settlement of slate-hung whitewashed cottages, lying in the shelter of Glen Dun where the river carves its way to the sea through one of the loveliest of the nine glens of Antrim, which dissect this wild, hilly countryside. The village has for long been a centre for poets and painters, and has many legends and folk tales surrounding it.

The Trust owns most of the village, with some of its buildings designed by Clough Williams-Ellis in the Cornish style as a memorial to Maud, first wife of Lord Cushendun. It also owns the dunes which have unfortunately suffered from the effects of sand extraction and erosion, but they have now been restored under an innovative programme supported by the local community.

The ruins of Castle Carra are near the Regency house of Rockport, the childhood home of Moira O'Neill, the poet of the Glens, and about three miles from the village is a Bronze Age passage grave, said to be the burial place of the poet Oisin.

On the north side of the glen nearby, Craigagh Wood conceals an old stone altar within the mixture of broadleaved trees and pines. Above Cushendun lie the extensive upland blanket peats of the Cushleake Mountains, also in National Trust care. The peats are rich in plants and insects typical of heather moorland, including *Sphagnum* moss, bog asphodel, black bog rush and cranberry. A population of large heath butterfly inhabits the area, and there are also red grouse and hen harrier.

⟨☆⟩ Cushendun accessible off A2; bus services to village; footpaths. Contact NT Northern Ireland Office for details of access to Cushleake.

P Car park in village.

★ WCs (including disabled); dogs on leads only; picnics; wheelchair access.

🏛 26 ha (64.5 acres) 23ml N of Ballymena, on east Antrim coast, via A2/B92.   [D248327]

Downhill   Co. Londonderry

The ruins of the eighteenth-century Downhill Castle can still be seen on this bleak headland overlooking the Atlantic Ocean, and the rotunda of Mussenden Temple, built in 1785 by Frederick Hervey, the Earl-Bishop of Derry, stands romantically poised on the edge of the cliffs complete with its impressive ashlar stone Corinthian columns and domed roof.

Midway between the mouth of the Bann and Magilligan Point, the site commands good views of Donegal, Portstewart Strand and the Antrim coast. A walled garden, dovecot, ice-house and storm-damaged mausoleum are further remains of an opulent lifestyle, although the headland is as dramatically wild as ever.

Remnants of the former heathland can be found among the farmland, and the maritime grassland of the clifftops is scattered with spring squill and heath spotted orchid. Seabirds such as fulmar and kittiwake nest on the cliffs. On the eastern border of the estate is a wooded glen with bluebell, wild garlic and ferns, as well as spotted flycatcher, willow warbler and goldcrest. Jackdaw and tree sparrow inhabit the ruins.

🚶 Grounds open all year; temple open seasonally; footpaths through woods and along cliff; limited access for coaches; station at Castlerock.

P Car park next to entrance on main A2 road.

★ Leaflet; WCs; picnics; facilities for disabled and paths through garden; dogs allowed on leads.

🏛 57 ha (141 acres) 1ml W of Castlerock, 5ml W of Coleraine on A2.
                                                                    [C758363]

Fair Head and Murlough Bay   Co. Antrim

This exceptionally beautiful and wild stretch of coast has a great variety of landscape and wildlife. The sheer, dolerite cliffs of the Fair Head promontory contrast strongly with the chalk and sandstone landslips of Murlough Bay.

The haunt of peregrine, buzzard, raven and the increasingly scarce chough, Fair Head is a landmark for miles around, with a wide range of vegetation resulting from its varied geology. There is a spectacular and steep path, known as the Grey Man's Path, down the centre of the promontory.

The plateau is covered with the dry and wet heath and grassland typical of acid soils. The small heath butterfly is common on the moorland, and wood tiger and emperor moths feed on the heather. Meadow pipit, skylark, linnet and stonechat inhabit the scrubby heather and bog myrtle, and the emergent and marginal vegetation around the three small lakes includes bog bean, white water lily, lesser spearwort and marsh marigold. A carpet of sedges and mosses covers the surrounding hollows.

The wooded slopes of Murlough Bay are notable for their rare lichens, mosses and ferns, characteristic of this damp western climate. The 'hanging' woodlands are dominated by rowan, downy birch, ash and hazel, with great wood rush, Wilson's filmy fern and bilberry. Other woodlands important in the landscape are plantation woods of ash, sycamore and beech. Chiffchaff and spotted flycatcher are among the many species of birds to be found in the woods.

Springs at the base of the cliffs are surrounded by damp-loving plants such as yellow flag, bog asphodel, bog cotton and *Sphagnum* moss. Damselflies and dragonflies dart over the damp hollows.

The chalk grassland in the south of the bay is rich with thyme, harebell, early dog violet and wild strawberry. The cliff scree is scattered with a number of rare plants such as spring sandwort, harebell, sheep's bit, bladder campion, stonecrop and St John's wort. Jackdaw, house martin, swift, rock and stock doves, kestrel and raven inhabit the cliffs, eider nest in the bay, and gannet dive off the shore. It is a good place to watch for whales, with occasionally pilots and killers as well as porpoises passing through the North Channel into the Irish Sea.

Relics of the area's industrial past include scattered lime kilns, coal mines and derelict cottages. At Benvan, overlooking the bay from the east, is a traditional Co. Antrim farm.

[🚶] Network of footpaths; circular waymarked path on Fair Head; paths in Murlough Bay. Bus service from Ballycastle.

[P] 3 car parks.

[★] Leaflet available from Causeway or Larrybane information centres; picnic areas.

[▣] 309 ha (764 acres) 3ml E of Ballycastle.   [D185430 and 199419]

Florence Court   Co. Fermanagh

Celebrated for its elaborate Rococo plasterwork, this impressive eighteenth-century house is situated against a backdrop of the imposing Cuilcagh Mountains. The surrounding parkland, designed by the Irish landscape gardener John Sutherland, is planted with clumps of oak, beech, sycamore, rhododendron and magnolia.

A saw mill, driven by a Victorian waterwheel, is a relic of the early woodland management. Other outbuildings include a forge and a carpenters' workshop. Whiskered bats and long eared bats are known to roost around the house.

Of particular interest for their wildlife, the damp, deciduous woodlands are contiguous with the Forest Park (managed by the Forest Agency of the Department of Agriculture). The luxuriant lichen, fern and moss communities include many rare species, and a number of uncommon plants such as bistort and broadleaved helleborine flourish in the rides and glades. Blackcap, woodcock and long-eared owl are among the many birds, and silver-washed fritillary, a woodland butterfly, has been recorded. Grasses, sedges and flowers border the paths around the estate.

[⚲] House and estate open seasonally; footpaths and bridleways; local bus service from Enniskillen.

[P] Car park at house; Forest Service car park by driveway.

[★] NT shop and restaurant; WCs (including disabled); wheelchair access to ground floor of house; holiday cottage in walled garden.

[⛰] 157 ha (388 acres) 8ml SW of Enniskillen, via A4 and A32 Swanlinbar road, 1ml W of Florencecourt village.   [H175344]

The Giant's Causeway   Co. Antrim

Immortalised in Irish folklore and legend, this geological phenomenon is internationally renowned for its impressive columns of exposed basalt, the result of volcanic activity millions of years ago. Fanciful names such as the Giant's Eyes, Chimney Tops, Onion Skins and Amphitheatre reflect the unusual formations. The towering, sculptured pillars, mainly hexagonal in shape, create an imposing landscape which has now been designated a World Heritage Site and National Nature Reserve.

As well as the rock structure itself, there are some beautiful bays overlooked by headlands from which there are good views of the north coast and the Hebridean Islands. Port-na-Spaniagh, off Lacada Point, is the site of the wreck of the Spanish galleass *Girona* which sank in 1588 after the ill-fated Armada was dispersed.

Affected by sea spray and driving winds, the clifftop vegetation includes maritime heath and grassland, two habitats which support a range of plants such as heathers, mountain everlasting, heath spotted orchid, creeping willow, heath bedstraw and devil's bit scabious. Sea pink and bladder campion carpet the slopes, and the occasional delicate sky-blue flowers of spring squill can sometimes be seen. The scarce sea spleen-wort also occurs.

The rocks are encrusted with lichens in shades of black, yellow and grey-green, and at the shady base of the cliffs woodland plants such as great woodrush, bluebell, wood stitchwort and red and white campion flourish. In the bays, wet flushes emerge from the cliff base, and grade to a mixture of sand, boulders and saltmarsh on the shore, which supports some rare northern plants such as oyster plant and Scots lovage.

The area is regionally important for its populations of breeding pere-grine, fulmar, buzzard and chough.

The rocks have attracted tourists for many years, including famous travellers such as Sir Walter Scott, and in the eighteenth and nineteenth centuries they were studied by geologists trying to find out about the origins of the earth. In the past, seaweed was dried on the old stone walls, and burnt in crude kilns to produce a residue rich in potash and iodine which was exported to Scotland.

The Causeway Coast Path runs for 14ml from the Blackfoot Strand, west of the Giant's Causeway, east and south along the clifftops to Dunseverick Castle and harbour. It continues along low cliffs and rocky shores to Portbraddan and thence long the extensive sandy beach of Whitepark Bay to Ballintoy harbour. A new path now links the harbour with Carrick-a-rede and Larrybane Head. The Coast Path offers spectacu-lar views and excellent opportunities to observe wildlife, but it is rough in places and can be very exposed in bad weather.

- [↟] Open all year; network of footpaths along coast; start of Causeway Coast Path; station at Portrush and bus service from Portrush and Ballycastle.
- [P] Car park (Moyle District Council) with special area for disabled visitors.
- [★] NT shop and tea-room in visitor centre (owned by Moyle District Council); WCs (including disabled); leaflets; audio-visual displays; guided walks; bus with hoist for disabled; ramps.

🖼 97 ha (239 acres) 9ml from Portrush on B146 Causeway to Dunseverick road, 2ml from Bushmills.   [C952452]

Kearney and Knockinelder   Co. Down

This property includes two miles of coastline looking towards the Isle of Man on the east side of the Ards Peninsula around the former fishing village of Kearney.

The green, rounded forms of drumlins (hills shaped by the retreating glaciers of the last Ice Age) give way to a plateau in the south and form a backdrop to the foreshore. Beyond the village, the coast includes cliffs, a low rocky foreshore, the three-hectare sandy beach of Knockinelder, and a small pocket of saltmarsh.

The path leads through lichen-covered slaty rocks and coastal grass-land studded with spring squill on the promontories. The small, sheltered bays are made up of shingle and saltmarsh, with the yellow horned poppy, an unusual plant of the area. Breeding birds along the coast include oystercatcher, rock pipit, shelduck and stock dove. The dramatic white form of the gannet can be seen diving out to sea, and tern, eider and wintering waders are common. Turnstone feed around the seaweed-covered rocks.

🚶 Footpaths.

🅿 Car park in village.

★ WCs; information centre.

🖼 17 ha (43 acres) 3ml E of Portaferry.   [J650517]

The Mourne Coastal Path   Co. Down

Leading through heathland, scrub and across wet flushes, the coastal footpath runs along a rocky shoreline at the base of boulder clay cliffs, with views across Dundrum Bay, Murlough Dunes and St John's Point. The mountain path follows the Bloody River Valley, a narrow glen leading up to Slieve Donard with a breathtaking panorama. Another section of the path runs for 2ml south from Bloody Bridge along the coast.

The heathland is dominated by western gorse and bell heather which attracts a diverse community of invertebrates, including a number of grasshoppers and butterflies, with marsh fritillary feeding on the devil's bit scabious. Bog myrtle, black bog rush, bog pimpernel and pale and common butterworts grow in the wet flushes. Yellowhammer, now scarce in Ireland, have been seen on the heath, and the viviparous lizard, the only terrestrial reptile native to the country, is present but uncommon.

A boulder beach, where yellow horned poppy and oyster plant can be seen, runs from William's Harbour to Dunmore Head. The rocks are covered in lichen, with some maritime grassland. There is a small fulmar colony, and black guillemot breed in holes in the rocks. Tern, gannet, Manx shearwater and common seal can be seen offshore. St Mary's Ballaghanary, a Celtic church, stands on the clifftop.

[⚲] Open access from A2. Bus services from Newcastle.

[P] Car park at Bloody Bridge.

[★] Local facilities; WCs.

[⚏] 21 ha (53 acres) S of Newcastle, E of Mourne Mountains.   [J389269]

The Mournes: Slieve Donard and Slieve Commedagh
Co. Down

The rounded granite masses of Slieve Donard and Slieve Commedagh form the highest peaks in the Mourne Mountains massif of south Down, which tower over the holiday resort of Newcastle, and true to the song really do 'sweep down to the sea'.

The Trust's holdings on the northern flanks of the mountains, together with the hills of Thomas' Mountain and Shan Slieve, are included in the Eastern Mournes ASSI and SAC. The mossy heath of the summit is of particular interest, and the lower slopes support a wide range of montane and western heath, with rare flowering plants and ferns. In late summer these slopes are ablaze with purple heathers. The jagged cliffs of Eagle Rock, overlooking the infant Glen River, were the last Northern Irish home of the sea eagle.

Prehistoric burial cairns are found on the summits of both mountains. Those on Slieve Donard are also associated with Saint Domangard, a disciple of St Patrick, who is reputed to have lived the life of a hermit on the mountaintop. No doubt he too enjoyed the spectacular views to the Isle of Man and to the English Lake District, which today reward the visitor for the climb from sea level to 852.4 metres.

These splendid views, together with the thrill of climbing the highest peaks in Northern Ireland, attract many thousands of walkers. Their impact on the floor of the Glen River valley has led in the past to erosion which the Trust is now controlling.

- 🚶 Open access; main point from Glen River path from Donard car park in Newcastle.
- Ⓟ Large car park in Newcastle.
- ★ Local facilities.
- ⊞ 526 ha (1300 acres) S of Newcastle.   [J365285]

Murlough Nature Reserve   Co. Down

The village of Dundrum lies within a beautiful landscape of dunes and a tidal estuary overlooked by the Mourne Mountains. The dunes and heathland of Murlough contain many interesting botanical and archaeological specimens; the dunes have been a site of human settlement over thousands of years, with archaeological remains from the Neolithic and Bronze Ages to early Christian Iron Age and medieval times.

The dunes were once the site of a vast warren where rabbits, introduced by the Normans, were farmed for meat and fur for the Dublin hatters.

The complex network of dunes, grassland, heath and scrub harbours an immense variety of wildlife, and in 1967 Murlough was designated Ireland's first Nature Reserve. It is now an ASSI and SAC.

The oldest dunes have been dated to over 6,000 years ago and the highest reach 36.5 metres. Beneath the dunes lie post-glacial 'raised' shingle beaches of great interest. The older dunes support fine examples of dune heath, a scarce and declining habitat supporting a rich variety of insects. Murlough is one of Ireland's most important butterfly sites with over twenty species recorded, the most important being the marsh fritillary, whose larvae feed on devil's bit scabious in the dune hollows. The dune grasslands support a wide range of plants including pyramidal and bee orchids, carline thistle and Portland spurge, as well as many tiny but rare dune animals. Breeding birds include skylark, meadow pipit and cuckoo, with whitethroat, reed bunting, stonechat and linnet in the scrub.

The mudflats of the Inner Bay are an important wintering site for dunlin, redshank, oystercatcher, curlew and Brent geese. Overwintering seaduck, divers and auks can be seen offshore and in summer there are concentrations of feeding terns, gannets and gulls, as well as seals.

[⚹] Main access point on A24; access to certain areas restricted April to September; network of footpaths open all year.

[P] Car park at access point next to A24.

[★] Visitor facilities and information centre open seasonally; guided walks (seasonal); education and special interest tours all year by arrangement; schools video on sale to teachers; boardwalk suitable for wheelchairs; dogs on leads only and prohibited in fenced areas.

[!] Military activity at north end of beach (not NT) is indicated when flags flying.

[⬱] 282 ha (697 acres) 2ml NE of Newcastle, 28ml S of Belfast on Dundrum to Newcastle road.   [J410350]

Portstewart Strand   Co. Londonderry

Protecting the mouth of the River Bann, this elongated sand spit is backed by one of the few dune systems in Northern Ireland. The long beach is very popular with holidaymakers, especially in the summer.

Many features of a mature dune system, an increasingly threatened coastal habitat, can be seen, with mobile and stable dunes, hollows (dune slacks) containing herb-rich grassland, dune scrub and saltmarsh.

The mobile dunes are colonised by sand couch, marram grass, and sand sedge. The established dune grassland is rich with flowers such as kidney vetch, bulbous buttercup, creeping thistle and wild pansy, with the calcareous nature of the sand encouraging a wide range of plants. The oldest dunes support bee and pyramidal orchids, and common centaury.

More than fourteen species of butterfly have been recorded, including small heath, dark-green fritillary and grayling. Mosses and lichens are also important in the more stable dunes. Sea buckthorn, although not native to Ireland, is now widespread. It provides an ideal habitat for warblers and reed bunting, and shelter for foxes and badgers.

Saltmarsh in the Bann Estuary attracts waders and wildfowl which feed on the intertidal mud.

[⚹] From Portstewart; station at Coleraine. Bus service from Portstewart.

[P] Parking on beach (at a charge).

[★] WCs; information at Warden's office on beach; horses and dogs controlled (dogs to be kept on leads on beach, dog litter area).

[⬱] 80 ha (197 acres) $\frac{3}{4}$ml NW of Coleraine, off A2.   [C720360]

Skernaghan Point, Island Magee   Co. Antrim

Situated on the northern tip of Island Magee at the entrance to Larne
Harbour, Skernaghan Point is an open headland enclosing Brown's Bay.
Low basalt cliffs, small coves and beaches fringe a domed grassy whaleback rich in flowers and insects on its lower slopes, where freshwater
flushes grade into maritime grassland, saltmarsh and rock crevice
communities. On the wetter ground black bog rush, northern marsh
orchid and bog pimpernel occur, with the drier slopes supporting lady's
bedstraw, milkwort and harebell. Gannet and terns can be seen feeding
offshore in summer.

[⋆] Open access; footpath onto the headland along the shore from Brown's
 Bay. Bus service from Larne.

[P] Public car park in Brown's Bay.

[★] Toilets (not NT) and seasonal kiosks in public car park.

[▦] 46ha (110 acres) 8¾ml from Whitehead via the B150 and B90. [J437034]

Strangford Lough   Co. Down

Linked to the Irish Sea by a narrow channel less than a mile wide, this
great sea lough is not only a most beautiful landscape of islands, water
and rounded drumlins or glacial hills, but also of international importance for its wildlife. The Trust owns or leases many islands and areas of
shoreline habitat, as well as most of the intertidal foreshore.

The 80,000 million gallons of sea water which rush through the
'Narrows' on each tide bring in marine life which feeds thousands of overwintering and summer-breeding birds. Two-thirds (more than 15,000) of
the world population of pale-bellied Brent geese spend the winter on the
lough after summers in the Arctic Circle.

Over 2000 species of marine animals have been recorded in several
unique marine communities in the lough, and include starfish, corals, sea
anemones, molluscs and crustaceans and worms. Among the large and
varied populations of birds are shelduck, teal, oystercatcher, godwit,
knot, curlew, redshank, wigeon, red-breasted merganser, cormorant and
mallard. The abundance of sand eels attracts flocks of tern (which breed
on the islands). Common and grey seals rest and breed on the isolated
rocky shores, and basking sharks and porpoises may be seen on the
incoming tide. The coastal rocks are encrusted with lichens and
seaweeds.

Around the shoreline, the variety of habitats depends on the tide and on the rivers feeding the lough. Coastal grassland of thrift and campion merges with heathland, shingle and sandy beaches, tidal mudflats and saltmarsh, with the sheltered islands, reefs and deep waters adding to the range. The lack of temperature extremes in this sheltered environment allows both southern and northern species to coexist.

[🚶] Unrestricted access by boat to Darragh, Taggart, Ballyhenry and Salt islands except where bird colonies are protected; footpaths around shore; bus service from Downpatrick to Strangford or Portaferry with connections from Belfast.

[P] Car parks at Castle Ward; several car parks around the lough.

[★] WCs (including disabled) at Mount Stewart and Castle Ward; Strangford Lough Wildlife Centre at Castle Ward; bothy on Salt Island for yachtsmen and groups; base camp at Castle Ward; picnics allowed on some properties (prohibited on nesting islands during breeding season); other activities (not necessarily NT), sailing, yacht and cruising clubs, birdwatchers' hides.

[⛴] 2185 ha (5400 acres) SE of Belfast via A22, A21, A20 and A25, car ferry from Portaferry to Strangford.   [J560615]

White Park Bay   Co. Antrim

A sweep of golden sand flanked by chalk cliffs marks a distinct change from the dark, tilted basalt stacks at the eastern edge of the bay and the cliffs of the Causeway coast to the west. The variation in the underlying rocks and soils is reflected in the variety of plants and habitats, which range from sand dunes through neutral clays and wet flushed areas to calcareous grassland and undercliff scree and scrub.

A broad stretch of lumpy grassland, wet flushes and scrub lies between the beach and the cliffs, and a narrow band of sand dunes is a refuge for some uncommon plants such as sea sandwort, fragrant agrimony, and Portland and sea spurges. The ancient chalk grassland contains a wide range of wild flowers and grasses, with orchids, lady's mantle, bird's foot trefoil, thyme, purging flax, lady's bedstraw and meadow crane's bill. Moonwort and adder's tongue are two unusual ferns to be found.

Bees, ants, grasshoppers and molluscs are among the many invertebrates which thrive on the coarser grassland, and brambles, hawthorn, elder and hazel scrub provide important nesting sites for willow warbler, whitethroat, sedge warbler, linnet and stonechat. The shaded slopes below the cliff, with conditions similar to those in woodland areas, harbour a variety of woodland plants such as wood anemone, primrose and common twayblade. Yellow flag, meadowsweet, water mint and marsh marigold flourish in the marshy pockets.

There is much of archaeological interest, including some megalithic tombs above the bay, and a Bronze Age burial mound along the sand hills.

🚶 Network of footpaths; Causeway Coast Path.

P Car park on clifftop.

★ WCs; nature trail.

🏞 72.5 ha (179 acres) 1½ml W of Ballintoy, 7ml NW of Ballycastle off A2.

[D023440]

South-West England I

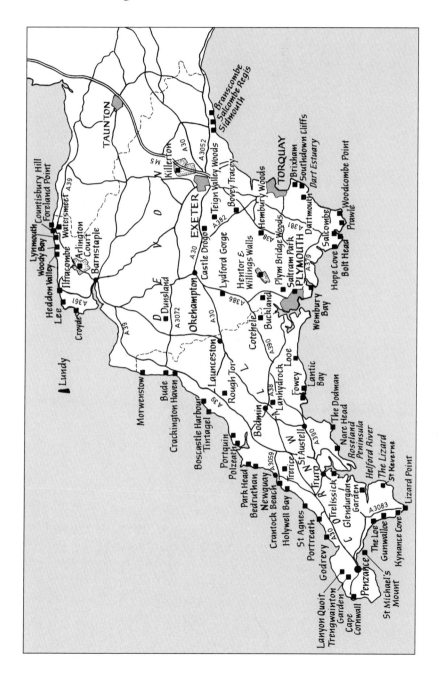

South-West England II

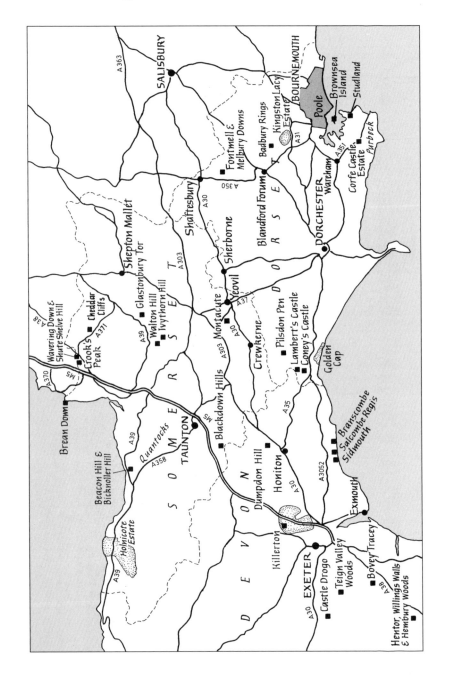

Southern England with Wiltshire

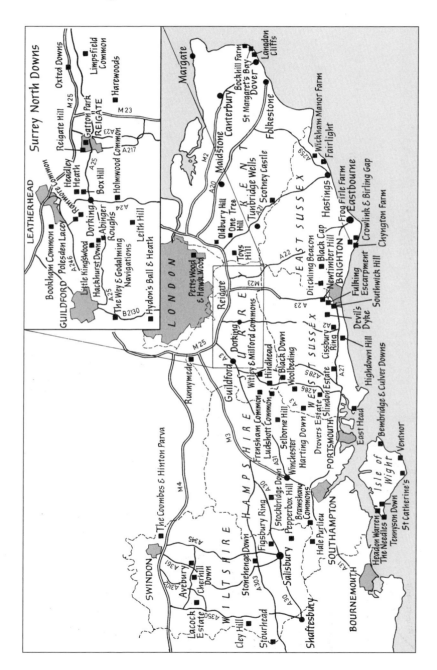

London, Thames Valley & Chilterns with part of Gloucestershire

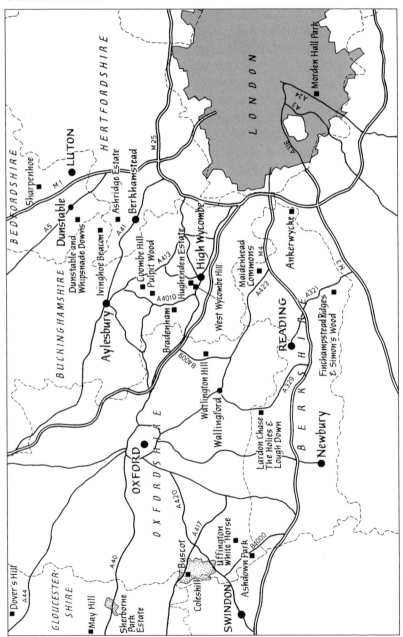

Eastern Counties

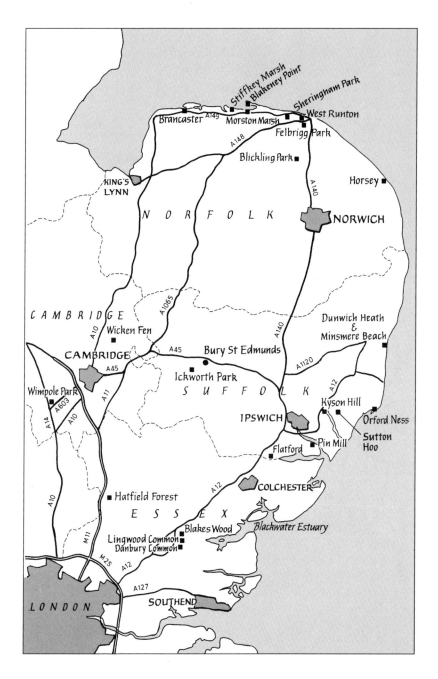

Central England with Merseyside

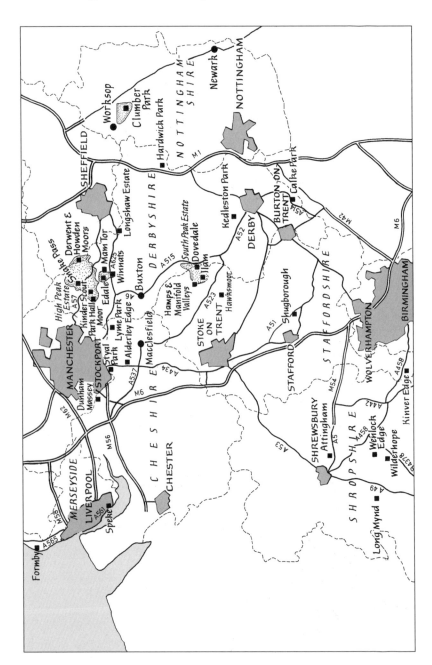

North-West England

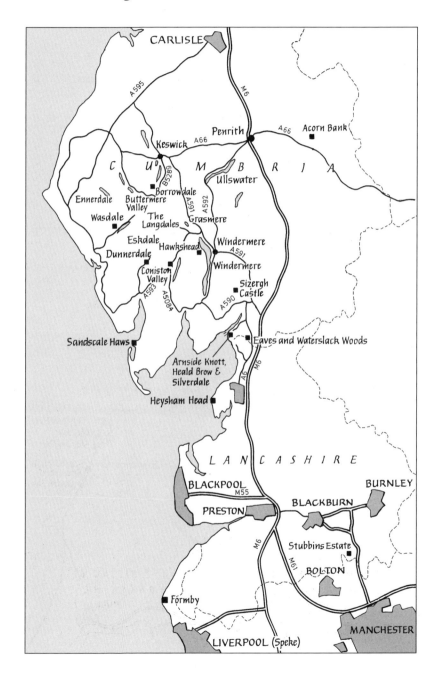

North-East England

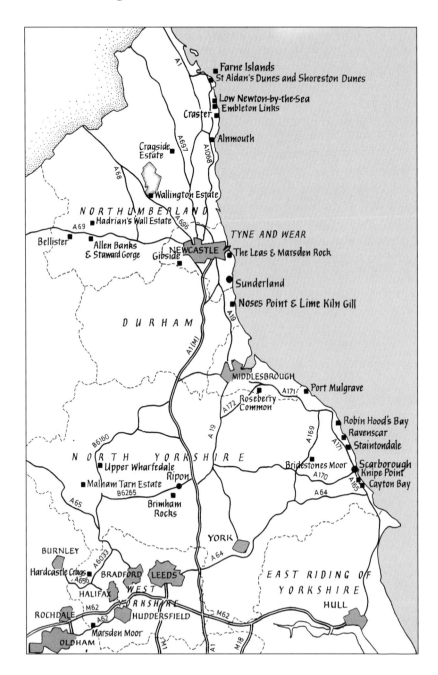

Farne Islands
St Aidan's Dunes and Shoreston Dunes

Low Newton-by-the-Sea
Embleton Links
Craster

Alnmouth

Cragside
Estate

A1

A697

A1068

A68

Wallington Estate

N O R T H U M B E R L A N D

Hadrian's Wall Estate

A69

A696

TYNE AND WEAR

Bellister

Allen Banks
& Staward Gorge   Gibside

NEWCASTLE

The Leas & Marsden Rock

Sunderland

Noses Point & Lime Kiln Gill

A19

D U R H A M

A1(M)

MIDDLESBROUGH

Port Mulgrave

A171

Roseberry
Common

A172

Robin Hood's Bay
Ravenscar
Staintondale

A19

A169

A171

B6160

N O R T H   Y O R K S H I R E

Upper Wharfedale

Malham Tarn Estate

Ripon

B6265

Bridestones Moor

A170

Scarborough
Knipe Point
Cayton Bay

A65

A64

Brimham
Rocks

A65

YORK

A64

BURNLEY

Hardcastle Crags

A6033

BRADFORD

LEEDS

E A S T   R I D I N G   O F
Y O R K S H I R E

A646

HALIFAX

W E S T
Y O R K S H I R E

HULL

ROCHDALE

M62

M62

A62

HUDDERSFIELD

Marsden Moor

OLDHAM

M1

A1

M18

North Wales with Shropshire

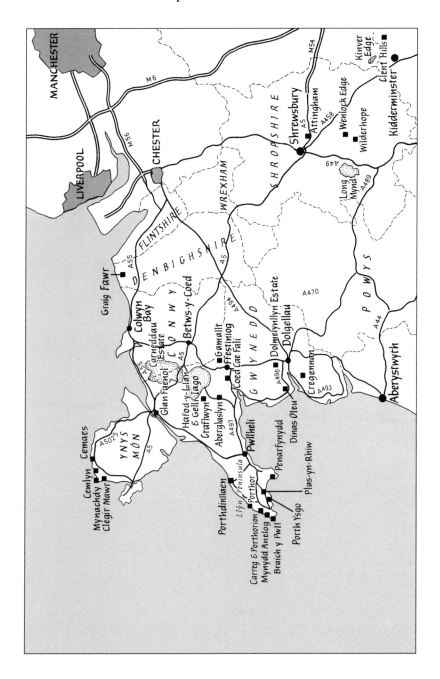

South Wales with Bristol, Bath, part of Gloucestershire, Herefordshire, North Somerset and Worcestershire

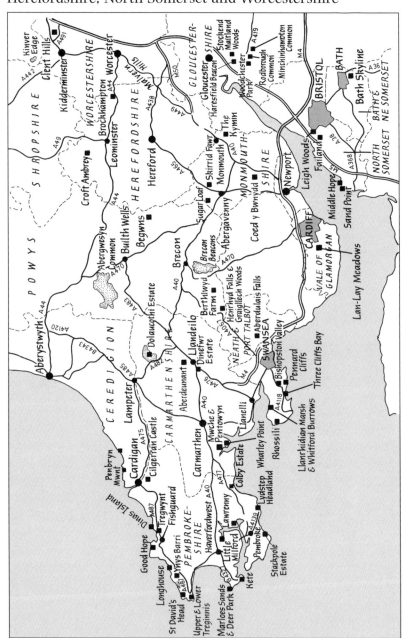

Northern Ireland

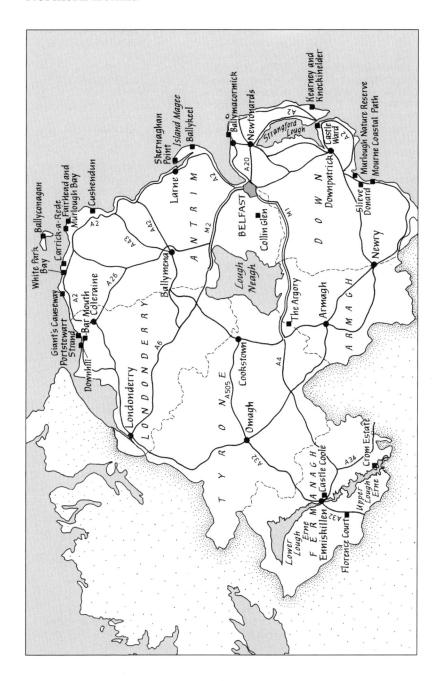

Index